Politics and religion in the modern world

Politics and religion in the modern world

Edited by
George Moyser

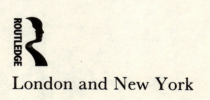

London and New York

First published 1991
by Routledge
11 New Fetter Lane, London EC4P 4EE

Simultaneously published in the USA and Canada
by Routledge
a division of Routledge, Chapman and Hall, Inc.
29 West 35th Street, New York, NY 10001

© 1991 George Moyser

Typeset by Selectmove Ltd, London
Printed and bound in Great Britain by
Biddles Ltd, Guildford and King's Lynn

British Library Cataloguing in Publication Data
Politics and religion in the modern world.
  1. Politics. Related to religion
  I. Moyser, George *1945–*
291.177

ISBN 0–415–02328–9

Library of Congress Cataloging in Publication Data
Politics and religion in the modern world / edited by George Moyser.
      p.   cm.
   Includes bibliographical references and index.
   ISBN 0–415–02328–9
   1. Religion and politics--History--20th century.   I. Moyser,
George.
BL65.P7P64   1991
291.1'77--dc20   91–2083
                                                                        CIP

Contents

List of tables and figures

Contributors

George Moyser is an Associate Professor of Political Science at the University of Vermont, USA.

John Madeley is a Lecturer in Government at the London School of Economics and Political Science, England.

Sabrina Ramet is an Associate Professor of Political Science at the University of Washington, USA.

Glenn E. Perry is a Professor of Political Science at the Indiana State University, USA.

Ian A. Talbot is a Lecturer in Languages, Politics and History at Coventry Polytechnic, England.

Adrian Hastings is a Professor of Theology and Religious Studies at the University of Leeds, England.

Kenneth Medhurst is a Professor of Political Science at the University of Bradford, England.

Jennifer Pearce is a Research Associate at the University of Bradford, England.

Kenneth D. Wald is a Professor of Political Science at the University of Florida, USA.

Preface

Political science, like most academic disciplines, tends to focus research according to fashion. There are, in any given period, areas of the subject that receive a lot of attention, and those which attract less. The study of religion and politics, in these terms, has moved rapidly in recent years from one of neglect to one of relatively intense scrutiny. Institutionally, one can see this in the swelling of the research committees and papers delivered at professional meetings both nationally and internationally. But this is, I suggest, no more than its due. Twenty years ago, a writer suggested that however imprudent it might seem to grapple with the complexities of the relationship between religion and politics, its importance demanded such an endeavour. Today, this is even more clear, and fortunately, it is being recognized. In contradiction to those in the western world who thought that secularization had removed religion from the realm of political affairs, it has remained a vital force. In First, Second and Third Worlds, one can find in most countries evidence that religion still has a substantial imprint, worthy of critical scrutiny.

This volume is a contribution to that task. Its theme, 'politics and religion in the modern world', captures its goal – to undertake a survey of the field of religion and politics over the last half century. This is, obviously, an ambitious task for one book. Inevitably, therefore, it cannot be definitive. The regions and countries covered are selective. Nevertheless, by focusing on key areas and countries, the authors collectively provide a substantial commentary on what has happened, and is happening, to religion and politics in the world today. Many of the contributions provide a holistic regional focus, such as on Latin America and Eastern Europe, to give a broad perspective. But they also incorporate detailed case studies of given countries so that the reader can appreciate some of the rich variety of particular national situations.

As editor, I would first of all like to thank those contributors for their time and labours in making this volume possible. Their individual expertise in their chosen regions gives the book a scholarly authority that could not be otherwise achieved, and for that they alone are responsible. The deficiencies and shortcomings of the whole, where they are perceived, are mine alone.

I would also like to thank Stella Moyser, Barbara McGray and Gail Hampton for their typing assistance, and the staff of the Bailey – Howe Library at the University of Vermont for helping me complete the occasionally incomplete reference. Last, but certainly not least, I wish gratefully to acknowledge the support and forbearance of the editor at Routledge, Peter Sowden. He first commissioned this volume a considerable time ago. Since then, the world of religion and politics has moved on in sometimes dizzying fashion, but he never lost hope that we would stop observing and start writing!

George Moyser
Burlington, Vermont

Chapter One

Politics and religion in the modern world: an overview

George Moyser

INTRODUCTION

It is very difficult in the modern world to ignore the presence of religion in public affairs. Virtually on a daily basis, the media provide instances demonstrating that the people, institutions, and ideas that make up the religious sphere have a continuing and important relevance to the political realm. A glance at the morning newspaper as I write is as good an illustration as any.[1] In it there is a story from Britain concerning a broadcasting bill going through one of the legislative stages on the way to becoming an Act of Parliament – the law of the land. The focus of the story is about the problems of drawing up new rules restricting access to television by religious institutions, rules that have caused 'a great deal of concern among Christians', according to a campaigner for religious programming. Another, from the Swiss sub-canton of Appenzell Inner-Rhoden, relates how male voters meeting in the annual *Landsgemeinde*, or town meeting, of this strongly Roman Catholic area had refused for the third time to give women the vote in local affairs. There is also a report from Harare, Zimbabwe, in which an Anglican priest, 'prominent in the ranks of anti-apartheid activists and a member of the African National Congress' was injured by a booby-trapped parcel, allegedly sent by right-wing political elements from South Africa. Perhaps most noteworthy of all is an article about reforms in Albania, famous for its attempt to eliminate systematically all trace of religion from its society. In this article, mention is made of a new generation of younger technocrats described as supporters of religion, and unwilling 'even in public, to state the official line that the Albanian people were "never religious"'.

These momentary examples could be extended almost indefinitely to others, both great and small. The role of the Christian Churches in legislative controversies over abortion; the *rapprochement* between the Kremlin and the Vatican; and the more familiar events in the Middle East where religion, in the shape of Judaism, Christianity and Islam, is a significant factor in the domestic and international politics of the entire region.

What they demonstrate, unequivocally, is that religion and politics have a lot to do with each other: they interact in a number of important but complex ways. Whether it is at the local, national or international level; whether it involves ordinary citizens, activists or major leaders; whether it concerns legislative institutions, pressure groups or competing political parties and ideologies; whether it is the First World of liberal democracy, the Second World of state socialism, the Third World of developing countries or the Fourth World of abject poverty, religion and politics relate.

This ongoing reality is, therefore, the basic motivation for this book. The view is taken, in other words, that 'secularization', or 'modernization', have not marginalized religion in the modern world – at least not to the extent that it ceases to have much relevance to politics, or politics to religion. Clearly, vast changes in the relationship have taken place even over the last few decades, but those changes have by no means sundered the connections.

It is, indeed, in that context that the second part of the title of the book 'in the modern world', has been cautiously added. This has narrowed the focus to relatively recent times and so given each contributor scope to provide greater detail about issues and events in given contemporary relationships between religion and politics than would otherwise have been possible. At the same time, it allows them room to indicate the dynamics of those issues and events and, not least, to set them in a broader historical context. Those dynamics and that context are always an essential part of understanding the whole.

To assist in that understanding, this introductory chapter sets out some general considerations which might be used to compare, contrast, and derive significance from the various case studies. To that end, we must turn first to basic definitional questions, for it is from definitions that clear, analytic understanding must proceed.

THE BASIC ELEMENTS

Politics

What is politics? A simple question, but one difficult to answer in a precise way. Nevertheless, if we are to begin to appreciate the various elements that make up the relationship between religion and politics, some answers, however imperfect, must be given.

In that spirit, one encyclopedia's definition is as good a start as any: 'a process whereby a group of people, whose opinions or interests are initially divergent, reach collective decisions which are generally regarded as binding on the group, and enforced as common policy.'[2] From this, we can derive a number of important elements and so flesh out what the realm of 'the political' is that 'religion' might engage.

First, politics is a process, a complex set of activities that form part of a 'group of people's' shared existence. The purpose of those activities is, as noted in the definition, essentially the making of collective decisions – the exercise of power. Our particular focus, therefore, is with the interconnections that exist between the religious life of the group and any or all of those activities, always bearing in mind that they take place within a broader social, cultural, economic and geographical context defined by the character of the group. But what 'group of people' are we talking about here? In principle, one could be speaking of a wide spectrum ranging from small primary groups such as family units, through to the entire human race. All to a greater or lesser degree have a corporate life, containing individuals to some degree divergent in opinion or interest. All, therefore, have formal or informal 'political' processes whereby collective decisions are made.

Hence, we might, indeed be interested in how 'religion' affects family decision-making, or the 'politics' of the workplace, or other groups of people. Indeed, one particular set of groups is that defined by religious membership. And so we might well ask how these groups formulate collective decisions. We might then also ask how those patterns impinge upon the way those groups engage in political processes outside the group. Studies have in fact been done on this, showing that such internal political practices do indeed affect the manner of external engagements. They also show that internal power arrangements tend to reflect patterns in the secular political world.[3] All of which serves to emphasize that the relationship between religion and politics is not a simple one; there are many complex features that must be taken into account.

Normally, however, 'politics' is reserved for decision-making processes among large spatial groups, collectivities of people that inhabit a given local, regional or, above all, national territory. Numerous studies have focused on the contribution of religion at each of these levels. At the small end of the spectrum, they include reports of the way religion intersects with the political processes of particular villages or cities – what some call 'communal politics'.[4] They also include many more that look at provinces or regions; many are very large and significant entities yet sufficiently distinctive to be an important focus of religious and political life in their own right.[5] But most common, perhaps, are 'country studies' of the relationship between religion and politics in sovereign nation-states.

In part, this is because of the nature of a 'nation', defined in one dictionary as follows:

> a nation is a body of people who see part at least of their identity in terms of a single communal identity with some considerable historical continuity of union, with major elements of common culture, and with a sense of geographical location at least for a good part of those who make up the nation.[6]

Hence, to the extent that religion is a part of that communal identity, that common culture, that historical continuity, so religion and 'nation' become closely entangled: religion can be a means through which a nation expresses its identity and aspirations.[7]

However, perhaps the key interest in nation-states lies in their sovereignty – their capacity, theoretically at least, to make binding and enforceable collective decisions for generally large aggregates of people. The world has become dominated by such entities, as is attested by the collapse of empires and the ending of colonialist regimes. Though in some regions, nation-states are initiating the creation of super-states, as yet power lies substantially at the national level. Thus it is national politics which in a sense counts the most and hence it is relationships between that politics and the religious sphere which generate major attention. This book, organized substantially in terms of national case studies, is testament to this.

At the same time, significant collectivities exist at the international level where, in consequence, interesting linkages with religion can be examined. Here we are dealing with such topics as the contribution of religious agencies as actors in international relations. We are also reminded at this level that religion expressed in the domestic political arena may spill over into cross-border disputes and other types of international difficulties.[8]

The second key element in a definition of politics besides the character of the collectivity is the process of decision-making itself. As noted, this entails the reconciliation of divergent opinions and interests in mechanisms of conflict resolution. How this is achieved varies considerably. In some contexts, it is a matter of the direct use of violence, coercion and terror. In others, methods based on historical tradition and custom may prevail. In yet others, a conscious attempt is made to devise a written formula, or constitution, that lays down clear legal rules whereby power is wielded.

The formal institutions at the heart of this process constitute 'the state', 'the set-up of authoritative and legitimately powerful roles by which we are finally controlled, ordered, and organized'.[9] It includes the agencies that make up the national political executive ('the government' narrowly construed), the legislative and judicial organs, and an administrative or bureaucratic apparatus ('the civil service'). The state also includes the means whereby its decisions are ultimately enforced – the coercive apparatus of police, militia, and army. Authoritative institutions at the sub-national level function analogously as 'the local state', although their power is subordinated to a greater or lesser degree to the national level. Similarly, the term should sometimes perhaps be stretched to include formally authoritative supranational institutions where there has been a significant transfer of decision-making from the national level. The European Community is a case in point.

It is because of the centrality of these state institutions to the political process that their relationship with religion has received close scrutiny. Indeed, 'church and state' was, for a long time, taken to be what 'religion and politics' was essentially all about. Connections between religion and the constitution form one important aspect. In the United States, for example, as in other countries, the relationship between religion and the national constitution has been an important focus of study.[10] The US constitution lays out the basic legal framework within which state institutions operate. In doing so, it also reflects important symbolic elements and ideological preferences. This in turn raises the question of the role accorded to religious bodies in the constitution, and the extent to which its symbols and values have a religious provenance. Similar considerations can also be raised in every other national context.

Constitutional studies, particularly in the United States, also draw into view the relationship between religion and the judiciary, which in that country has a major responsibility for deciding constitutional issues.[11] Beyond that, such a focus raises the whole question of the contribution of religion to understandings of the law. In many Islamic countries, for example, the contribution is very explicit.[12]

The other state institutions also may have important links with the religious sphere. Studies have looked at the religious motivations of legislators, for example, as well as their treatment of a wide range of issues that relate specifically and directly to religion.[13] It is true, of course, that religious outlooks may have a bearing on any or all issues on a given legislative agenda. But the impact of religion is perhaps most visible in law-making within such areas as education, the family, sexuality, and capital punishment. The same can be said of the other central apparatus of the state – the political executive of presidents and prime ministers, cabinets and councils of ministers.

Politics, however, is much more than the exercise of power within the state apparatus. Indeed, one of the problems of defining 'the state' lies precisely in the fact that power and influence over decisions is often diffused well beyond these officially authoritative institutions. As part of the play of power, agencies and individuals outside the state seek to affect the nature of the collective decisions – public policies – as they are made. Indeed, some achieve a status that can rival and even overshadow officially-designated institutions. This necessarily extends the scope and complexity of the relationship between religion and politics. It is indeed about far more than 'church and state'.

In recognition of the broader political reality, political scientists tend to speak as much, if not more, about 'the polity' or 'the political system' rather than 'the state'. As David Easton, and others, have conceived the term, it includes all those who generate 'inputs' – demands, resources and support – as well as the authorities who 'allocate', that is make and implement decisions.[14] For present purposes, these other elements may be divided into three: political parties, pressure groups, and the mass of citizens itself. What then has religion to do with them?

The relationship between religion and political parties has, in itself, been the subject of numerous inquiries. These include, *inter alia*, the religious composition of their mass base, the religious outlooks of party activists and leaders, and the religious character (or lack of it) of the party's ideology and programme.[15] Of course, such studies have achieved particular prominence in the Second World, where the ruling Marxist parties are constitutionally recognized as the leading force in society and the state itself. The key relationship in those contexts has been that between Church and party and, in particular, the policy adopted by the party towards those religious bodies.

Pressure groups have been a rich, if generally less decisive, part of the story. These are typically defined as structures, formal or informal, that try to influence public policy without (unlike most parties) seeking to become themselves the political office-holders in the state. Only in exceptional instances, most notably the military, do they come to hold the reins of power. Religious groups themselves may become institutional pressure groups promoting their particular views of issues on the current public agenda. This may take the form of lobbying the legislature, making contacts with the executive apparatus, or even going to court. It may also entail building and using links with political parties and forming alliances with other like-minded pressure groups. Not least, action may extend to the mobilization of religious adherents, the formation of religiously-inspired political movements, and the attempt to sensitize public opinion through the mass media.[16] In extreme instances, at least in the modern world, religious leaders may even actively seek office themselves. But equally, there are religious groups who seek no engagement at all in the political realm, who see it as a corrupt and corrupting arena.

At the grass roots of the pyramid of power are the mass populace. Though in many ways the least powerful in the play of power, here too a rich array of interconnections exist between the religious and the political. Perhaps the most significant act is that of voting which, at least in competitive systems, is the major means through which citizens as individuals come to participate in the play of power. Under this heading a variety of important questions are raised. To what extent, for example, are voting decisions founded upon, or influenced by, religious criteria? A classic study of western party systems revealed that religion retained a remarkable saliency in fixing voting alignments.[17] This is not to claim, however, that overtly religious issues and identifications are necessarily always at the centre of the voting decision. But it is to say that religion continues to play at least a passive role in influencing voting behaviour in many countries, being interwoven with ethnic, linguistic, racial and sometimes economic interests. To put it another way, religious groups may form moral and indeed political communities, shaping and mobilizing their members' electoral activities as they react to the candidates, parties and issues within the campaign.[18]

Mass political behaviour is by no means, of course, confined to voting, even if it is the commonest mode of expression in many countries. One other particularly significant activity is that of protest. Hence, as with voting, we might inquire as to the religious roots of this phenomenon, and indeed of even more 'extreme' activities grouped under the term 'political violence'. To the extent that religion functions as a mechanism of social control and political integration, the relationship is a negative one. A study in Britain conducted by the author, for example, found this to be the case: religious adherence generally reduced the propensity for protest.[19] However, in other milieux, it is apparent that religion can serve to promote very active rejection of government policies and personnel – as in the case of the peace movement, or abortion, for example. Furthermore, religion can be the means of focusing and intensifying alienation from an entire political regime which can lead to political violence and insurgency. This type of linkage can be found not only among liberation movements of the left but also to some degree of the extreme right.[20]

Although political actions may be the most visible imprint that citizens make in the political system, those actions reflect important underlying beliefs, values and opinions – the mass political culture. This, too, extends the relationship between politics and religion. To what extent, for example, are religious orientations linked to the national political culture and/or given subcultures? Are religious belief systems, such as they are at the mass level, systematically associated with ideological dispositions in the political realm? In general, the answer seems to be positive. In numerous countries and contexts, religion and politics do indeed connect in this way. Religion and nationalism, fundamentalism and political conservatism, and, not least, the political witness of those committed to liberation theology are all examples.[21]

From the foregoing, it is apparent that 'making collective decisions for a group of people' is a complex, multi-faceted matter. From local level to international level, and from ordinary citizen to political elite, the modern polity encompasses a wide range of elements susceptible to religious influence. But what is the character of the religious side of the equation? How might we define its basic essence (if we can) and what does this further reveal about the linkages under review?

Religion

In one usage, the term 'religion' simply specifies extant world religions – Buddhism, Judaism, Islam, Christianity and so forth. But this begs the question – what distinguishes these 'religions' from other 'isms' like fascism or Marxism, or indeed from magic and superstition? A more generic approach is called for and this sees religion as being defined in terms of one or more of three related themes said to be characteristic of religion and the religious experience: the notions of transcendence, sacredness and ultimacy.[22] Transcendence emphasizes the religious as being associated with a supernatural reality, in the sense that within the mundane world *homo religiosus* 'encounters powers that are impressively greater than (transcendent to) his own'.[23] In this way, the religious order is seen as having a pre-eminent claim over the believer and the social order of everyday life. This in turn extends to an influence over the political domain when collective decisions concerning that social order are being made.

Sacredness is a second theme, emphasized by Durkheim in his now classic distinction between the sacred and the profane:

> Sacred things are those which the interdictions protect and isolate; profane things, those to which these interdictions are applied and which must remain at a distance from the first. Religious beliefs are the representations which express the nature of sacred things and the relations which they sustain, either with each other or with profane things.[24]

This has been a very influential approach. For example, Berger argues that 'religion' should be demarcated as those systems of belief that invoke a 'sacred canopy'.[25] Paden also suggests that 'the term religion is generally used to mean a system of language and practice that organizes the world in terms of what is deemed sacred.'[26] To the extent that the sacred is used by people 'as the organizing points of reference for defining their worlds and lives',[27] this too entails a relationship with the social and political domain. The feeling of extraordinary power evoked by 'the sacred' compels the believer to try to order 'the profane' in a manner consistent with those greater imperatives.

The same might also be said of the idea of religion as ultimacy. This has been propounded in terms of religion as articulating the core values of society which address the very foundations of meaning through a sense of superordinate purpose and significance. As Bellah puts it, religion 'relate[s] man to the ultimate conditions of his existence'.[28] In that way, religion as ultimacy also commands the believer; it sets all other aspects of human existence beneath, and in the context of, that ultimate concern. Politics, once more, is made relative to, and is validated by, religion. But religion, by its very claims, also becomes subject to the exercise of political power.

How this dialectic is worked out varies greatly from religion to religion, and even with given religious belief systems, widely different 'political theologies' are espoused. In a classic study of the problem, Niebuhr speaks of a dialogue between Christ and culture, the sacred and the profane which 'proceeds with denials and affirmations, reconstructions, compromises, and new denials'.[29] And as if to underscore these ambiguities, he then goes on to outline as many as five different answers as to how Christ and culture come together. But, important as these themes are in understanding how religion and politics fit together from a religious viewpoint, there is clearly more to it than that. Though belief may be at the core of the religious experience there are other aspects which need to be brought into view in order to grasp the varied ways in which religion reaches out to the political realm.

First, religion is also a matter of personal experience and, not least, of action or practice.[30] This adds visibility to religion, in terms of rituals, such as prayer and religious ceremony, a visibility which can become deeply enmeshed with the political realm. One thinks, for example, of the symbolic religious anointing of the British monarch at the coronation, or the use of prayer to invoke the support of the deity in connection with some governmental policy or the interweaving of political and religious ideas in the American pledge of allegiance.

In many instances, religious ceremonies necessitate the designation of particular places or buildings as sacred arenas in which these activities are conducted – temples, mosques, shrines, synagogues, churches and the like. Indeed, in popular culture, some equate 'religion' with those physical appurtenances. Here too, points of contact with politics arise, as the conflicts surrounding the Golden Temple at Amritsar and the Babri Mosque in Ayodhya, Uttar Pradesh (both in India), or the Ka'bah at Mecca, in Saudi Arabia, all attest. Albeit in different ways, the same might be said of Westminster Abbey and St Paul's Cathedral in England.[31]

As these sacred places suggest, religion does not simply have meaning at the individual level, it also, like politics, has a corporate or communal character. This, in turn, presents another level at which religion and politics engage. Here it is a matter of group solidarities. It is also a matter, in many contexts, of inter-group tension and conflict. Both solidarities and conflicts may have a religious element, revolving around shared or discrepant images of the sacred. But in addition they also may acquire other elements, either cultural (ethnicity, language, race, etc.) or economic (wealth, occupation, class, etc.), or a complex mixture of both. That is why, so often, inter-group 'religious' cleavages are complex divisions to analyse. Once more, it points to the need to set the relationship between religion and politics in its proper social, cultural and economic context.

To speak of a community of believers is to imply, more often than not, some role differentiation, between rank and file believers and those who take some leadership position, as priest or prophet, pastor or spiritual guide. In Catholicism, role differentiation has resulted in a highly elaborated ecclesiastical institution with numerous levels of authority and a multiplicity of component agencies, both intra-national and international. In Hinduism, on the other hand, there is very little role differentiation, and hence very little of what could be called a specifically Hindu religious institution. But where institutionalization takes place, the relationship between those religious elements and the political world tends to become very diverse and varied. The Roman Catholic Church, despite its centralization of authority in the person of the Pope and the organs of the Vatican state, is a case in point.

Clearly therefore, to bring together the political and religious spheres in all their varied aspects and then to discern significant patterns and trends within 'the modern world' is not a simple task. But, in attempting it two final points are perhaps worth emphasizing. First, there is something of a distinction to be drawn between looking at the relationship in terms of the impact of religion on politics, and that of politics on religion. In so far as we are concerned with the way in which power is exercised in society, then the relationship tends to be focused on how religious believers, leaders and institutions influence the play of power. But, in all contexts, and not least the Second World, it is also a matter of how political authority treats religion. Both causal directions need to be held in view.

The second and perhaps more fundamental point is that these

various linkages change their general character over time. In other words, they have a dynamic aspect, an evolutionary pattern. It is to this important topic that we now briefly turn.

PATTERNS OF CHANGE

In the preceding pages, the tacit assumption has been made that religion and politics constitute at least analytically distinct spheres of meaning and action. In traditional cultures, however, this was in practice generally not the case. (It is only with modernization and its associated process of secularization that religion became distinguishable from politics. As a result, in those societies less touched by modernization, religion and politics still retain a close, overlapping relationship.) Indeed, some religions and religious outlooks specifically try to deny the compartmentalization of religion and politics, a dualism which is common in modern western cultures.[32] It is therefore appropriate to consider first these earlier arrangements which still provide a significant context in many nation-states today.

The traditional, or pre-modern, relationship between religion and politics was one in which the two were closely integrated, one with the other. Religious beliefs and practices underpinned and entered into the heart of the political process, supporting and sustaining the exercise of power. But, by this very token, political concerns also extended throughout the religious sphere. The two formed, in effect, one co-terminous set of beliefs and actions. It was a system in which social and political life was touched at virtually all points by religious considerations. Smith characterized it in the following terms:

> The sacred permeates the principal social institutions. Laws are divine commands, based on sacred texts or otherwise revealed to man. Where social classes and orders are ranked hierarchically, this pyramidal social system is divinely ordained. All education is religious in content and transmitted by religious specialists. Divine regulations govern economic behavior and ecclesiastical centers frequently wield extensive economic power. Above all, government is sacral. Religion and government, the two major society-wide institutions of social control, form an integrated religiopolitical system.[33]

This pattern applied to Buddhist, Hindu and Islamic societies. In the medieval west it was a basic feature wherever the Roman Catholic

Church was in the ascendancy. It was also normative among tribal societies and within ancient civilizations.

There were, however, some variations around this basic pattern, depending upon the particular institutional features of given religions and polities. The key factor lay in whether religious authority and political authority was exercised by the *same* leadership or by complementary but *distinct* leaders. The former, 'the organic model', is more characteristic of historic patterns within Islamic and Hindu cultures. By contrast, a 'church model', representing distinct religious and political structures, is more typical of earlier arrangements involving Christian and Buddhist institutions.[34] Where such differentiation occurred, a greater variety of power relationships between religious and political structures became possible. In some societies, integration was achieved on the basis of the political authorities extending control over the religious institutions. (The eastern Orthodox societies discussed in Chapter 3 represent such a pre-modern tradition.) In others, the religious leadership created a theocratic form of decision-making. In yet others both co-existed in a pattern of symbiotic parity. (Here, the history of the Papacy in relation to the Holy Roman Empire is instructive.)

In the modern world, however, the situation is now generally much changed. The detailed arrangements of the integrated pattern are mainly of significance as an historical and cultural legacy. But their echoes can be found in contemporary patterns and assumptions. In Britain, for example, the monarch is still technically both head of state – the political realm – and Supreme Governor of the Established Church of England. Many still view Christianity (and especially Anglicanism) as an important normative ingredient of social and political identity. The pattern can also be seen vestigially in the Shinto rites conducted at the funeral of Emperor Hirohito, stripped by the US government of his status as a near-deity only at the conclusion of the Second World War. And in relatively traditional Nepal, King Birendra is still seen as an incarnation of the Hindu God Vishnu by the more traditional sectors of society.

One of the few remaining important examples of the pattern is, perhaps, Saudi Arabia. The Saudi state itself came into being on the basis of an eighteenth-century alliance between a political leader, Muhammad ibn Saud, and a muslim activist, Muhammad ibn Abd al-Wahhab. Present-day Saudi Arabia retains the centrality of this religious element in its state affairs: there is no secular constitution and few secular laws. Furthermore, the basis of the legal system is the *shari'ah*, the 'Straight Path' of muslim life, derived from the *Qur'an* and the life of the Prophet Muhammad.[35] The Saudi (and Nepali) case is, however, exceptional. Over the last century, and especially in the period since 1945, the substance of such arrangements has in most cases been drained away.

The key process that has contributed to this end is secularization, seen by Smith as 'the most fundamental structural and ideological change in the process of political development.'[36] As a concept, however, it is somewhat controversial, being viewed by some as anti-religious, rather than neutral, in nature.[37] Equally problematic is the variety of specific meanings given to the term by different authors.[38] Yet others object to secularization being construed as a strictly linear, uni-directional process. Nevertheless, despite these problems, it does point to a seemingly general trend whereby societies around the world have gradually moved away from being focused around the sacred and the numinous. In that sense it does indicate a certain loss of power and authority of religion in society and, in consequence, indicates a slow transformation in the basic relationship between politics and religion.

Some sense of the nature of the changes this process entails can be seen if we distinguish some of its constituent parts. These include the following:

1   Constitutional secularization: the process whereby the official character and goals of the state cease to be defined in religious terms, or whereby religious institutions cease to be given special constitutional recognition and support.
2   Policy secularization: the process whereby the state ceases to regulate society on the basis of religious criteria, and expands the policy domains and service provisions of the state into areas previously the reserve of the religious sphere.
3   Institutional secularization: the process whereby religious structures lose their political saliency and influence as pressure groups, parties, and movements.
4   Agenda secularization: the process whereby issues, needs and problems deemed relevant to the political process cease to have overtly religious content, and whereby solutions developed to resolve those issues are no longer constructed on the basis of religious principles.
5   Ideological secularization: the process whereby the basic values

and belief-systems used to evaluate the political realm and to give it meaning cease to be couched in religious terms.

It is, in short, a multi-faceted process whereby the political and the religious partially disengage from each other. This in turn creates tensions as political power is reformulated in new terms and the religious domain constructs new and somewhat different relationships with society and the state.

Such tensions are further heightened by other developmental processes. For example, the politicization of the mass population through the extension of the suffrage presents novel challenges to both religious and political leaders. The growth of the mass media also disturbs traditional patterns of religious and political communication. The state, and even religious leaders, also face far-reaching problems of social and economic development which undermine established power relationships.

Some idea of what these general changes entail can be seen in three models proposed by Medhurst and representing different stages in the modification of the integrated polity.[39] The first he calls 'the confessional polity'. Political leaders continue to legitimate their rule in religious terms but do so, in an increasingly pluralistic context, by giving official preference to one religious option. Equally, religious leaders mobilize support against threats to their communal hegemony. The intended result is to hold back the tide of pluralism so as to preserve as much as possible of the traditional monistic pattern that served the established political and religious elite alike. Colombia and Iran, and in some respects Ireland too, are offered as contemporary examples.

A further pattern arises when secularization removes religion as the major basis of the political system. The state comes to view the forces of religion as just one group among many contesting for power. It therefore becomes in Medhurst's words, a 'religiously neutral polity'. It should be emphasized, however, that secularization does not *eliminate* religion from the political realm. It is more a matter of religious communities finding themselves in a more politically pluralistic context in which their particular agendas and claims are given less recognition. It is a context, therefore, in which those religious bodies turn, where possible and appropriate, to parties and/or pressure groups to defend and promote their interests.

So far, the impression may have been given of an inevitable one-way movement towards an age in which religion and politics will cease to have any effective claims over each other. However, history does not seem to support this. Without suggesting that religion will

ever return to the centrality accorded it in pre-modern eras, there
seems good reason to believe that the relationship between religion
and politics has not and will not become moribund. For example,
Second World polities have been far from indifferent to the political
claims of religion. This is encapsulated in Medhurst's final model,
dubbed 'the anti-religious polity'. This is in some respects the mirror
image of the traditional integrated arrangement – the active attempt
by the state to eliminate any religious presence within the political
arena. In most cases (notably in Albania, referred to at the beginning
of the chapter), moreover, the state tried to eradicate any visible
public religious presence whatsoever. Society and polity were to
be reconstructed on an entirely secular ideological basis of Marxist
materialism without any religious institutions, symbols, or practices.
Yet these various attempts to eliminate religion have failed. Indeed,
in some instances, political oppression seems to have the opposite of
the intended effect.

Even in liberal-democratic polities, it is by no means clear that
religion and politics continue to lose mutual relevance. Hadden and
Shupe go so far as to propose a cyclical theory of secularization
in which the process of removing the sense of the sacred from
society contains the seeds whereby religion is eventually revived
and revitalized.[40] This-worldly, secularized answers to the meaning
and purpose in life, they imply, are alienating and unsatisfying.
Hence, they see religious ideas finding fresh relevance and power,
albeit possibly within new structures and patterns of belief: a kind
of post-secular religion for a post-secular society.[41]

Whether these ideas stand up to the test of history remains to be
seen. Some forms of religion do continue to decline and the forward
movement in the secularization of political life can be detected
in many places. But, at the same time, there are also signs of
growth and revival, a resurgence that renews and reinvigorates the
religio-political relationship.[42] Islamic fundamentalism, reacting to
overly-secularized western values, is a case in point. As I write,
Sheikh Abassi Madani's Islamic Salvation Front has achieved a
decisive electoral victory over the ruling National Liberation Front in
Algeria. In many Second World countries, secular Marxism has been
decisively rejected. And in the First World, new religious movements
are creating novel but potentially significant political pressures. In
all these ways, therefore, we must indeed retain a healthy scepticism

about the rapid and early demise of the relationship between religion and politics. Let history be the judge of that while we get on with the study of what is clearly a far from comatose subject.

THE REGIONAL AND COUNTRY STUDIES

The first contribution, Chapter 2 by John Madeley, discusses religion and politics in Western Europe, with particular emphasis upon its most populous constituent nation-state, the Federal Republic of Germany. As he notes, we are essentially speaking here of a relationship between Latin Christianity and liberal democracy. We are also speaking of a relationship, therefore, in which the religion takes an incarnational and Church-like form: God intervening in history and society through a distinct set of ecclesiastical institutions.

Those institutions, however, vary in the different countries of the region. In some, Roman Catholicism is in the ascendancy, in others the Protestant Church, in yet others there is a rough balance. This latter situation was true of West Germany, for example, which comprised 42.9 per cent Roman Catholic and 42.6 per cent Evangelical Protestant (mainly Lutheran) adherents. After unification with East Germany, a traditionally Protestant area, in October 1990, however, the numerical balance once more slightly favours Protestant denominations by approximately 42 per cent to 35 per cent. But the political dangers such an ascendancy once posed under the Second Reich (1871–1918) no longer obtain. In part, this is because in Germany, as elsewhere in Western Europe, there has been a slow diminution of active church commitments. This process has reduced but by no means eliminated the political role of religion, which remains, in Madeley's view, a diminished but still significant force.

The nature of that impact is detailed at many levels. There are constitutional and legal arrangements, reminiscent of the integrated polity, that continue to tie Church and state together in varying degrees. One German manifestation of this is the Church tax whereby the state collects what are in effect membership subscriptions and distributes the proceeds to the relevant denominations. There is also a rich array of pressure groups and, above all, political parties who represent an evolution toward a confessional, and now more religiously neutral, polity. These groups, together with the Churches themselves, make contributions to a range of more traditional public issues, such as educational policy, and legislation on abortion and divorce. The continuing vitality of the religious input is further emphasized by the involvement of Christian activists in the 'new politics' of environmentalism, disarmament and aid for the Third World. Not least, in Germany, the Churches and their leaders played a role in assisting the process of national re-unification.

In Eastern Europe and the Soviet Union, the dominant pattern for most of the time since 1945 has been one of the 'anti-religious polity'. As Sabrina Ramet points out in Chapter 3, the state's policy has been to privatize religion so that it makes no contribution to the public realm. In the Soviet Union, for example, the Council for Affairs of Religions ensured that religious activities were highly restricted. A majority of churches were closed and all social, educational and charitable works were prohibited. In Albania, perhaps the most extreme case, religion was officially abolished: the 1976 constitution eliminated all religious organizations and the ruling party forbad all public religious rituals.

The ascent to power of Mikhail Gorbachev has, however, begun to transform the relationship between religion and politics in the Soviet Union. During the celebration of the Christian Millennium in Russia in 1988, Gorbachev met with the Holy Synod of the Russian Orthodox Church and began the process of applying *glasnost* and *perestroika* to the religious domain. This culminated in a new law on 'Freedom of Conscience and Religious Organizations' approved by the Supreme Soviet in 1990. The law, if fully implemented, will end state funding for atheistic propaganda, allow the establishment of Sunday schools and other proselytizing activities, and even permit religious services to be held within the armed forces. In short, it would confirm the changed posture of the state towards religious organizations in the Soviet Union which so far has only appeared in more ad hoc and informal ways. In Eastern Europe, equally drastic changes have occurred. The arrangements of atheistic state-socialism have largely collapsed. In Poland, for example, the Roman Catholic Church has regained its full legal status, removed forty years before. Even in Albania, although as yet only partly untouched by democratization, changes in the attitude of the state towards religion can be detected. In short, the age of the anti-religious polity is largely dead in Europe. A new age, in which religion can once again operate as a relatively legitimate political force, seems to have dawned.

In the Middle East, as Glenn Perry indicates in Chapter 4, politics and religion have long formed a close, intimate relationship at every level. Indeed, for Islam, there is ideally no sphere of religion separable from the political, no 'Islamic Church', only the state itself. In practice, however, modernization, nationalism and westernization, have created a situation within which religion has had both a somewhat autonomous status and a complex, and at times very violent, relationship with the political arena. This is not least true of Egypt and Iran, the two countries given particular attention in Perry's essay.

Thus, in Egypt, one finds religiously inspired conflicts at the most fundamental level. The 1952 Revolution itself, which formed the present state arrangements, was in part inspired by the Islamic ideology of the Muslim Brothers. However, the relationship between the state authorities and the Muslim Brothers has always been a traumatic and full of conflict. Leaders of the Muslim Brothers have been imprisoned and executed; and militant Islamic factions were responsible for assassinating political leaders, including President Sadat. On the other hand, Islamic forces have also entered the 'conventional' political arena in the shape of electoral alliances with political parties, alliances that have found considerable success. In this way, religious perspectives on such policy areas as the family, education and the law have achieved some political resonance. Meanwhile, however, fundamentalist groups continue to rail against what they see as the apostate political leadership of the country.

Iran, of course, has been the epicentre of such radical ideas. There, the forces of a militant Islam collided with the modernizing and westernizing regime of Reza Shah and ended in the 1979 Revolution. Since the advent of a quasi-theocratic Islamic Republic, religion has been at the very centre of Iranian political life. Religious parties and authorities (scholar–jurists) have dominated the national political leadership. Equally, religious differences between moderates and hard-liners over the handling of the government's agenda are a key element in the struggle for political power. As the events surrounding the publication of *The Satanic Verses* by Salman Rushdie show, religion continues to play a very powerful role in Iranian politics and elsewhere in the Islamic world.

The same is also true of India, as is revealed in Ian Talbot's discussion in Chapter 5. Although officially a secular state, secularization has *not* led to the marginalization of religion in Indian political life. On the contrary, both before, during and after Independence, religion has intruded into the political domain at every level. It has been the basis of Indian communalism, and communalism has in turn been an important contributor to the formation of political loyalties. The result has been a public arena in which, if anything, religion has gained in importance in recent years rather than declined. Radical Hindu groups, such as the Rashtriya Swayamsevak Sangh (involved in the assassination of Mahatma Ghandi) and Vishwa Hindu Parishad, exercise considerable influence at the mass level. Issues, such as the control of religious sites, the regulation of religious rituals (notably *sati* and *cunari*) and the application of religious laws have produced controversy and violence. Equally, militant muslims in Kashmir have agitated for its Islamicization while similar experiences have also marked the Sikh community in the Punjab. Not least, the Indian government of V.P. Singh was itself brought down in 1990 over a dispute between rival religious communities. All in all, Indian politics will no doubt continue to be heavily influenced by religion as the country moves forward through the myriad problems of social, economic and cultural change.

As Adrian Hastings demonstrates in Chapter 6, Southern Africa is also an arena in which religion and politics have entered into relatively close relationships. In Zimbabwe, one of three country studies included, the Anglican Church formed what Hastings calls an unofficial or quasi-establishment for Rhodesians. This, however, ended when Robert Mugabe came to power since when the Churches have enjoyed a varying but never particularly influential position. In Mozambique, a 1940 Concordat had given the Roman Catholic Church an even more clearly privileged position. But it too suffered a loss of political authority when the Marxist Frelimo movement came to power. Indeed, the new rulers' anti-religious policy, compounded by the country's involvement in an internal civil war, have resulted in a situation in which the Churches' very existence has been threatened.

The most significant regional power, however, is South Africa which receives Hastings' greatest attention. The story since 1945 is in part one of a close confessional association between the Dutch Reformed Church, or more accurately the *Nederduitse Gereformeerde Kerk* (NGK), and the white Afrikaner Nationalist ascendancy. But it is also a story of Churches organizing opposition to a regime committed to racial apartheid. Religious leaders, like Dr Allan Boesak of the reformist *Nederduitse Gereformeede Sendingkerk* and Archbishop Desmond Tutu, Primate of the Anglican Church in South Africa, have been leaders in confronting the Nationalist government. On the other hand, right-wing Church-based movements like the *Afrikaanse Protestante Kerk* (a breakaway from the NGK) and the Gospel Defence League, continue to support political hard-liners seeking to prevent further erosion of apartheid arrangements. In these ways, varied Christian understandings about human rights and the character of society have made a distinctive, though not necessarily decisive contribution to public debate.

Since the demise of President Botha, and his replacement by a more moderate reformist President, F.W. de Klerk, and above all since the release of Nelson Mandela and the unbanning of the African National Congress, the central oppositional role of the South African Council of Churches has somewhat diminished. At the same time, there is no doubt that in the future, as further pressure builds towards a truly non-racial and democratic state, the Churches will continue to exercise a political voice that will be heard both at home and abroad.

Conflicting pressures of political stability and social justice, and Churches divided within and among themselves, are also a hallmark of the contemporary relationship between religion and politics in Latin America, which Kenneth Medhurst describes in Chapter 7. The traditional pattern, common to the region, is still to be found best exemplified in Colombia, a pattern recalling the Christendom model of the medieval Church.[43] Officially, the Roman Catholic Church claims the adherence of the vast majority of the Colombian population. That salient social position is reflected in arrangements with the state whereby the Church is given special recognition through a Concordat (originally signed in 1887) in return for its support of established social, economic and political elites. In recent times, however, the relationship has been strained by modernizing trends which have undermined both state and religious authority. Further pressure has been created by powerful drug cartels who have injected a degree of violence into public life to which neither the Church nor the state have yet responded effectively.

In contrast to Colombia, the impact of modernization in trans-forming Church outlooks and political linkages are fully evident in Brazil. Medhurst stresses the significance of the Second Conference of Latin American Bishops, held at Medellín in 1968, in focusing Church attention on the powerful forces of change operating in the region, and the need seriously to address the socio-political critique presented by exponents of liberation theology. This provides the central theme for the dilemmas faced by the Church in balancing a high political profile and oppositional role with a more traditional, quiescent and apolitical posture. It also provides the context for the aggressive response of authoritarian governments in Brazil, Chile and elsewhere.

These tensions and conflicts are raised to particularly acute levels in El Salvador, the Central American country examined by Jennifer Pierce in Chapter 8. The traditional role of the Church was as a passive agency of social control, building upon yet earlier pre-Christian Mayan arrangements. Politics, as Pierce notes, was equated with opposition to the state, not support for it – a familiar theme in other countries. But in El Salvador over the last fifteen years that is the form the Church contribution has taken. In the decade and a half, Pierce documents a radicalization of Church leaders face to face with a repressive and reactionary regime; a regime that sponsored death squads which executed priests, lay religious activists and other opposition figures. It also led, in March 1980, to the assassination of the Archbishop of San Salvador, Monseñor Oscar Romero. Since 1981, a guerilla movement has further polarized the political situation and raised tensions to even greater heights. Romero's successor, Monseñor Rivera y Damas, has tried to play a conciliatory role between guerillas and government, not always with success. Indeed, the killings of Church clerics have continued and debates about the proper role of religious groups in this strife-torn situation has divided both Church and polity alike. The result is that both Roman Catholic and Protestant Churches will no doubt continue to play a central part in the political life of El Salvador.[44]

We turn finally to Chapter 9 by Kenneth Wald on Canada and, principally, the United States. As he notes, the relationship between religion and politics in the two countries is not the same, although both draw substantially upon a European, and therefore Christian, heritage. In Canada, the fundamental cultural linkage of religion is between francophone Quebec and the Roman Catholic Church, and between anglophone Ontario and the Anglican Church. Both Churches serve as badges of ethnic identity in those two most populous provinces of the Canadian federation. Politically, there are also links between religious communities and national political parties, but secularization has weakened the connection very considerably. Secularization has also reduced the standing of the Roman Catholic Church in Quebec politics. However, there remain many issues on the Canadian political agenda to whose resolution religious organizations make some contribution. These range from traditional concerns such as abortion, divorce and capital punishment to free trade and the looming constitutional crisis over Quebec's status as a distinct society.

In the United States too, as Wald argues, secularization may have modified, but has certainly not greatly diminished the relevance of religious factors to political struggles. He suggests in fact that the American experience neither proves nor disproves the claims of secularization. Better, he concludes, to speak simply in terms of change. In that context, American religion has become more fragmented and voluntaristic. Equally, Church denominations have experienced contradictory growth paths: 'mainline' Churches have substantially declined while more conservative evangelical denominations have grown. Politically the key religious cleavage is not between Protestants and non-Protestants but between theological conservatives and liberals.

Indeed, within the polity, a clear religious imprint can be detected in every facet. At the level of the political culture, religious beliefs make a contribution; at the constitutional level, issues of Church and state still remain contentious. And within the arenas of pressure group politics, electoral politics and policy-making, religion takes a substantial part. Roman Catholic bishops assert their views on nuclear weapons and the rights of the unborn; powerful Jewish groups lobby on behalf of Israel; born-again evangelicals turn 'liberal' into a term of political derision. All of which reinforces the view that if 'events in the past three years cap an extraordinary decade of religious – political developments'[45] in that arguably most modern and developed of societies, the United States of America, then indeed the study of religion and politics has a rosy future the world over.

NOTES

It should be noted that many of the citations in the notes below, drawn particularly from the American and British experience, are only illustrative of the scope and character of the relationship between religion and politics. For more detailed references to many of the themes alluded to, see the notes appended to each of the substantive chapters.

1   See *The Times*, (London) 30 April 1990.
2   D. Miller (1987), 'Politics', in *The Blackwell Encyclopaedia of Political Thought*, Oxford: Blackwell, p.30. A more concise definition along the same lines is offered by R. Hague and M. Harrop, who simply say that

'politics is the process by which groups make collective decisions'. See their *Comparative Government and Politics: An Introduction* (1987) 2nd edn, Basingstoke: Macmillan Education, p.3.

3 See, for example, the study of the Church of England's internal patterns of decision-making by K.N. Medhurst and G. Moyser (1988), *Church and Politics in a Secular Age*, Oxford: Clarendon Press, especially Part 2.

4 Many of the studies of local politics find a place for the role of religion. See, for example, the classic American study by K. W. Underwood (1957), *Protestant and Catholic: Religious and Social Interaction in an Industrial Community*, Boston: The Beacon Press. In Britain, and from a church point of view, see *Faith in the City: A Call for Action by Church and Nation* (1985), London: Church House Publishing and G. Wheale (1985), 'The parish and politics' in G. Moyser (ed.), *Church and Politics Today*, Edinburgh: T & T Clark, Ch. 7.

5 See, for example, the study of Quebec, an important and 'distinct society' in Canada, by G.F. Rutan (1989), 'A field burnt over: The Catholic Church in the contemporary Quebec polity', American Political Science Association Annual Meeting, Atlanta, Georgia. Among regional studies in the United Kingdom, see particularly E. Moxon–Browne (1983), *Nation, Class and Creed in Northern Ireland*, Aldershot: Gower and A. Elliot and D.B. Forrester (1988), *The Scottish Churches and the Political Process Today*, Edinburgh: Centre for Theology and Public Issues.

6 D. Robertson (1986), *The Penguin Dictionary of Politics*, Harmondsworth: Penguin Books, p.223.

7 Studies of religion and nationalism are legion. See, for example, the historical and modern studies in S. Mews (ed.) (1982), *Religion and National Identity*, Oxford: Blackwell. See also P. Ramet (ed.) (1989), *Religion and Nationalism in Soviet and East European Politics*, Durham: Duke University Press, F.R. von de Mehden (1963), *Religion and Nationalism in Southeast Asia*, Madison: University of Wisconsin Press, and P.H. Merkl and N. Smart (1983), *Religion and Politics in the Modern World*, New York: New York University Press. For a recent study of religious nationalism in the United States, see D. Chidester (1988), *Patterns of Power: Religion and Politics in American Culture*, Englewood Cliffs, NJ: Prentice Hall, Ch. 3. On Britain, see D. Jenkins (1975), *The British: Their Identity and their Religion*, London: SCM. Press.

8 See, for example, E.O. Hanson (1987), *The Catholic Church and World Politics* Princeton: Princeton University Press. For a study of religion in foreign policy see A. Geyer (1990), *Christianity and the Superpowers; Religion, Politics and History in US–USSR Relations*, Nashville: Abingdon Press; for international relations, see, for example, J.K. Roth (1987), 'The prices of peace: Religion and politics in Western Europe', in R.L. Rubenstein (ed.), *Spirit Matters: The Worldwide Impact of Religion on Contemporary Politics*, New York: Paragon House, Ch. 4. Two studies of the Middle East are K.C. Ellis (1987), *The Vatican, Islam and the Middle East*, Syracuse: Syracuse University Press and A.R. Taylor (1988), *The Islamic Question in Middle East Politics*, Boulder, Co: Westview Press.

9 Robertson, op. cit., p.307.

10 For a historical review, see T.J. Curry (1986), *The First Freedoms: Church and State in America to the Passage of the First Amendment*, Oxford: Oxford University Press; see also F.J. Sorauf (1976), *The Wall of Separation: The Constitutional Politics of Church and State*, Princeton: Princeton University Press and, for a recent essay, A.J. Reichley (1989), 'Religion and the constitution', in C.W. Dunn (ed.), *Religion in American Politics*, Washington DC: CQ Press Ch. 1. For an English case study, see A. Dyson, '"Little else but the name" – reflections on four church and state reports' and P. Cornwell, 'The Church of England and the state: Changing constitutional links in historical perspective', in Moyser, op. cit., Chs 12 and 2.

11 For a recent report, see R.S. Alley (ed.) (1988), *The Supreme Court on Church and State*, Oxford: Oxford University Press.

12 See for example, J.L. Esposito (1987), *Islam and Politics*, 2nd edn, Syracuse: Syracuse University Press, and I. Goldziher (1981), *Introduction to Islamic Theology and Law*, trans. by A. and R. Hamori, Princeton: Princeton University Press. For a western study, see St.J.A. Robilliard (1984), *Religion and the Law: Religious Liberty in Modern English Law*, Manchester: Manchester University Press.

13 See, for example, P.L. Benson and D.L. Williams (1986), *Religion on Capitol Hill: Myths and Realities*, Oxford: Oxford University Press; C. Davies (1989), 'Religion, politics and the "permissive" legislation', in P. Badham (ed.), *Religion, State, and Society in Modern Britain*, Lewiston, NY: Edwin Mellen Press, Ch. 18 and P.G. Richards (1970), *Parliament and Conscience*, London: George Allen & Unwin.

14 Easton's early formulation of the general idea of a 'political system' is set out in D. Easton (1953), *The Political System*, New York: Knopf. See also his subsequent volume, *A Framework for Political Analysis* (1965), Englewood Cliffs, NJ: Prentice-Hall. A short version is available in his article 'An approach to an analysis of political systems' (1957), *World Politics*, vol. 9, pp.81–94.

15 See, for example, D.E. Smith (ed.) (1971), *Religion, Politics and Social Change in the Third World*, New York: Free Press, section 6. The Roman Catholic Church has been noteworthy for its use of parties to exert influence and defend its interests. See R.E.M. Irving (1979), *The Christian Democratic Parties of Western Europe*, London: Royal Institute of International Affairs and George Allen & Unwin and J.H. Whyte (1981), *Catholics in Western Democracies: A Study in Political Behaviour*, Dublin: Gill and Macmillan.

16 Pressure group studies are legion. See, for example, A.D. Hertzke (1988), *Representing God in Washington: The Role of Religious Lobbies in the American Polity*, Knoxville, TN: University of Tennessee Press and L. Sandon, 'Who speaks for America? Religious groups and public policy formation' in Rubenstein, op. cit., Ch. 2. On England, see Moyser, op. cit. Part 2.

17 See R. Rose and D. Urwin (1969), 'Social cohesion, political parties and strains in regimes', *Comparative Political Studies*, vol. 2, no. 1, pp.7–67. See also A. Lijphart (1979), 'Religious vs linguistic vs class voting: The "crucial experiment" of comparing Belgium, Canada, South Africa and

Switzerland', *American Political Science Review*, vol. 73, no. 2, pp.442–58 and K. Janda (1988), 'Region and religion as factors underlying support for national political parties', 14th World Congress of the International Political Science Association, Washington, DC.

18   See K.D. Wald, D.E. Owen and S.S Hill (1988), 'Churches as political communities', *American Political Science Review*, vol. 82, no. 2, pp.531–48; D. Knoke (1974), 'Religion, stratification, and politics: America in the 1960s', *American Journal of Political Science*, vol. 18, no. 2, pp.331–46; and K.D. Wald, 'Assessing the religious factor in electoral behavior', in Dunn, op. cit., Ch. 9. For a case study, see P. Converse (1966), 'Religion and politics: The 1960 Election', in A. Campbell, P. Converse, W. Miller and D. Stokes, *Elections and the Political Order*, New York: Wiley, Ch. 6. On Britain, see J.M. Bochel and D.T. Denver (1970), 'Religion and voting: A critical review and a new analysis', *Political Studies*, vol. 18, no. 2, pp.205–19; W.T. Miller and G. Raab (1977), 'The religious alignment at English elections between 1918 and 1970', *Political Studies*, vol. 25, no. 2, pp.227–51; and K.D. Wald (1983), *Crosses on the ballot: Patterns of British voter alignment since 1885*, Princeton: Princeton University Press.

19   See G. Moyser (1989), 'In Caesar's service? Religion and political involvement in Britain', in Badham, op. cit., Ch. 19. See also S. Barnes, M. Kaase, *et al.* (1979), *Political Action: Mass Participation in Five Western Democracies*, Beverly Hills: Sage, pp.118–9.

20   See, for example, A. Kee (1986), *Domination or Liberation: The Place of Religion in Social Conflict*, London: SCM Press.

21   See, for example, A. Kee, ibid. For an empirical study, see Medhurst and Moyser, op. cit., Ch. 11. See also D. Chidester, *op. cit.*, especially Part 1, and K.D. Wald, *Religion and Politics in the United States* (1987), New York: St. Martin's Press, Ch. 3

22   See W.G. Comstock *et al.* (eds) (1971), *Religion and Man: An Introduction*, New York: Harper and Row, pp.21–4.

23   ibid, p.25. See also, R. Robertson (1970), *The Sociological Interpretation of Religion*, Oxford: Blackwell.

24   Quoted in Comstock, *op. cit.*, p.21.

25   See P. Berger (1969), *The Sacred Canopy*, Garden City, NY; Doubleday.

26   See W.E. Paden (1988), *Religious Worlds: The Comparative Study of Religion*, Boston: Beacon Press, p.10.

27   ibid., p.11.

28   Quoted in Paden, ibid, p.11. See also R. Bellah (1969), 'Transcendence in contemporary piety', in D. Cutler, *The Religious Situation*, Boston, MA: Beacon Press.

29   See H.R. Niebuhr (1951), *Christ and Culture*, New York: Harper and Row, p.39. For a general introduction to the field of political theology, see D.B. Forrester (1988), *Theology and Politics*, Oxford: Blackwell. See also G. Tinder (1989), *The Political Meaning of Christianity: An Interpretation*, Baton Rouge, LA: Louisiana State University Press.

30   See C.Y. Glock and R. Stark (1965), *Religion and Society in Tension*, Chicago, IL: Rand McNally, Ch. 3. See also M. Argyle and B. Beit-Hallahmi (1975), *The Social Psychology of Religion*, London: Routledge &

Kegan Paul.

31 Westminster Abbey is, of course, the site of British coronations. St Paul's Cathedral was also the occasion of a political dispute between the Church of England and the Government over the conduct of a religious service to mark the end of the conflict with Argentina over the Falkland Islands in 1982. For details, see H. Montefiore (1990), *Christianity and Politics*, London: Macmillan, Appendix 2, pp.91–6.

32 See R. Panikkar (1983), 'Religion or politics: The western dilemma', in Merkl and Smart, op. cit., Ch. 3.

33 See D.E. Smith (1970), *Religion and Political Development*, Boston, MA: Little, Brown, p.6.

34 ibid., pp.7–8.

35 On Saudi Arabia, see A. Al-Yassini (1985), *Religion and State in the Kingdom of Saudi Arabia*, Boulder, co: Westview Press. See also Esposito, op. cit., pp.100–11.

36 Smith, op. cit., p.2.

37 See D. A. Martin (1969), *The Religious and the Secular*, London: Routledge & Kegan Paul, p.9.

38 See M. Hill (1973), *A Sociology of Religion*, London: Heinemann, Ch. 11. See also K. Dobbelaere (1981), 'Secularization: A multi-dimensional concept', *Current Sociology*, vol. 29, no. 1, especially, pp.11–2.

39 See K. Medhurst (1981), 'Religion and politics: A typology', *Scottish Journal of Religious Studies*, vol. 2, no. 2, pp.115–34.

40 See J. K. Hadden and A. Shupe (1986), *Prophetic Religious and Politics: Religion and the Political Order*, vol. 1, New York: Paragon House, p.xv.

41 See also R. Falk (1988), 'Religion and politics: Verging on the postmodern', Occasional Paper No. 4, City University of New York, Center on Violence and Human Survival.

42 See, for example, E. Sahliyeh (ed.) (1990), *Religious Resurgence and Politics in the Contemporary World*. Albany: State University of New York Press.

43 For a discussion of the Christendom model, see W. Ullman (1961), *Principles of Government and Politics in the Middle Ages*, London: Methuen. See also Forrester, op. cit., Ch. 1.

44 For a recent study of Protestantism as a growing force in Latin American in general, see D. Martin (1989), *Tongues of Fire: The Explosion of Protestantism in Latin America*, Oxford: Blackwell.

45 A.D. Hertzke, in Mews (ed.) (1989), *Religion in Politics: A World Guide*, Harlow, England: Longman, p.298. See also A.J. Reichley (1986), 'Religion and the future of American politics', *Political Science Quarterly*, vol. 101, no. 1, pp.23–47.

Chapter 2

Politics and religion in Western Europe

John Madeley

INTRODUCTION

One of the classic themes of sociology focuses on the role of religion as a kind of social glue or cement which binds the constituent elements of societies together and so underwrites the social order. Conservative thinkers of the nineteenth century in particular pointed to religion as an (or occasionally *the*) essential foundation of any society or civilization and the founding fathers of the modern social sciences, with the conspicuous exception of Marx, placed the study of the social impact of religion close to the centre of their concerns. Despite its pedigree, the relevance of this view to modern society is, however, far from obvious and the political history of the countries of Western Europe in the modern period suggests rather that the impact of the religious factor has generally been as much to undermine as to underwrite the stability of the social and political order.

While the discipline of sociology has often stressed the secular functions of religion in all types of society, it was until quite recently fashionable among political scientists to believe that the religious factor had ceased to have much impact at all – whether in the direction of conflict or consensus – on the contemporary politics of the western democracies. There was a widespread assumption that the trends toward industrialization, urbanization and cultural secularization which Europe had pioneered in the nineteenth century had led to the complete displacement of religion from any central role in public life. If religion itself had not dissolved away in the cold light of Reason, as Enlightenment thinkers had once expected, it was surely much more marginal for the modern European with an essentially secular and materialist approach to life and politics. After 1945 in particular, the political agenda seemed to revolve almost entirely around the humdrum business of 'who gets what, when, how'. The great moral and ideological questions about the merits and demerits of socialism and capitalism, communism and fascism, which had so exercised politicians, commentators and activists in the interwar period, seemed to have lost their purchase on the public mind – a fact doubtless accounted for in large part by the complete discrediting of fascism during the Second World War, the stigmatization of communism with the onset of the Cold War and the west's rapid economic recovery.

In the 1960s, however, two things happened which undermined this set of assumptions. First, there was the re-emergence of ideological conflict and political turbulence around a wide range of issues which did not seem, except to the most unreconstructed of reductionists, understandable purely in terms of class or group competition for material benefits. Questions relating, for example, to the political role of ethnicity, race, religion and gender or to the implications of western-style 'modernization' for economic development across the globe, national self-determination, peace and environmental protection raised disturbing questions about whether people's concerns had changed or whether previous assumptions about the nature of those concerns had been inadequate. Second, a number of studies led political scientists to re-examine the orthodox assumptions about the secularity and materialism of politics in the liberal democracies. In 1967 for example, S.M. Lipset and Stein Rokkan published a seminal survey of the origins and development of social cleavage patterns underlying the characteristic structures of western party systems, which argued for a new understanding of the non-economic springs of modern politics.[1] They showed that not only had religion and other sources of cultural differentiation been of prime importance in the foundation of the European party systems in the late nineteenth century but that the effects of this early impact had been extended into the most recent period by virtue of a sort of 'freezing' of the party systems which had occurred some time in the 1920s.

While they seemed to require some revision of the conventional view of the historical importance of religion, these claims were not of course incompatible with the deeply rooted assumption that the religious factor was in some way archaic – a survival from some earlier era; indeed, the implication of Lipset and Rokkan's analysis in particular was that its importance derived almost entirely from the twist given to modern developments by the outcome of events as distant as the Reformation and the French Revolution. Two years later, however, Rose and Urwin underlined the contemporary significance of the religious factor when their examination of the social bases of political parties led them to the surprising conclusion that, contrary to previous assumption, 'religious divisions, not class, are the main social basis of parties in the Western world *today*'.[2] This was only one of a number of studies which 'rediscovered' the political impact of the religious factor at about this time and since then a number of publications have been concerned with the question of assessing and accounting for the strength of the religious factor in the politics of the liberal democracies.[3]

One of the notable aspects of Rose and Urwin's analysis was the use of a number of alternative survey criteria for identifying the presence of the religious factor in different national contexts; in some it was a matter of confessional affiliation, most often whether respondents were Catholic or Protestant; in others a matter of attitude to the Church(es) or the clergy, in particular whether respondents were pro- or anti-clerical; and in yet others a 'behavioural' criterion was used, in particular whether or not (or how frequently) respondents attended religious services. It might be objected that this involved a double (or treble) counting of the religious variable which was likely to skew the analysis and undermine its validity, but it seems more appropriate to observe that the different use of membership, attitudinal and behavioural criteria in different contexts only represented an appropriate recognition of the complexity of the factors governing the inter-relationship of religion and politics.

One of the factors which becomes clear on even the most cursory survey of the subject is that the population of Western Europe is differentiated both within and between its various political regions on a number of criteria affecting the structure, content and location of religion, which are at least potentially relevant to politics. First, there are the confessional differences between the Catholic and the several varieties of Protestant Churches, denominations, sects and cults with their particular traditions of social and political thought. Second, there are the religious differences internal to the main confessional traditions – differences of observance, belief and opinion, including those directly related to conflicting political viewpoints. Third, there are the different patterns of Church–state relations which have been of central importance in determining the relationship at both mass and elite levels between different groups of religious activists and adherents on the one hand and between the religious and those of no religion on the other. In addition to these 'religious' dimensions account must also be taken of the impact of multifarious other social, economic and cultural forces which vary greatly from one national context to another. Fortunately, Lipset and Rokkan's developmental model has helped to make sense of these complexities in so far as they have affected the development of modern party systems, by providing a framework for identifying the main dimensions of difference and relating them to the historical conjunctures at which they were generated.

It would, however, be wrong to overemphasize the complexity of the West European case by stressing too much the diversity of factors which have cumulatively intersected at different points in time. Seen in a wider comparative context the relative simplicity of the case might be the first impression. After all, the following survey of the main interconnections of religion and politics in postwar Western Europe will concern itself almost exclusively with the Latin form of Christianity and its local variants in the context of the liberal democratic arrangements which have obtained almost everywhere since 1945. On the one hand, after the virtual annihilation of European Jewry during the holocaust and despite the immigration of significant numbers of people of non-European cultural traditions, the most influential linkages between religion and politics have until recently concerned Christian Churches, denominations and groups deriving from the western or Latin tradition. And on the other hand, with the exception until the mid-1970s of the Iberian peninsular, politics has, in the manner of liberal democracy, been almost entirely a matter of parliaments, parties and pressure groups.

More significant perhaps than the multifarious differences between the regions of Western Europe, which must necessarily be a central focus of attention in what follows, is the trend toward cultural secularization which can be observed over the last few generations almost everywhere. As the contents of this book indicate, by comparison with other parts of the world, society and politics in contemporary Western Europe *is* in fact marked by an extra-ordinarily high level of secularization; with the exception of the continuing struggle in Northern Ireland and occasional dramatic episodes like the 1984 demonstrations in Paris on behalf of religious schools – and the 'religious content' of such exceptional cases can easily be disputed – religion seems to account for very much less political conflict or consensus in the 1980s than it did, for example, in the 1880s. This said, it is still remarkable – and was until relatively recently largely unremarked – just how much the religious factor continues to obtrude into the world of politics, where, by long-standing liberal-democratic prejudice, it has no legitimate place.

EUROPE AS A WHOLE

The first remarkable fact is that the religious geography of Europe has changed little since the end of the wars of religion in the seventeenth century; the boundaries between areas dominated by populations of, severally, the Roman Catholic, Lutheran/Evangelical, Calvinist/Reformed, and Anglican confessions still by and large run where they were fixed about three hundred years ago. The fact is all the more remarkable because the political boundaries which define the territorial limits of Europe's states have undergone considerable change over the same period so that the religious and political lines of demarcation no longer coincide in the way they once did. The political map of Europe, not least the line which has since 1945 divided it into its western and eastern parts, has thus been overprinted on a set of religious territorial divisions which it only in part reflects, with the consequence that the various parts of contemporary Western Europe differ from each other not only by confession but also by degree of confessional diversity.

An important reason for the relative fixity of the religious or confessional map is to be found in the nature of the Westphalian settlement of 1648 which brought to an end not only the Thirty Years' War but also the century or more of religious wars which had followed in the wake of the Reformation. That settlement, with its decisive recognition of the principles of secular sovereignty, finally established the rule, first assayed almost a century before, that it was for the political authorities to decide which religion should be established in a particular territory. One effect of applying this rule was to reinforce tendencies to religious uniformity *within* political units (while recognizing religious differences as between them) and over time to entrench the different confessional forms of Christianity in the culture of Europe's various national population groups. The rule did not of course entail granting a significant degree of religious liberty to any other than 'the prince'; indeed the inclusion of decision-making in religious matters within his jurisdiction meant that the disciplines of religious monopoly could be enforced, where the prince so decided, with even greater rigour than before. Thus the Huguenots in France, the victims of the Inquisition in Spain or the occasional religious dissidents of Lutheran Scandinavia all suffered at the hands of princes who long after 1648 continued to see in the maintenance of religious conformity an essential support of the existing social and political order.

Table 2.1 traces the continuing legacy of these early-modern developments in the very uneven distribution of Europe's main confessions. The overwhelming predominance of Christians in the population of all the countries is of course a legacy from the much earlier period of Europe's conversion but the patterning of dominance as between the different confessional forms of Christianity dates from approximately 1648 and continues to provide the basis for the most natural division of the whole area into four groups of countries. Two of the groups are characterized by the overwhelming predominance of a single confession – in Scandinavia, Lutheranism and in the southern part of the continent, Roman Catholicism – while the other two, the British Isles and the Continental countries of mixed confession, are constituted of countries divided between at least two confessions, even though in each case only one or other of the Protestant confessions has been historically dominant. An important corollary of this four-way division is that in the two groups of countries which are by and large confessionally homogeneous there has been no basis for the type of political conflict between confessional groups which has been of considerable importance in the groups of countries of mixed confession. A more controversial aspect of this classification is the degree to which, and the way in which, the political culture of the various countries has been affected by the nature of the different confessions. Despite the interest of such influential scholars as Weber and Troeltsch in these issues it remains a matter more of conjecture than of well-founded argument whether or how the traditional political quiescence of Lutheranism as against, say, the more combative, almost 'republican', spirit of Calvinism has affected the politics of the different parts of Protestant Europe. The magnitude of the impact of Roman Catholicism on the politics of all the countries where its adherents form the majority or a large minority is on the other hand less open to doubt, although variations in the strength, nature and timing of that impact does raise questions about how much is contributed by the intrinsic nature of Catholicism and how much by contextual factors.

By the late eighteenth century the basic patterns of confessional affiliation were still firmly entrenched although some experiments in religious toleration had been attempted in Britain and in those

Table 2.1 The populations of the West European states by religion & confession, 1980
(All figures expressed as % of total population)

	All Christians	Membership of historically dominant confession	Membership of other main confession(s)	Non-religious and atheists	Others
SCANDINAVIA					
Denmark	95.9	95.0 (L)	0.6 (C)	3.6	0.8
Finland	94.4	92.5 (L)	1.2 (O)	5.5	0.8
Iceland	97.3	96.4 (L)	0.7 (C)	2.1	0.8
Norway	98.1	97.6 (L)	0.3 (C)	1.7	0.4
Sweden	70.9	67.6 (L)	1.4 (C)	28.7	0.3
BRITISH ISLES					
United Kingdom	86.9	56.8 (A)	13.1(C)	9.5	20.6
England	–	69.0 (A)	14.0(P) 10(C)	5.0	2.0
Scotland	–	67.0 (CV) 1964	16.0(C) 9(P)	5.0	3.0
Wales	–	45.0 (A)	40.0(P) 6(C)	4.0	5.0
N. Ireland	–	25.0 (A)	38.0(P) 25(C)	2.0	12.0
Rep. of Ireland	99.5	95.3 (C)	3.7(P)	0.4	0.6

CONTINENT: MIXED RELIGION					
Netherlands	85.7	41.8 (CV)	42.6 (C)	12.1	3.5
Switzerland	97.4	42.9 (CV)	52.8 (C)	1.9	2.4
West Germany	92.8	46.7 (L, CV)	43.8 (C)	4.6	4.9
CONTINENT: CATHOLIC					
Austria	96.6	88.8 (C)	6.2 (P)	2.7	2.3
Belgium	90.9	90.0 (C)	0.4 (P)	7.5	2.1
France	80.1	76.4 (C)	2.0 (P)	15.6	6.0
Italy	83.6	83.2 (C)	0.4 (P)	16.2	0.2
Luxembourg	94.4	93.0 (C)	1.3 (P)	4.9	0.8
Portugal	95.3	94.1 (C)	0.8 (P)	4.6	0.5
Spain	97.0	96.9 (C)	0.1 (P)	2.9	0.1

Note: A = Anglican, C = Roman Catholic, CV = Calvinist,
L = Lutheran, O = Russian Orthodox, P = Protestant (in column 4 also
        includes Anglican)

Source: Numerical data derived from D.B. Barrett (ed.) (1982), *The World Christian Encyclopaedia*, Oxford: Oxford University Press.

parts of the Continent where rulers influenced by the Enlightenment flourished in the 1700s. The coming of the French Revolution and the diffusion of its impact across Europe, however, inaugurated a new era. While the 1648 settlement had made both for religious unity and conformity *within* Europe's constituent political units and for diversity *between* them, the tendency of the French Revolution was to divide national populations internally in terms of attitude and behaviour relating to religion and politics. Its impact was particularly marked in Catholic Europe where the Church had retained much of the privilege, wealth and even, on occasion, power which had been stripped from it elsewhere at the time of the Reformation; this, in addition to the close association of its leadership with the monarchy and aristocracy against whom the revolutionaries and republicans directed their main assault, would have made it an obvious target even if Enlightenment thinkers had not already identified it as an 'infamous thing' which should be crushed in the interests of Reason and Progress. In France itself after a series of radical reforms had been imposed on the Church, an attempt was actually made to destroy it altogether. While the de-Christianization campaign of Year 1 (1793–4) failed and was not again attempted in Western Europe, a great gulf opened up in France and elsewhere in Catholic Europe between the partisans of the Church and of the Revolution. Nor did the gulf get much narrower over the succeeding century; between the 1840s and the 1870s it widened again as the Church responded to the rising tide of European liberalism with increasing intransigence and from the 1880s to 1914 French politics witnessed a series of bitter set piece battles between 'the two Frances'. The contemporary emergence of socialist movements with a strong Marxist bias gave the clerical–anti-clerical struggle added impetus as the two forces fought for influence among the industrial working class, which was being called into existence by the other great transforming process of the time, the industrial revolution. Nor are these observations of mere antiquarian interest in an examination of religion and politics after 1945; the legacy of the bitter struggles between clerical and anti-clerical forces has continued until recently to exert a considerable influence on both the form and content of mass politics in Europe, its force only diminishing sharply in the 1960s.

While the epicentre of these religio-political upheavals was principally in Catholic Europe no part of Western Europe was left unaffected by controversy about the issue of dismantling the old systems of confessional monopoly. Everywhere the terms of the old Church–state alliances were progressively relaxed during the nineteenth century as liberal and radical forces fought for the introduction of, successively, religious toleration, religious liberty and religious equality. The recognition of these principles involved breaking the link between citizenship and adherence to a dominant creed, accepting the rights of individuals to choose their own religious orientation (or none) and, finally, removing the barriers to equality of civil status which attached to religious differences.

By contrast with Catholic Europe opposition to these trends among Protestant populations came less from the leadership of the established Churches than from revivalist movements or groups who objected to the dilution of the faith tolerated by relatively easy-going Church elites. One consequence of these various developments was a growing pluralism of religious, anti-religious and religiously indifferent belief and behaviour as the secularizing impact of modernization processes and the various countervailing movements of religious revivalism and liberal reform undermined the religious uniformity which had characterized the old monopoly system. As has already been seen this pluralizing tendency did not go so far as to 'wash out' the predominant confessional colouration of the different countries and regions of Europe however. One of the reasons for this was that religious revivalism in the various Protestant and Catholic areas tended to take forms peculiar to the dominant traditions – pietism in the Lutheran cultures, Methodism and its various offshoots in the Anglican, and one form or other of precisionism or evangelical revivalism in the Calvinist. None the less by the time in the late nineteenth century when the liberalization and democratization of the political systems finally admitted mass electorates to involvement in politics, the population of most of the European states showed a previously unwonted variety in matters of religion and non-religion and in most of them this variety was more or less directly reflected in the character of the parties and party systems which arose to channel (and contain) that involvement.

There is of course no *a priori* reason why differences in matters of religion should be translated into differences of political loyalty or behaviour but conditions at the time of the first emergence of Europe's mass political parties (approximately 1870 to 1920) were such that in very few parts of Europe did the religious factor fail to leave its mark. Nowhere had the legacy of the old discriminatory Church–state arrangements been completely liquidated, whether in terms of remaining elements of religious privilege and underprivilege, or of variable propensities to take account of religious groups' claims in making arrangements for new public services such as education or of the simple inertial tendency for new organizations to develop in such a way as to reproduce and reinforce old religious group loyalties. The force of these different circumstances varied greatly, however, between the different parts of Europe.

In Catholic Europe, where opposition to the traditional Church–state arrangements took the form of a clash between 'coherent and massive secularism' and 'coherent and massive religiosity',[4] the liberal political traditions deriving from the French Revolution ranged themselves with the rising force of continental socialism against the often disparate groups on the right who retained a loyalty to the Church. The conflict over the control and content of public education which for a time became virtually endemic in Catholic Europe was thus just another battle in the ongoing war between anti-clericalism and clericalism, secularism and religiosity. In Europe's other confessionally homogeneous area, Scandinavia, with its Lutheran state churches, a different source of opposition to the traditional arrangements derived from the groups of religious revivalists and dissenters who occasionally combined with more secular elements to resist the influence of the old establishment. This meant that instead of the stark bipolar confrontation between secularism and religion which made such a deep and lasting impact on the situation in Catholic Europe, the basic controversies on Church–state issues in the Protestant north were more easily and more quickly composed; by 1920 indeed they had largely ceased to affect patterns of political competition, although, as will be seen, other related issues such as temperance and the control of sexual mores, have continued up to the present time to generate significant political consequences.

In the two groups of countries of mixed religion other, more complex patterns developed at the formative stage of Europe's modern party systems. Here of course the potentially relevant religious differences also included the confessional one between groups which, after centuries of discrimination on the one hand and privilege on the other, often defined their community identities in religious terms. In the British Isles, until 1921 a single state comprising four distinct nationality groups, there was a strong tendency for national and confessional differences to reinforce each other; thus Irish nationalists and to a lesser extent the Scots and

Welsh often looked to the distinctiveness of their national–religious traditions for a bulwark against the Anglican-dominated culture of the old social and political elites.

From the 1800 Act of Union to the 1921 Irish Treaty both main islands, Britain and Ireland, were under the undivided rule of London and the Catholic majority in Ireland had to wage a bitter struggle to achieve recognition of their rights first as Catholics and then as members of a separate nation; O'Connell's campaign for Catholic rights in the 1820s in fact led to the creation of Europe's first mass Catholic reform movement of any significance and was an important source of inspiration to liberal Catholics on the Continent.[5] Once O'Connell's campaign had succeeded the religious issues tended to be replaced by more secular nationalist concerns, but the confessional divide between Catholic and Protestant communities within Ireland continued to define the principal basis for the rival nationalist and unionist movements – something which, notoriously, continues to be the case today in Northern Ireland, the one part of the island to remain part of the United Kingdom after 1921. In the Republic of Ireland on the other hand, where Catholicism had become so closely identified with the nationalist cause before 1921, there has been no basis for a non- or anti-Catholic party; the Irish Republic thus exemplifies the paradox that in a country where one religion is overwhelmingly dominant it may well fail to register as a source of political conflict (not least, of course, because no party *dare* oppose religion or the Church).[6] On the island of Britain religion has also by and large failed to register as an important aspect of party politics since around the time of the First World War even where, as in the case of many parts of England, Scotland and Wales, there has been a historically strong, second axis of opposition, namely that between the religious establishment and dissent (Church and Chapel). Whereas earlier religion was of considerable importance in dividing conservative from liberal supporters in all three countries on issues such as education or Church establishment, the rise to prominence of the Labour party with its new political agenda of class-related issues largely erased the political traces of religious antagonism.[7] The fact that in addition Labour, like the Liberal party before it, was not tainted by secularism in the manner of continental socialism meant that in Britain, as in most of Scandinavia, the political impact of the religious factor waned considerably after 1918.

In the mixed religion territories of the Continent the old contrast between privileged Protestant majorities and disadvantaged Catholic minorities provided early occasion for the creation of political groups or alliances to fight for the interests of Catholics; indeed in Belgium just such a movement was involved, in alliance with local liberals, in seizing national independence from the Protestant-dominated Netherlands almost a century before Irish Catholics achieved a similar feat. In the territories which, unlike Belgium, continued to be of mixed religion, however, the religious factor operated in contexts which combined the distinctive features of the three other groups of countries – the secular–religious axis of Catholic Europe, the establishment–dissent oppositions of Scandinavia and even on occasion the conflicts which resonated sub-state community identities in religious terms as in the British Isles. The outcome was a multiplex system of religious tensions and oppositions arrayed variously across the political space of the different countries in a remarkable variety of combinations. For the purposes of this brief survey it must suffice, however, to resolve the patterns into their basic elements, that is the principal religious–political constituencies which, though occasionally internally divided, acted and interacted as more or less solidary groups: the Catholics, the liberals (usually secular Protestants), the conservatives (usually establishment Protestants) and the dissenting or fundamentalist Protestants. In addition to these elements the formative period of the party systems also of course saw the emergence on the left of, first, the socialists and then, after 1917, the communists each with their own brand of anti-clerical animus to add to that of the liberals.

Table 2.2 summarizes in schematic form the underlying dimensions of religious–political opposition obtaining in the different groups of countries at the time that the modern party systems were created, i.e. over the period 1870–1920. It illustrates the reasons for both the particular strength of the religious factor in all the continental countries and the degree of complexity of the situation in those of mixed religion. Over this period in the continental groups the translation of the religious factor into politics meant that whereas in 1870 only Germany had a denominational party, by 1920 every country except France had one[8] – and in the Netherlands, where the full complexity of religious–political tensions was first translated into the shape of the party system, there were already several denominational parties. As Lipset and Rokkan pointed out in their pioneering study of the development of party systems and voter alignments it was the political translation of these and other cleavages which set the pattern for decades to come; 'the party systems of the 1960s reflect, with few but significant exceptions, the cleavage structures of the 1920s.'[9] The patterns of political opposition achieved a degree of permanency because, at some point in the 1920s, a 'freezing of major party alternatives' occurred in the wake of the extension of the suffrage, and this freeze survived the political turmoil of the 1930s, the traumas of the Second World War and persisted for a further twenty years after 1945.[10]

One of the main reasons for the long persistence of these basic patterns of party competition is that, especially in Continental Europe, they represented the translation into politics of cleavage lines which, despite their early origins, had gained a new vitality and force through the spread of modern forms of mass organization. Over the period when the parties were coming into existence there was also a tendency for all major groups involved in electoral competition, and the Catholics and socialists of the Continent in particular, to develop dense organizational networks to cater for the needs and aspirations of their members in the economic, social and cultural fields as well as the political. These organizations became the institutional embodiment of, and support for, more or less distinct political subcultures which tended at the extreme to constitute almost complete, mutually exclusive subsocieties – segments of the national societies to which they belonged and which, at the limit, they collectively more or less constituted. In the confessionally mixed areas the mutual insulation was often spatial, as the boundaries between different areas of subcultural dominance continued to run along the geographical fault lines of the mid-seventeenth century. In response to the challenges of industrialization, urbanization and geographical mobility, however, these old distinctions were also reproduced in non-spatial, associative form through the development of the proliferating organizational networks. Of the Netherlands where this process of segmentation or *verzuiling* progressed furthest it could be said that by the 1920s the wider national society had for certain purposes almost ceased to exist as Catholic, Calvinist and secular subcultural organizations competed with each other to cater for almost every need of the segments into which the population was exhaustively divided.[11]

The development of parties *pari passu* with this type of social and cultural segmentation was, like segmentation itself, much less pronounced in Scandinavia and the British Isles. Where it did occur at all, as in the case of the (non-sectarian) Labour or socialist camps,

Table 2.2   The religious factor in West European Politics, 1870–1920, by region

| | Religious factor dimensions | | |
	Secular–religious [(XXX)]	Catholic–Protestant [(XX)]	Establishment–dissent [(X)]
Scandinavia			X
British Isles		XX	X
Continental Mixed	XXX	XX	X
Continental Catholic	XXX		

Note: The number of Xs indicates the relative weight or impact of the different dimensions, i.e., the degree to which they have tended to generate strong and long-lasting tensions in the political arena.

it was not reinforced by the mutual antagonism and rivalry with powerful religious constituencies evident in much of the rest of Western Europe; the impact of the religious factor, which gave such an impetus to segmentation on the Continent, had, as noted, declined greatly by 1920. The principal exception to this generalization in the period after 1920 has been in Northern Ireland, the one part of the British Isles where a confessional contrast continues to divide the community into mutually antagonistic subcultural groups and the mutual reinforcement of rival religious and ethnic identities lends a particular virulence to the conflict. Another, much less dramatic exception is to be found in Norway, where the Christian Peoples' Party emerged first in one region in 1933 and then at national level in 1945 to give new life to a native tradition of fundamentalist protest which ranges itself as much against the secularism and indifference of the right as of the left. In this case there was an exceptional combination of the existence among the revivalists of a remarkably strong network of organizations supporting a dissident religious subculture, an unusual degree of anti-religious sentiment on the left and a failure on the part of the right to attract the support of the revivalists.

Among the Protestants of continental Europe only the Dutch with their advanced form of segmentation produced significant religious parties but amongst the Catholic populations the exceptional cases were those which failed to foster important parties of religious inspiration before 1920; in the Benelux countries and in Germany,

Austria and Switzerland Catholic parties had already established themselves in national parliaments, and, in most cases, in government by 1920. Even in Italy, where the papacy had expressly forbidden full political involvement on the part of Catholics up to the time of the First World War, a Catholic party emerged in 1919 with over 20 per cent of the votes. The main exception, as already noted, was in France, where, even though the contest between clericals and anti-clericals had contributed much to the fissile material of politics throughout the nineteenth century, numerous attempts to found a Catholic party were frustrated as other unfinished business of the country's turbulent political history continued to divide Catholics into mutually hostile factions. Yet another attempt was made in the 1920s shortly after a similar experiment in Spain, where the same sort of obstacles also stood in the way of launching a major Catholic party; in both cases however the attempt again failed.[12]

Even though Europe's party systems might be said to have 'frozen' between the 1920s and the 1960s, the end of the Second World War did mark an important new departure for Europe's religious parties, particularly on the Continent (see Table 2.3). All of the predominantly Catholic parties with the exception of the Swiss underwent significant changes in or around 1945, either altering their name (and with it most often their rules and programmes) or, as in the case of Germany, France and Italy, actually being completely remodelled. The significance of these changes was that they signalled a shift from what might be called denominational or confessional politics to the politics of Christian democracy. This shift was signalled not least in the changes of name: whereas in the interwar period not one of the religious parties was known by the Christian democratic label (only one, the Austrian Christian Social party, even approximated to it), in the postwar period this nomenclature became almost universal among the predominantly Catholic parties. Ironically, the only important Catholic party which by 1980 was not known by either the Christian democratic or Christian social label was the Austrian party which in 1945 had adopted the label Austrian Peoples party (APP) in order to dissociate itself from the authoritarian traditions and dubious record of its predecessor. In or around 1945 the old parties of Belgium (CSP) and Luxembourg (CSP) and the new parties of Germany (CDU/CSU) and Italy (DC) adopted one or other of the two labels. In Switzerland, where non-involvement in the war meant that 1945 was not, as in most of the rest of Europe, a time for new beginnings, the (Catholic) Conservative Peoples party did not make a change of name until

1957, when it became the Conservative Christian Social party, only to change it once again in 1971 to the Christian Democratic Peoples party (CDPP). Finally, even the Catholic Peoples party of the Netherlands followed the trend in 1976 when it joined with the two main Calvinist parties to form the new Christian Democratic Appeal (CDA). Of the Protestant religious parties more generally, only the small Swedish Christian Democrat party (CD) adopted a variant of the continental – and predominantly Catholic – label, the others preferring to retain their more distinctive original names: Christian Peoples party (Norway and Denmark), Christian League (Finland), Protestant Peoples party (Switzerland), Anti-Revolutionary party and Christian Historical Union (Netherlands until 1976).

The shift from denominational to Christian democratic politics involved much more than a re-christening however; it also entailed at least four other changes of importance. First, it involved an attempt to remove any ambiguity about the parties' commitment to liberal democracy in preference to more authoritarian forms of government or social organization such as, for example, those indicated by Pope Pius XI's endorsement of corporatist ideas in 1931. This new, or newly emphatic, commitment often took the form of statements to the effect that (liberal) democracy was the system of government most in agreement with the dictates of Christianity and that, accordingly, it should be supported against its enemies. Second, it involved ceasing to concentrate on attending to the *interests* of a Church or client religious community and directing attention instead toward promoting the *values* of Christianity as such (in so far as these were thought to have political relevance). Third, there was a change from reliance on the leadership (or even dictation) of clerical hierarchies to a reliance instead on independent, elective lay leaderships which could claim a legitimate independence of judgement in the political arena. And fourth, the shift meant broadening the parties' electoral appeal beyond the constituency of the faithful and openly attempting to attract the support of anyone, regardless of religious standing, who could be persuaded to support the parties' aims and policies. These were all important changes which did much to affect the form and content of postwar politics. It is none the less worthy of note that only the fourth change entailed any attempt to transcend the established cleavage lines inherited from the prewar era.

The religious parties were well placed to benefit from the particular circumstances of the immediate postwar period. Nazism had demonstrated with dramatic brutality that the extremism of a political right which eschewed traditional Christian values was quite as destructive and barbarous as any threat from a secularist left. In many countries, furthermore, groups of religious activists had been able to demonstrate their attachment to both national and democratic values through involvement in wartime resistance movements and this demonstration of their bona fides lent a new credibility to their commitment to Christian democracy. In addition a revival of interest in religion as a focus for the reconstruction of normal life after the traumas of war gave the new and the rejuvenated religious parties a fair wind; their stress on Christian values, the rule of law and respect for the family were attractive to many on the centre-right who feared what the surge in support for the more left-wing parties might usher in. By hewing to a centrist line with often strongly reformist and occasionally anti-capitalist elements new-style Christian democrats were also able to appeal to moderate left-wing elements, particularly those with religious attachments.

For most of the religious parties the first twenty years after the war was for all these reasons a period of unparalleled electoral success; in Italy and Germany the Christian democrats soon achieved the status of dominant parties in this period, while in almost all the other continental democracies their counterparts maintained the position of largest or next-largest party often making themselves virtually indispensable in coalition governments.[13] Even in France, where religious parties had always previously been bedeviled by a combination of secular–religious polarization between left and right and the fissiparousness of the right, it seemed that at last the right conditions for the launch of an important religious party had come into existence in the immediate postwar period. The Popular Republican Movement (MRP) was launched within months of the liberation by a group of Catholic militants with common experience in religious youth organizations and the resistance, and at its second election in June 1946 the party managed to take more votes than any other party. Unfortunately the favourable conditions of the immediate postwar months did not last long as Gaullism soon re-emerged as the major movement of the right, severely undercutting the MRP's standing with the more traditional Catholics. Although it continued at a modest level of support throughout the IVth Republic and took a leading part in its many governments, the MRP faded after 1958, its constituent parts dissolving into the shifting political alliances of the centre while most traditional Catholics aligned themselves with the Gaullist right.

Table 2.3 Confessional religious and anti-religious parties of Western Europe

Country	Religious party	Founded (renamed)	Highest vote (1945–1985)	Other parties rated cohesive by religion, (Rose and Urwin, 1969) with highest vote (1945–1985)	
SCANDINAVIA					
Denmark	Christian Peoples Party	1970	5.3 (1975)	SPP 11.3	(1981)*
Finland	Christian League	1958	4.8 (1979)	FDPU 23.2	(1958)*
Iceland	–				
Norway	Christian Peoples Party	1933	12.4 (1977)	CP 11.9	(1945)
Sweden	Christian Democrats	1964	1.8 (1970)	CP 6.3	(1948)
BRITISH ISLES					
United Kingdom	–			–	
England	–			–	
Scotland	–			–	
Wales	–			–	
N. Ireland				UL 23%	(1968)†
				UUL 54%	(1968)†
Rep. of Ireland	–			–	
CONTINENT: MIXED RELIGION					
Netherlands	[Anti-Revolutionary Party	1879	12.9 (1946)]	Lab P 33.8	(1977)
	[Christian Historical Union	1908	9.2 (1948)]	Lib P 17.9	(1977)
	[Catholic Peoples Party	1926 [1945]	31.7 (1956)]		
	Christian Democratic Appeal	1976	32.0 (1979)		
	Political Reformed Party	1918	2.4 (1952)		

	Party name	Founded	Vote % (year)	Other parties — vote % (year)
Switzerland	Christian Democratic Peoples Party	1896 [1957–71]	23.4 (1963)	SD 27.0 (1955)*
	Protestant Peoples Party	1919	2.2 (1979)	RD 24.1 (1979)*
	Christian Democratic Union/	1945	50.2 (1957)	SPD 45.8 (1972)
West Germany	Christian Socialist Union			FDP 12.8 (1961)
CONTINENT: CATHOLIC				
Austria	Austrian People's Party	1891 [1945]	49.8 (1945)	SP 51.0 (1979)
Belgium	Christian Social Party	1884 [1945]	47.7 (1950)	Soc 37.3 (1954)/ Lib 21.6 (1965)
				CP 12.7 (1946)/ V 11.1 (1971)
France	Popular Republican Movement (MRP)	1945	28.1 (1946)	Gau 31.9 (1962)/SP 37.8 (1981)
				CP 28.6 (1946)/RSP 15.2 (1956)
				Con II 15.3 (1956)
Italy	Social Democratic Centre	1966 [1976]	ca.9.0 (1979)	PCI 34.4 (1976)/PSI 20.7 (1946)
	Christian Democrats (DCI)	1945	48.5 (1948)	MSI 8.7 (1972)/Rep 4.8 (1946)
Luxembourg	Christian-Social Party	1919 [1945]	42.4 (1954)	SP 41.4 (1951)/CP 15.5 (1968)*
Portugal	Centre Socialist Democratic Party	1975	16.7 (1976)	CP 19.5 (1979)*
Spain	+			CP 10.8 (1979)*

Notes: † Data from survey
* Attributions additional to those made in Rose and Urwin (1969). Those for Denmark and Finland are made on the basis of comparability with Norway and Sweden. Swiss cases are determined by secondary analysis of data in H. Kerr (1974), 'Switzerland: social cleavages and partisan conflict'. *Sage Professional Paper in Comparative Political Sociology*, 1,06,002.
+ There is a very small Christian democrat party in Spain (as there is also in Portugal) which takes less than 2 per cent of the vote. More importantly, up to one third of the deputies of the Union of the Democratic Centre (35.0 per cent in 1979) are reckoned to be Christian democrats of one sort or another.
Party names as given in and (except where familiar) abbreviations derived from T.T. Mackie, and R. Rose, (1984), *The International Almanac of Electoral History*, 2nd edn., (London: Macmillan.) Electoral data also from same source.

Among most of the Protestant populations of Western Europe religious parties continued to be either marginal, as in Switzerland, or completely absent, as in England, Scotland and Wales; religiously active people distributed themselves instead across the political spectrum according to their political as opposed to their religious predilections, which were generally regarded as irrelevant to the main concerns of politics. As exceptions to this general pattern, however, in the Netherlands the two main Calvinist parties managed to maintain a fairly stable level of support into the 1960s, at a level only slightly below that of the interwar period. The one Protestant country where the Christian democratic wind did blow in 1945 was Norway where the CPP managed to break through at national level, aided in large part by the same favourable conditions which prevailed elsewhere, not least the resistance experiences of a number of religious figures. The principal object of surprise in the Norwegian general election of 1945, the CPP was found to be more solidly based than most contemporary observers believed, as the party successfully established itself over the following years until by 1973 it had become the third largest party in the country.

Despite developments in Norway and the Netherlands, the contrast between the Protestant and Catholic parts of Europe remained remarkable. Nor was this a matter merely of there being more parties on the Continent with religious names or identities. As the last column of Table 2.3 indicates, after 1945 continental Europe also had a large number of ostensibly non-religious parties for which the religious factor was of very particular significance; these were the parties for which either confessional affiliation, religious behaviour or attitudes to religion provided a 'factor of cohesion' and, most often, an element of political self-identification. In the case of most of the parties listed the religious factor operated in reverse as it were, religion or the Church entering into party politics as a focus of enmity on the part of anti-clerical forces still prosecuting the struggles which had been to the fore in the nineteenth century. However archaic these struggles seemed, the evidence is clear that their impact on patterns of electoral choice made them of continuing significance in the postwar era.

The survival of the anti-clerical element in continental politics was encouraged by the fact that the attempt on the part of many Christian democrats to make a break with the clericalism of the past only succeeded in part. Indeed, Whyte refers to the whole period from 1920 to 1960 as the peak period of what he calls closed Catholicism, when Catholic parties co-existed with Catholic social organizations (such as trade unions, farmers' organizations, etc.), all under strong clerical guidance – not least at election times.[14] He argues that the postwar attempt of the Catholic parties to begin again on a more open and less confessional basis was foiled in part by countervailing forces which actually made for a revival of closed Catholicism. In addition to the factors which helped to boost the prospects of all religious parties, such as the eclipse of former right-wing parties, the further extension of women's suffrage and the onset of the Cold War, Whyte points to other circumstances which helped to reinforce the earlier habits of confessional or denominational politics: the distinctiveness of Catholic social doctrine, the continuing strength of the organizations of Catholic Action, the re-emergence of the schools issue in a number of countries and 'the renewed willingness of some national hierarchies to give strong guidance to their flocks'.[15] The conclusion is that despite the virtual disappearance of the clerical deputy from the parliamentary scene,

> [on] the whole, it seems true that, at least in Germany, Italy and the Low Countries, electoral intervention by the Catholic hierarchies was more continuous and intensive in the period 1945–60 than in any previous period of equivalent length.[16]

The anti-clericalism of those on the left against whom these interventions were generally directed might be seen then as more than just a hangover from earlier times; it represented an understandable response against the continuation of what was seen by many, including many Christian democrats, as unwarranted clerical 'interference' in politics.

One of the secrets of Christian democracy's success in the twenty years after 1945 was a degree of ideological diffuseness which made the political content of its programmes and policies difficult targets for anti-clericals to aim at. Its claim to stand for Christian principles, democracy, economic liberalism and social progress (and *against* communism) failed to distinguish it in substantive terms from any but the most extreme political alternatives, while helping it to retain the support of socially heterogeneous electorates which had supported the prewar religious parties. The radical strains which were in evidence in the immediate postwar period were soon drowned out as Christian democratic participation in government confronted party leaders with the difficulty – and the electoral unpopularity – of actually implementing radical changes. Most of the parties continued none the less to accommodate groups and tendencies of diverse political tempers and in some cases this was done by tolerating the proliferation of more or less organized factions. Thus in Italy factions named after various prominent party figures differed not only in terms of how progressive or conservative they were but also in terms of ideas about how the party should relate to the Church; intergralists argued for a close reliance on the hierarchy and a stress on the party's specifically Catholic orientation while autonomists, who tended to predominate in the leadership, argued that the party should keep the Church at arm's length and present itself as 'the party of Catholics but not a party of Catholics pure and simple'.[17] Although there were costs and dangers in ideological diffuseness, it was turned to good electoral effect as the parties made a virtue of being non-doctrinaire and spread their appeal to the most diverse sections of the electorate; in so doing they pioneered the winning formula later copied by others of the ideologically open and socially diverse 'catch-all party'.[18]

After the golden years of 1945 to 1965, the late 1960s and early 1970s were a period of relative decline for continental Christian democracy, however, as a number of factors combined to undermine their electoral standing amidst a general thaw of party systems and voter alignments. First, there was the significant drop in levels of Church membership and orthodox religious practice which occurred during the 1960s. One recent author concluded that:

> From about 1967 the Churches were in a state of crisis in most parts of Western Europe. There was a general decline in church attendance; many churches lost members. . . . Even in Britain, where the churches were already relatively weak, the years 1965–70 saw a larger percentage decline in membership than any previous period this century; in many Catholic countries – the decline in the religious indices in the later 1960s and early 1970s was more spectacular, and the effects of these years far more traumatic.[19]

Second, the unsettling effects of the Second Vatican Council with its encouragement of a new pluralism within the Church and a new openness to the world, embracing not just other Christians but non-believers also, tended to undermine the cohesiveness of the Catholic bloc which most Christian democratic parties, for all their commitment to openness, had regularly relied on. Third, the Christian democrats' principal political rivals on the left, having discovered the electoral attractiveness of a non-doctrinaire approach, tended to abandon their anti-clerical rhetoric along with other Marxist baggage and this had the effect of shifting them towards the centre of the political spectrum where they were able to attract the support of Christian democracy's more reformist elements.

The result of these combined tendencies was that 'during the sixties and early seventies Catholic parties and social organizations were becoming less powerful or less confessional or both', in other words 'closed Catholicism' was, finally, entering a steep decline.[20] Several parties, for example, in the Benelux countries experienced a large loss of votes, while in France the MRP finally expired as an independent political force. Other parties, for example those in Germany and Austria, fared better 'but only by dint of diminishing their confessional character'.[21] The most spectacular collapse of a religious party occurred in the Netherlands, however, where, as noted earlier, the apparatus of confessional segmentalism had long lent impressive support to a complete range of confessional parties. There the Catholic Peoples party's vote fell from 31.9 per cent in 1963 to 17.7 per cent in 1972 as the proportion of all Catholics supporting it fell from 85 per cent to 38 per cent.[22] The Protestant CHU and ARP were also in decline at the time (although the latter had lost most support in the first decade after the war) and in 1976 they agreed to pool their resources with the Catholic party in order to present a common, Christian democratic front to the electorate. Finally, four years later the three parties actually abandoned their separate identities and formed the new Christian Democratic Appeal.

Curiously it was also during the decade from the mid-1960s to the mid-1970s that in Scandinavia, where previously a religious party had established itself only in Norway, new religious parties appeared on the political scene. Sweden's Christian democrats fought their first national election in 1964, two years before Finland's Christian League and seven years before Denmark's Christian Peoples party did the same thing. As Table 2.3 indicates none of these new formations became major parties, unlike their established counterpart in Norway. All of these signs of new life were none the less symptomatic of important changes occurring along the traditional borderline which, particularly in the Lutheran cultures, is expected to insulate the worlds of politics and religion from each other. The reason why these signs of new life should appear in Scandinavia just as the religious parties of other areas of Europe were encountering one sort of crisis or another is to be found in the changed balance in the salience of Church–state issues on the one hand and politics-of-morals issues on the other. The importance of the former during the formative period of the modern party systems had helped to facilitate, and in Scandinavia to frustrate, the emergence of religious parties. In most of continental Europe, Church–state conflicts, particularly over religion in the schools, had tended to bind members of a particular religious tradition together in defence of Church interests, but in Scandinavia, where the religious activists were divided into a range of different voluntary associations and denominations, such questions had tended to be a source of division. In the 1960s, however, when the frozen patterns of the party systems started to thaw, the classic Church–state questions were hardly anywhere prominent on the political agenda; instead, almost everywhere significant politics-of-morals issues, relating for example to drugs, pornography or abortion were at least periodically to the fore and here the large religious constituencies of the Continent tended to be torn internally, while the small constituencies of religious activists in Scandinavia found themselves united in the face of advanced programmes of liberalizing reform.[23]

Since the early 1970s continental Christian democracy has enjoyed something of a revival in its fortunes although this has tended to be in spite of, rather than because of, changes occurring within the religious sphere. In Irving's opinion the revival instead owes something to changes in the economic climate which began in the mid-1970s and put a premium on prudent housekeeping, and also to different party managers' efforts at reforming and strengthening their political machines. 'These factors', he adds, 'have helped to compensate for the erosion of the traditional Catholic, rural and female electorate, which for long formed the basis of Christian Democratic strength and stability'.[24] In Italy two referenda on politics-of-morals issues, on divorce in 1974 and on abortion in 1981, pointed up both the unwillingness of religious parties to run the errands of the Church and the unreliability of Catholic voters' support for the Church's restrictive stands on such issues. As Furlong commented in 1982, it remains an open question what influence groups with a strong commitment to promoting the Church's stands on such issues could have 'in a DC increasingly dominated by pre-occupations of governmental stability and clientilist distribution of public resources, in which religious issues merely add one variable to the complexities of coalition formation with lay parties'.[25] His own conclusion was that the Christian Democratic Party had effectively become a conservative party 'whose Catholic inspiration is scarcely visible either in its policy output or in its electoral programmes and only marginally in the speeches and writings of its leaders'.[26]

Whether or not Christian democracy generally should be regarded as a political tradition which does little more than add a religious aura or sanction to political conservatism has been much debated. While Fogarty in the 1950s argued that it could only be true to its sources of inspiration (could only really *be* Christian democracy) if it pursued policies of radical change and reform, most commentators have assigned it to the centre of the political spectrum, if only to distinguish it from other traditions such as that of the continental liberals which on central economic questions have often been more to the neo-liberal right. There are those, however, who follow Furlong and conclude that, while Christian democrats might well repudiate the conservative label, 'in terms of their political principles and policies, the nature of their political support and their political position *vis-à-vis* other major European political parties, they can be identified as conservatives of the pragmatic and reformist tradition'.[27] Such debates have in large measure revolved around alternative views about the meaning of the term conservative (particularly on the Continent) or the precise reference of left–centre–right labels. It can be argued, however, that in the last quarter of the twentieth century the principal challenge to the Christian democratic tradition is not to place itself advantageously so as to catch any political winds blowing from or towards left, centre or right, but to avoid capsize in the newly-choppy and turbulent waters of electoral volatility. In this respect the example of Germany is of particular interest because of the common view that Christian democracy there is overwhelmingly conservative in its emphasis.

GERMANY

The relationship between religion and politics in Germany is of particular interest for a number of reasons. First, as the western part of the country where the Reformation began, it is the only part of Europe where all three of the major confessions of the continent have been continuously represented ever since: Catholics, Lutherans and Calvinists have all had areas of local dominance in what was until the nineteenth century a veritable patchwork of small states. For Germany, in fact, the principal significance of the 1648 settlement, apart from the fact that it marked the end of the devastating Thirty Years War, was that it extended to Calvinists the application of the Augsburg rule which had up to then applied only to Catholics and Lutherans in the Holy Roman Empire. This basic confessional diversity was furthermore increased rather than decreased in the early nineteenth century when the (originally Calvinist) Hohenzollern monarchy forced through an ecclesiastical union of Lutherans and Calvinists in its territories. Nor did the cross-confessional phenomenon of revivalism do anything to simplify the picture; rather, it added a degree of internal diversity to the existing confessional communities which articulated new tensions between liberal elitist and more orthodox, popular religious traditions. In summary then, not only does the territory of the Federal Republic of Germany (FRG) belong to the group of mixed religion countries, it is historically perhaps the most mixed of them all.[28]

Second, the territory of the FRG also spans large areas of both very high and very low levels of religiosity. When Thomas Luckmann argued that 'church-oriented religion has become a marginal phenomenon in modern society' he did so on the basis of studies undertaken largely in certain Protestant areas of West Germany which 'have long been among the most secularized in the Christian world'.[29] Other parts of the Federal Republic, on the other hand, such as Bavaria or parts of the Rhineland, belong to that extended area which Fogarty identified as Europe's religious heartland where levels of orthodox religious observance have historically been very high.[30]

Third, as has already been noted, Germany is also the country where the political potential of the religious factor was first realized and transposed into the forms of modern party politics: the Zentrum was in some ways as much a model of party organization for Europe's Catholics as was the SPD for Europe's socialists. In a number of respects they both resembled each other, not least by developing rival organization networks on segmental lines to the point where they almost became states within the state. This tendency both to innovate and to ape one another has finally been carried into the politics of the FRG as the CDU and the SPD have jointly pioneered the techniques and the ideological agnosticism of 'catch-all party politics' on the Continent.[31]

By the first decade of the twentieth century the disadvantages of cultural and political segmentalism were already appreciated by some Catholic leaders; in 1906 one of them argued in a famous pamphlet that it was necessary for Germany's Catholics to leave the fortified tower or ghetto which they had built for themselves if they were to maximize their influence (*Wir müssen aus dem Turm heraus*) but this suggestion was not successfully acted on until after the Second World War. The Centre party (Zentrum) had not in fact started as an expression of 'political Catholicism' – in its very first years it had even attracted the support of a small group of Protestants around Ludwig von Gerlach – but the onset of the *Kulturkampf* in the early 1870s had soon reduced it to a *de facto* confessional party.[32] In 1874 it managed to mobilize the support of almost the entire Catholic electorate of the Reich in defence of Church interests against Bismarck's campaign, a feat probably never equalled by any other confessional party in Europe.

Within the majority Protestant community there were few attempts to emulate the Centre party and launch a specifically religious party. Prussian conservatism paid tribute to Stahl's defence of divine right monarchy against democracy and continued to attract the support of many orthodox believers well into the Weimar period, while more liberal Protestants (adherents of what is known as *Kulturprotestantismus*) cast their votes for various centrist parties. In the 1890s, however, the Conservative party effectively opted to become an agrarian interest party rather than a Christian conservative party.[33] The great majority of Protestants who belonged to the established Churches did not of course suffer from disadvantages by virtue of their religion, unlike the Catholics in the 1870s, and accordingly little incentive existed for the creation of a confessional Protestant party. In addition, Lutherans in particular were historically committed to the view that religion and politics were two separate spheres which should not be allowed to impinge on, or interfere with, each other.[34] There were none the less some exceptions which proved the rule of the Protestants' confessional nullity in politics. Thus, for example, in 1878 Adolf Stocker founded a Christian Social Workers party which was to survive in one form or another for approximately thirty years and during Weimar a small Christian Service party also flourished. Both of these parties can be seen as responses on the part of Protestant religious activists to the challenges of militant secularism, represented from the 1870s by the SPD and after 1917 by the Communist party as well. All of these parties and their related organizations were suppressed during the Third Reich so that 1945 involved an almost completely new beginning.

At the collapse of the Third Reich and the end of the Second World War the country was faced with the need for massive reconstruction.

So far as the Churches were concerned not the least of the challenges was the need to come to terms with the recent Nazi past, the war guilt attributed to the whole nation by the Potsdam Agreement and the even deeper sense of collective guilt provoked by the final disclosure of the Nazi regime's most barbarous atrocities. The revulsion against Nazism had created a vacuum which the Churches were well-placed to fill; there was a general desire to return to traditional standards such as the rule of law and personal and political freedom. Furthermore, as the only sources of public authority to survive the Nazi collapse, the Churches were generally entrusted by the occupation authorities with a wide range of civil functions. Since they were also the only important organizations to span the four occupation zones they tended for the same reasons to take on the role of the sole legitimate voice for the whole German nation.

In 1945 one of the lessons of the recent past was how much Christians of different confessions actually had in common with each other. The incipient division of the country between east and west was considerably altering the confessional balance between Catholics and Protestants; whereas the former had previously been in a clear minority position, they now moved towards near parity within West Germany. As elsewhere in Europe the experience of common suffering and struggle had also helped to create a new basis for co-operation across earlier, traditional boundaries. In particular among the Protestants, who had previously provided much of the support for right-wing nationalist parties, there was a significant number who had discovered a commonality of Christian values with the Catholics from whom they had earlier been politically separated. Disabused by recent experience of the Lutheran tradition of obedience to authority and political quiescence, those who had supported the Confessing Church, in particular, during the Nazi period, looked for a way of building support for an active politics of Christian inspiration. Meanwhile many Catholics were determined to resist rebuilding the Zentrum's political tower or ghetto which in the past had not only repelled non-Catholics but had also during the Weimar Republic progressively failed to attract the support even of practising Catholics. Had there still been issues which divided Catholic from Protestant on Church interest grounds there might have been some real incentive to revive the confessional division in politics but these issues were soon settled. The Basic Law of 1949 returned to the separation of Church and state and the guarantees of religious freedom, which had obtained under Weimar, while at the same time allowing the continuation of generous systems of financial support through the levying of Church taxes by the general tax authorities.

The organizational origins of the CDU are to be found as early as mid-June 1945 in the formation of groups in Berlin and Cologne. The individuals who came together were of the most diverse religious and political backgrounds having before 1933 been supporters of not only the Centre party but also the conservative DNVP (Deutsche-Nationale Volkspartei) and the liberal DDP (Deutsche Demokratische Partei) and DVP (Deutsche Volkspartei). They included Christian socialists (Dirks), Catholic trade unionists (Kaiser, Arnold), conservative Protestants of the nationalist tradition (Dibelius, Schlange-Schoeningen), conservative Catholics (Adenauer) and leaders of the Confessing Church (Heinemann). As a French commentator remarked rather dismissively in 1946, 'this party is socialist and radical in Berlin, clerical and conservative in Cologne, capitalist and reactionary in Hamburg, and counter-revolutionary and particularistic in Munich.'[35] It was with this diversity in mind that the party eventually adopted the title of Christian Democratic (in Bavaria, Social) Union, thereby making a virtue out of its necessity to appeal to, and to unite, a broad spectrum of opinion.

In the years 1947 to 1949 the new party's individual identity began to emerge; it was then that crucial developments occurred and decisions were taken affecting where it would stand on the left–right spectrum, what weight confessional considerations would carry and what sort of organizational form it would take. As chairman of the first CDU organization in the British zone, where *Land* parties had been licensed a year earlier than elsewhere, the conservative Catholic Konrad Adenauer was from the beginning at the centre of events, playing a key role in fixing the party's image and character. Not the least significant of his achievements was the dilution of some of the ideological commitments made by some of the party's founders, thereby ensuring that it remained pluralistic, non-doctrinaire and pragmatic.

In the early months Christian socialist ideas had been much to the fore; even though in 1931 the Pope had virtually declared Christian socialism to be a contradiction in terms, the exigencies of the immediate postwar situation made a commitment to planning, nationalization and 'economic justice' attractive in West Germany as much as elsewhere in Europe at the time. Accordingly the regional Berlin, Cologne, Bad Godesberg and Frankfurt programmes of 1945 were distinctly leftist in slant. With the ideas, as well as the parties, of the right generally discredited, the Ahlen programme as late as 1947 also incorporated sharp criticisms of capitalism, which was presented as being not only intrinsically corrupt but also in large measure responsible for Hitler's rise to power. Two years later, however, Adenauer was able to preside over what turned out to be a decisive shift to a much more conservative economic philosophy, when the Düsseldorf programme, on which the party fought its first general election in 1949, committed it to building a 'social market economy', a blend of free enterprise and social provision based on insurance principles. It was this new economic policy, favoured by the Protestant economist and economics minister, Ludwig Erhard, which, together with the boost delivered by Marshall Aid, laid the foundation for the country's 'economic miracle' and helped to underwrite the CDU/CSU's electoral success. Within a few years of its foundation the CDU, under Adenauer's leadership, had changed from being a left-leaning reformist party to being a party of the centre-right whose conservatism in economic policy was only augmented by its successful absorption of potential right-wing rivals. By the 1960s indeed it had in one view become 'the party of all those who were suspicious of "socialism" and "collectivism" in the broadest senses of these words'.[36]

One of the features which distinguished the CDU/CSU from all other Christian democratic parties in Western Europe at the time of its foundation was of course its genuinely cross-confessional basis. Although it has throughout its history received considerably greater support from Catholics than from Protestants, the party has always retained an important Protestant element, and to reflect this the distribution of leadership positions over the party's first two decades was so arranged as to include an equal number of Catholics and Protestants. Indeed, confessional differences were also taken into account in the formation of the coalition cabinets; the CDU/CSU's allocation of ministerial posts was balanced in such a way that there was parity between the two confessions within the government as a whole, once the affiliation of ministers from all parties had been taken into account. From the mid-1960s this principle of confessional parity has been eroded, with Catholics enjoying a numerical preponderance on the executive and in the parliamentary group. The trend is explained more by a decreased sensitivity to confessional backgrounds in the 1960s than by any metamorphosis towards a Catholic party of the old, prewar type. The pragmatic cast of the party was beyond doubt by the 1960s, encapsulated as it was in the 'double compromise' which had underlain its successes in government and at the polls: the compromise between Protestantism and Catholicism, which resolved into little more than a vague emphasis on Christian principles, and the compromise between capital and labour, middle and working classes which was enshrined in the commitment to the 'social market economy'.

As the dominant party of government from 1949 to 1969 the CDU/CSU was influenced greatly by the character of its leadership, headed for most of this time by Adenauer. It was in its first years a remarkably loose-jointed organization; having grown from its base in the various zones and *Länder*, the CDU only actually became a fully federal party at its first national congress in 1950 and even then the federalist leanings of many of the *Land* associations stood in the way of setting up a powerful national secretariat of the type desired by Adenauer. Paradoxically, however, the weakness of the party in the country only served to strengthen the standing of Adenauer's leadership. Indeed by the early 1960s the CDU was seen by many commentators as little more than a *Kanzlerwählerverein*, an association for the election of the chancellor, the main purpose of which seemed to be to contest elections on behalf of its leadership and then wait in the wings for another four years as Adenauer exercised to the limit his constitutional right to lead and direct national policy according to his own lights.[37]

The electoral basis for the Christian Democrats' success was the combination of support from a relatively solid Catholic constituency, inherited from the days of the Centre, with the support of conservative Protestants whose attachment tended to be more a matter of pragmatic choice on the basis of the party's policy than of confessional loyalty or other religious motivations. Left-leaning Protestants, whose religious ties were often little more than nominal, at first provided the main electoral support for the CDU/CSU's main rival, the SPD, but after the 1959 Bad Godesberg conference decision to abandon anti-clericalism that party moved to attract religious people of either confession who might support its aims, whatever their grounds for so doing. In the early 1960s the ferment of change within the Catholic Church had the effect, of making the choice of left-wing alternatives by Catholics more legitimate, thereby undermining the unity and cohesion of German Catholicism which the more conservative members hierarchy, such as Cardinal Frings of Cologne, had long been at pains to preserve. The pastoral letters issued at election times tended to become less politically pointed; whereas in the 1950s stress was usually laid upon assessing the Christian credentials of particular candidates and parties when choosing between them, by the early 1970s the pastoral injunction tended instead to be simply in favour of voting and thereby performing one's citizen duty. As if to confirm the basis for this stand, in 1971 the Catholic bishops' conference announced that as a general principle the Church should refrain from speaking out on issues where there was no clear biblical guidance. This progressive withdrawal from the habit of broadcasting its own political judgements and wishes on the one hand and the effect of the internal controversies unleashed by, for example, Pope Paul VI's encyclical on birth control in 1967 on the other, severely undermined the cohesiveness of German Catholicism when it was already being weakened by declining church attendance and an increase in mixed marriages. In 1969 the consequences of all these changes became evident when a marginal decline of the CDU/CSU vote and a new increment in support for the SPD at the general election of that year led to the latter taking over from the former the role of principal party of government; after twenty years with the CDU/CSU as the senior partner in an unbroken succession of cabinets, the SPD took over the same role for the years 1969 to 1982.

The defeat of 1969 was a severe blow for the Christian Democrats. Many saw it as another mark of the general trend towards cultural and political secularization which seemed to be underway almost everywhere in Western Europe; parties such as the CDU/CSU which had traditionally relied (if only in part) on the political loyalty of religious groups were bound to suffer when those groups became either smaller or less cohesive. Nor had the West German party made any serious attempt to resist the general trend, seemingly preferring to join it instead; during the 1960s, despite the pleas and warnings of the Catholic hierarchy, it had presided over a steep reduction in the number of single-confession public schools and had even gone along with a liberalization of laws relating to homosexuality, blasphemy and adultery.[38] The party was from the start only partially reliant on a relatively solid Catholic vote however; it is interesting to note that the CDU/CSU was the only 'religious' party which Rose and Urwin, using West German data from 1967, did not rate as cohesive in terms of religion – its attachment to 'catch-all' politics was thus clearly reflected in the make-up of its electoral support.[39] As a broad, pragmatic party of the centre-right it was however well-placed to benefit when the tide of opinion turned back in favour of more conservative policies and attitudes in the mid-1970s. Among the factors which helped to turn the tide were the international economic crises associated with the oil-price increases of 1973 and 1979 and the resurgence of political violence and terrorism, not least on West German soil.

The overall 'swing to the right' which helped West Germany's Christian Democrats and was evident in much of northern Europe was not the only, or even the most striking, political trend which occurred in the wake of these developments however; there was also the emergence, particularly among the country's 'post-materialist' youth, of a wide range of campaigning groups and organizations devoted to the promotion of 'new politics' issues such as nuclear disarmament, women's rights, environmental pollution and concern for the plight of the Third World. Many of these groups included significant numbers of religious (mainly Protestant) activists, whose vocal presence tended to accelerate the 'political decomposition' of the religious constituencies, but the response of the general population to the new activism with its tactics of direct action and attention-grabbing initiatives was actually to become more conservative.[40] As the principal political vehicle of conservative values (secular as well as religious) the Christian Democrats were thus able to benefit doubly from the political turbulence of the 1970s and 1980s despite the continuing trend of cultural secularization. Greatly strengthened also by a reform of the party's organization, the CDU/CSU was finally returned to government in 1982 by courtesy of the FDP, which chose to switch coalition partners, and a year later the Christian Democrats achieved their second-highest ever electoral level of support.

As this account implies, the resurgence of the Christian Democrats owed most to factors unrelated to developments in the religious sphere; it was certainly not a consequence of some latter-day revival of religion. On the other hand it was not hindered by the fact that left-liberal proposals for reform in areas of particular sensitivity to the Churches and the more religious sections of the population also called forth a widespread conservative reaction. In 1972 the SPD–FDP coalition's proposal to liberalize the abortion law aroused predictably strong opposition among both Catholics and orthodox Protestants and inaugurated a long cycle of campaigning and public agitation on the issue. As if to add more fuel to such fires of religion-related controversy the FDP in 1974 published a series of theses and proposals under the title 'Free Churches in a Free State'. Amongst the proposals canvassed were the abolition of the Church tax in favour of an entirely voluntary system of membership dues, the removal of public subsidies and fiscal privileges and the introduction of a rule that public education should be religiously neutral. Upholders of traditional Catholic teaching were also further provoked by the liberalization of the divorce laws in 1977 and in the 1980 election there was a sign that the Catholic hierarchy was about to return to its old ways when a pastoral letter deplored not only the decline of moral standards but also the high level of the federal government's borrowing. This highly controversial lapse into old habits of direct political 'interference' seems to have been an aberration, however, and the 1980s saw markedly less controversy than the previous decade so far as the more directly religion-related issues were concerned. One reason for this was that by the time they decided to enter a coalition with the Christian Democrats in 1982 the FDP had dropped their commitment to reform Church–state relations (although it was clear that they would not agree to a repeal of the liberal reform of abortion and divorce legislation). One recent analyst argues that regardless of surface appearances which might imply its decline or decay the religious dimension has continued since 1949 and continues still to provide a significant factor underpinning the relative stability of voting patterns in Germany, at least on the right.[41]

CONCLUSION

The impact of the religious factor in the politics of Western Europe is often seen as an anachronistic survival from a pre-modern era. In so far as it has operated as a source of social cleavage and political differentiation, instead of a source of undisputed social and political authority, it has, however, failed to provide the social glue or cement which Durkheim and others regarded as its prime social function in traditional societies. It is true that the origin of the broad confessional differences which have resonated in the politics of several nations is to be found in the early-modern – and certainly the pre-industrial – era, although the other sources of religious–political cleavage between clerical and anti-clerical or religious and anti-religious (or religiously indifferent) population groups are at least in part products of the industrial age. And as has been seen these cleavages continue to be reflected in the patterns of mass politics of some countries (not least in Germany).

At the level of party systems and voter alignments the role of religion has been particularly prominent in much of Western Europe. For the first twenty years after the war cleavages between sections of the several populations identified by criteria of religious affiliation, attitude or behaviour continued to be reflected in the patterning of party support and, consequently, in the character of the parties themselves. This connection between religious differences and the choice of political alternatives at elections, having been established during the formative period of the party systems, survived into the 1960s largely through the operation of the inertial forces which survived the traumas of the Second World War. Even parties such as the CDU/CSU, which emerged for the first time after the war, have been seen to reflect the continuing impact of older religious cleavages as inherited electoral loyalties to earlier confessional parties were transferred to the new. In the British Isles and Scandinavia on the other hand the impact of the religious factor on voter alignments in this period was of political importance at national level only in the exceptional cases of Northern Ireland and parts of Norway, the class factor otherwise being overwhelmingly dominant. People who attached importance to religious matters in these societies tended to distribute their votes between parties either without reference to religious considerations or according to differing views as to the implications for political action of their religious concerns. Those who adopted this approach exemplified what Fogarty in the 1950s identified as the Anglo-Saxon type of Christian democracy in contrast to the continental type which was characterized by voters opting, along with others of the same religious stripe, for parties identified with distinct religious traditions.[42]

Since the 1960s politics in Western Europe has been characterized by unwonted levels of electoral volatility and old political loyalties have tended to be eroded. Two main types of explanation have been offered for the sea change which has occurred; it either marks a transitional process of *realignment* from the relatively stable conditions which existed when competing class and religious cleavages patterned the vote, to some future stable state when other cleavages may have established themselves, or it signals a loss of function for parties as such, a *dealignment* of voters and parties, as other types of organization such as public bureaucracies, the electronic media or pressure groups perform tasks previously undertaken by political parties.[43] If either of these explanations are borne out Christian democracy is likely to face a crisis along with all of Europe's other established party-political traditions. This does not mean that the impact of religion on politics would necessarily diminish further, although a continuing decline in the political cohesiveness of religious groups would mean that, even if there were to be no further decline in the actual size of those groups, their impact is likely to be more diffused. It is quite possible, however, that on one measure at least, the impact of religion could in fact increase as 'political Christians' engage themselves for and against the 'new politics' of peace, environmental, development and other issues. There are already signs of such diversity as was discussed in the last section.

It is also possible, however, that the thinkers of the Enlightenment were partly right and that as the part of the world where western Christianity, liberal democracy, the modern nation-state and industrial capitalism first took recognizable form (before they were exported to, or imposed upon, other parts of the world), Western Europe is now also pioneering entry into a post-religious age. If this turns out to be so, the post-Christian era in Europe itself will, in all probability, not so much see the disappearance of Christianity as its return instead to the socially and politically marginal position it occupied before Constantine elevated it into the official religion of the Roman Empire one-and-a-half millenia ago.[44] From this position Christians of different stripes will doubtless continue to make a distinctive contribution to the political life of societies to which they belong – all the more distinctive perhaps because of their marginality and almost certainly with more of an impact than their even more marginal forerunners before Constantine were either willing or able to achieve. In doing so, however, they are likely to find themselves as only one among a number of different minority constituencies attempting to make their voice heard; the triumphalist days when the Christian Church could claim the allegiance and obedience of men of power as well as their subjects are surely gone forever.

In Western Europe at least, religion's contribution to political life seems already to have changed from that of being a straitjacket, which for a long time constrained political movement, to that of being a coat-of-many-colours, which might yet add to the liveliness of political debate and the diversity of its sources of inspiration.

NOTES

1   See S.M. Lipset and S. Rokkan (1967), 'Cleavage structures, party systems and voter alignments', in S.M. Lipset and S. Rokkan (eds) *Party Systems, and Voter Alignments*, New York: Free Press.

2 See R. Rose and D. Urwin (1969), 'Social cohesion, political parties and strains in regimes', *Comparative Political Studies*, vol. 2, no. 1, p.12, emphasis added.
3 See A. Lijphart (1971), *Class Voting and Religious Voting in European Democracies*, Glasgow: University of Strathclyde Occasional Papers, see also R. Rose (ed.) (1974), *Electoral Behaviour: A Comparative Handbook*, London: Collier–Macmillan; D. Martin (1978), *A General Theory of Secularization*, Oxford: Basil Blackwell and J. H. Whyte (1981), *Catholics in Western Democracies*, Dublin: Gill and Macmillan.
4 See Martin, op.cit., p.6.
5 See J-M. Mauyeur (1980), *Des Partis catholiques à la Démocratie chrétienne XIXe–XXe siècles*, Paris: Armand Colin, pp.23–4.
6 See J.H. Whyte, 'Ireland: Politics without social bases', in Rose, op.cit., pp.619–51.
7 See K. Wald (1983), *Crosses on the Ballot: Patterns of British Voter Alignment Since 1885*, Princeton: Princeton University Press.
8 See Whyte (1981), *Catholics in Western Democracies*, Dublin: Gill and Macmillan, p.63.
9 Lipset and Rokkan, op.cit., p.50.
10 ibid.
11 See A. Lijphart (1968), *The Politics of Accommodation: Pluralism and Accommodation in the Netherlands*, Berkeley: University of California Press.
12 On France, see R.E.M. Irving (1973), *Christian Democracy in France*, London: George Allen & Unwin and on Spain see S.G. Payne (1984), *Spanish Catholicism: An Historical Overview*, Madison: University of Wisconsin Press.
13 See R.E.M. Irving (1979), *The Christian Democratic Parties of Western Europe*, London: Royal Institute of International Affairs and George Allen & Unwin. For a more recent overview see J.T.S. Madeley (1986), 'Prophets, priests and the polity: European Christian democracy in developmental perspective', in J. Hadden and A. Shupe (eds), *Prophetic Religions and Politics: Religion and the Political Order*, New York: Paragon House, Ch. 18.
14 Whyte, op.cit., Ch. 4.
15 ibid., p.88.
16 ibid., p.91.
17 Irving, op.cit., p.77.
18 See O. Kirchheimer (1971), 'The waning of opposition in parliamentary regimes', in R. Rose and M. Dogan (eds), *European Politics: A Reader*, London: Macmillan.
19 H. McLeod (1981), *Religion and the People of Western Europe*, Oxford: University Press, pp.134–5.
20 See Whyte, op.cit., p.111.
21 ibid., p.100.
22 See H. Bakvis (1981), *Catholic Power in the Netherlands*, Kingston and Montreal: McGill–Queen's University Press, p.2.
23 See J.T.S. Madeley (1977), 'Scandinavian Christian democracy: throwback or portent?', *European Journal of Political Research*, vol. 5, no. 3, pp.267–86.

24   Irving op.cit., p.xxi.
25   P. Furlong (1982), 'The Italian Christian democrats: From Catholic movement to conservative party', *Hull Papers in Politics*, no. 25, Hull: University of Hull Department of Politics, p.40.
26   ibid.
27   See Z. Layton-Henry (ed.) (1982), *Conservative Politics in Western Europe*, New York: St. Martin's Press, p.17.
28   See F. Spotts (1973), *The Churches and Politics in Germany*, Middletown: Wesleyan University Press, p.291.
29   See McLeod, op.cit., p.137.
30   See M.P. Fogarty (1957), *Christian Democracy in Western Europe 1820–1953*, London: Routledge and Kegan Paul, pp.7–9.
31   See O. Kirchheimer, op.cit., pp.280–96.
32   See K. Buchheim (1953), *Geschichte der Christlichen Parteien in Deutschland*, Munich: Kösel Verlag.
33   ibid., p.281.
34   See E. Troeltsch (1931), *The Social Teaching of the Christian Churches*, trans. by O. Wyon, London: George Allen & Unwin.
35   G. Pridham (1977), *Christian Democracy in West Germany*, London: Croom Helm, p.23.
36   Irving op.cit., p.121.
37   See A.J. Heidenheimer (1960), *Adenauer and the CDU: The Rise of the Leader and the Integration of the Party*, The Hague: Nijhoff.
38   See Spotts, op.cit.
39   See Rose and Urwin, op.cit., p.59.
40   See K.L. Baker, R.J. Dalton and K. Hildebrandt (1981), *Germany Transformed: Political Culture and the New Politics*, Cambridge, MA: Harvard University Press, p.295.
41   See F. Pappi (1984), 'The West German party system', *West European Politics*, vol. 7, no. 4, pp.7–26.
42   See Fogarty, op.cit., p.10.
43   See R. Dalton, S. Flanagan and P. Beck (eds) (1984), *Electoral Change in Advanced Industrial Democracies*, Princeton: Princeton University Press.
44   See A.D. Gilbert (1980), *The Making of Post-Christian Britain*, London: Longman.

Chapter 3

Politics and religion in Eastern Europe and the Soviet Union

Sabrina Ramet

INTRODUCTION

Great historical changes have often been associated with changes in religion. Whether one thinks of the emergence of patriarchal religion, or the replacement of the Olympian religion by Christianity, the spread of Islam in Arabia and the Near East, the conversion of the Mongols from Islam to Buddhism, the Protestant Reformation and subsequent Catholic Counter-Reformation, or in this age, the reforms of the Catholic Church's Second Vatican Council and the encouragement which that inadvertently gave to liberation theology, the resilience or ennervation of specific religious forms has had direct consequences for people's attitudes about authority, social roles, social mores and concepts of liberation and progress. Moreover, as social behaviours and political roles have changed, religious organizations have often adapted themselves to the changing environment, even as new religions appear in response to new demands.

When the communists took power in the USSR in 1917 (and in Eastern Europe after the Second World War), they understood the first part of this correlation – that religious forms have political consequences – but did not fully appreciate the second part – viz., that political changes may elicit successful adaptive behaviour on the part of Churches. They therefore adopted policies designed to erode religion, believing, mistakenly, that secularization was a simple process and ignoring the fact that the chief result of secularization is not the disappearance of religion but the shattering of the religious monopoly, and hence, in consequence, the mushrooming of alternative faiths.

The communists underestimated the adaptive resilience of religious organizations and thus they concluded, mistakenly, that in the effort to achieve social homogenization, they could assault both religious culture and national culture without reinforcing the strong organic bonds that tie them together. The history of communism has demonstrated, however, that efforts to suppress aspects of indigenous culture (as most graphically illustrated in the programmes of Russification, Bulgarianization and Romanianization) highlight the internal ties connecting those aspects; in practice, those efforts have thus underscored the nationalist aspect of religious organizations. The communist effort to depoliticize religion backfired, and actually deepened its politicization.

This chapter will focus specifically on the relationship between the religious policy and nationalities policy of the communist regimes of Eastern Europe and the Soviet Union as it existed up to 1989–90 when most of the communist regimes began to fall. In particular, I shall argue that for that period there is a direct correlation between regime policy *vis-à-vis* nationalism and regime policy *vis-à-vis* religion. A regime policy hostile to nationalism and national heritage is apt to be associated with a policy that throws the Church into an opposition posture. On the other hand, a regime policy supportive of nationalism tends to be associated with a co-optive relationship with the relevant Church. Since there is usually only one Church which is closely associated with the national heritage of any given people, this correlation is usually clear enough. It becomes more complicated when a given national group has long historic ties with two or more Churches to the extent that more than one Church may be viewed as the 'national' Church (as in the case of the Hungarians, the Romanians, the Latvians, and arguably, the Ukrainians).

RELIGIOUS COMPOSITION OF THE AREA

There is no reliable data on religious affiliation in Albania, where religion was officially banned between 1967–90. (It might be noted that in Albania, the last East European country to be significantly affected by the 1989–90 revolutionary tide, religion is once again re-surfacing into the public domain. Reports from Albania indicate that the authorities allowed a Catholic mass to take place at Rrmajit in November 1990, which was attended by at least several hundred people. It was led by a priest who had recently been released from prison where he had been held for twenty five years.) But surveying the other eight countries of the region, one finds conservatively close to 227 million adherents of various religious organizations today. Of these, the largest number (89 million) are Orthodox, with about two thirds of them living in the USSR (50 million Russian Orthodox and 5 million Georgian Orthodox). The second largest group is the Catholic Church, with some 69 million members in the region; 36.8 million of these live in Poland. The Muslims are the third largest group, with 49 million in the area; almost all of them (44 million nominal Muslims) live in the Soviet Union. There are also 12 million Protestants and Seventh Day Adventists, 4 million Armenian Apostolics, 1.6 million Jews, 590,000 Buddhists and 133,000 members of Apostolic congregations, not to mention smaller numbers adhering to other religious organizations.

Table 3.1   Religious groups numbering 2,000 or more, in the USSR and Eastern Europe

(All figures are from 1988, unless otherwise stated)

USSR

Orthodox	
Russian Orthodox	50 m.[1]
Georgian Orthodox	5 m.[2]
Armenian Apostolics	4 m.
Old Believers	3 m.[3]
Muslims	14–50 m. (nominal)[2]
Catholics	5–10 m.
Jews	1.5 m.
Lutherans	570,000[4]
Pentecostals	100–300,000
Hungarian Reformed	80,000
Reformed Church of Trans carpathia	70,000[4]
Seventh Day Adventists	32,000
True Adventists	32,000
Mennonites	15,000
Reformed Church of Lithuania	10,000[5]
Pentecostal Zionists	10,000[5]
Ind. Mennonite Brethren	5,000
Methodists	2,200
Other Christians	
Jehovah's Witnesses	10–20,000[4]
Molokans	10,000[4]

Buddhists	590,000
Bahai	4,000[6]
Hare Krishna	3,000
Murashkoites	2,000[5]
Innozenti	2,000[5]

German Democratic Republic
Protestants
   Evangelical–Lutherans

	7.7 m. (nominal)[3]
	5–5.5 m. (government estimate of actual #)
Methodists	28,000
Baptist Federation	20,000
Reformed	15,000
Old Lutherans	7,500
Evangelical–Lutheran Free	3,050
Moravian Church (Unity of Brethren)	2,600
Catholics	1.05m.
Apostolic Communities	
New Apostolic	100,000
Apostolate of Jesus Christ	12–14,000
Shepherd and Flock	7,000
Community in Christ Jesus (Lorenzianer)	5,000
Apostolate of Juda	3,000[7]
Catholic–Apostolic	2,000
Reformed Apostolic	2,000
Other Christian	
Jehovah's Witnesses	25–30,000
Seventh Day Adventists	9,000
Christian Community (Christengemeinschaft)	5,000
Mormons	4,700
John's Church (Johannische Kirche)	3,500
Muslims	2,000[8]

Poland

Catholics	36.8 m.[1]
Catholic-Splinter	
Old Catholics	25,000
Polish National Catholics	25,000
Catholic Church of the Maravites	4,000[9]
Orthodox	855,000[4]
Protestants	
Lutherans	70,000
United Evangelical	10,000

Methodists	8,000
Baptists	7,000
Reformed	4,000
Other Christian	
Jehovah's Witnesses	100,000
Seventh Day Adventists	7,000
Union of Free Bible Scientists	2,043[9]
Jews	8,000[5]
Muslims	2,000[11]
Hare Krishna	Unknown: possibly 2,000

Czechoslovakia

Catholics	
Roman Catholics	10,024,361[11]
Greek-Rite Catholics	353,991[4]
Protestants	
Hussite	500,000
Slovak Evangelical	369,000
Czech Brethren	230,000
Reformed, Slovakia	100,000
Silesian Evangelical	48,000
Church of Brethren	6,000
Moravian Church (Unity of Brethren)	6,000
United Methodists	5,200
Darbyists	5,000[5]
Baptists	4,000
Orthodox	20–30,000[4]
Other Christian	
Jehovah's Witnesses	7,680[5]
Seventh Day Adventists	7,000
Old Catholics	3,000[4]
Unitarian	2,000
Czech Apostolic	2,000
Jews	5,000[5]
Muslims	2,000[8]

Hungary

Catholics	
Roman Catholics	6,339,978[4]
Greek-Rite Catholics	322,800[4]
Protestants	
Reformed (Calvinist)	1.9 m.
Lutherans	430,000
Baptists	20,000
Pentecostals	7,000[2]
Methodists	2,000
Free Christians	2,000[4]

Other Christians
    Unitarians   15,000[12]
    Nazarenes   7,000[10]
    Seventh Day Adventists   4,761[5]
    Jehovah's Witnesses   4,500[12]
Jews   80,000
Orthodox   40,000[4]

Yugoslavia
Catholics
    Roman Catholics   6,677,490[4]
    Greek-Rite Catholics   48,760[4]
Orthodox
    Serbian Orthodox   8 m. (nominal)[4]
                                4 m. (probable actual)
    Macedonian Orthodox   600,000–1 m.[3]
    Romanian Orthodox (in Voj
      vodina)   5,000[5]
Muslims   3.8 m.[11]
Protestants
    Slovak Lutherans   51,000
    Slovene Lutherans   20,000
    Pentecostals   11,300
    Lutheran Church of Croatia,
      Bosnia-Herzegovina and
      Vojvodina   4,950[4]
    Methodists   4,000
    Baptists   2–3,000
    Calvinists   22,406[5]
    Hungarian Lutherans   2,000[11]
Other Christians
    Seventh Day Adventists   10,600
    Jehovah's Witnesses   10,000
    Old Catholics   5,000[12]
    Church of God   4,000[5]
    Nazarenes   2,000[5]
Jews   Less than 6,000

Romania
Orthodox
    Romanian Orthodox   15.5 m.[3]
    (of which, Lord's Army   = 400,000[9])
    Old Believers   40,000[5]
    Serbian Orthodox   36,000[5]
Catholics
    Roman Catholics   1.39 m.
    Greek Catholics   .75 m.
Protestants
    Reformed   715,000
    Pentecostals   200–250,000

Baptists	200,000
German Lutherans	137,000
Brethren	40–50,000
Plymouth Brethren	45,000
Hungarian Lutherans	32,000[1]
Other Christian	
Unitarians	70,000
Jehovah's Witnesses	55–60,000
Seventh Day Adventists	50,000
Armenian–Gregorian	7,000[5]
Muslims	38,000
Jews	22,000

Bulgaria

Orthodox	6 m.[9]
Muslims	1.05 m.[10]
Catholics	70,000
Armenian Apostolic	16,000[5]
Protestants	
Pentecostals	2,000–10,000
Congregationalists	1,500–5,000
Darbyists	3,000[5]
Other Christians	
Church of God	4,000
Seventh Day Adventists	3,000
Jews	Less than 5,000
Hare Krishna	Unknown: perhaps 2,000

Notes:

1	1986
2	1979
3	1974
4	1984
5	1982
6	1970
7	1983
8	1971
9	1980
10	1987
11	1981
12	1978

I am grateful to James Critchlow, Joseph Pungur, Gerd Stricker, and Philip Walters for reviewing the data and providing corrections, up-dated figures and emendations. They are, of course, not responsible for any inaccuracies that may remain.

Sources: East German and Yugoslav data derive from on-site interviews and data collection in 1987 and 1988, and from the following sources: W. Kaul (1984), *Kirchen und Religionsgemeinschaften in der DDR – Eine Dokumentation*, Rostok-Warnemunde: Institute for Marxism–Leninism, pp.5–6; *Zahlenspiegel Bundesrepublik Deutschland Deutsche Demo-*

kratische Republik: Ein Vergleich (1988), 3rd edn, Bonn: Federal Ministry
for Inter-German Relations, p.97; and H. Kirchner (ed.) (1987), *Frei-
kirchen und Konfessionelle Minderheitskirchen*, East Berlin: Evangelische Verlagsenstalt. Most other figures are taken from individual
chapters in the following: P. Ramet (ed.) (1988), *Eastern Christianity
and Politics in the Twentieth Century*, Durham: Duke University Press;
P. Ramet (ed.) (1990), *Catholicism and Politics in Communist Societies*,
Durham, NC: Duke University Press; S. Ramet (ed.) (forthcoming),
Protestantism and Politics in the Soviet Union and Eastern Europe.
Some figures for East European Jews come from: *Neue Zürcher Zeitung*
(1982), 15–16 August, p.6; M. Pollack (1982), 'Anti-Semitism in Poland',
The Tablet, 30 January, pp.99–100; T. Beeson (1982), *Discretion and
Valour: Religious Conditions in Russia and Eastern Europe*, rev. edn,
Philadelphia: Fortress Press; *Radio Free Europe Research* (1985), 3
May. Some figures for Muslims come from S. Balic (1979), 'Eastern
Europe: The Islamic dimensions', *Journal of the Institute of Muslim
Minority Affairs*, vol. 1, no. 3, p.31; *Keston News Service* (1987),
no. 272, p.31; F. De Jong (1986), 'Islam at the Danube: History and
present-day conditions of the Muslim community in Romania', *Religion
in Communist Dominated Areas*, vol. 25, no. 3, p.136; 'News in brief'
(1977), *Religion in Communist Lands*, vol. 5, no. 4, p.272; *The Times*
(1985), (London), 8 February, p.10, 16 February, p.6, 20 February, p.9,
and 17 April, p.9; *Vestnik Statistiki* (1980), (Moscow), no. 7, pp.41–2; and
Z. T. Irwin (1989), 'The fate of Islam in the Balkans: A comparison of four
state policies', in P. Ramet (ed.), *Religion and Nationalism in Soviet and
East European Politics*, rev. edn, Durham: Duke University Press. Other
data are derived from: *Keston News Service*; E. Voss (ed.) (1984), *Die
Religionsfreiheit in Osteuropa*, Zollikon: GZW Verlag; J. Broun (1988),
Conscience and Captivity: Religion in Eastern Europe, Ethics and Public
Policy Center, Washington, DC.

In several countries, one Church predominates both in terms of numbers of adherents and, in consequence, in terms of mobilizable political power. In the former German Democratic Republic (GDR), the Evangelical Church, which numbers between 5 and 7.7 million members, dwarfs all other Churches and the relationship between this Church and the state has often set the tone for other Churches in the GDR. In Poland, this position is occupied by the Catholic Church, and the identification of Poland with Catholicism is so strong that loyalty to the Church is frequently viewed as a question of patriotism. In Czechoslovakia and Hungary, the Catholic Church is again clearly the preponderant ecclesiastical body, but in these countries there are also substantial Protestant minorities which lay claim to a role in having shaped the national culture and national heritage. In Romania, fully 15.5 million persons belong to the Romanian Orthodox Church; the next largest Church, the Roman Catholic Church, is far behind, with only 1.39 million believers. And in Bulgaria, it is again the Orthodox Church which is in a numerically auspicious position. In Yugoslavia, by contrast, no single Church can lay claim to the loyalty of even half of the population. The Serbian Orthodox Church may be the largest body, with perhaps as many as 8 million adherents. The Catholic Church is close behind, with 6.7 million Roman and Greek-rite Catholics. Yugoslavia's 3.8 million-strong Islamic community as such has tended to be less political than the Catholic and Orthodox Churches, although there have been some noisy controversies over the years.[1]

A TYPOLOGY OF NATIONALISM

Regimes may construct policies to deal with religion and nationalism, as they find them, but they can rarely rewrite the past so successfully that the meanings associated with their identities are lost. For that reason, I believe it will be useful to outline a brief 'typology of nationalism', identifying the chief examples of each type.[2]

Nationalism is simultaneously an orientation towards one's own ethno-national community, including its history, culture and religion, and an orientation towards the outside world. The different orientations possible along these two axes account for five modal types of nationalism. These are: *heroic* nationalism, in which mythology stresses the successful struggle against external challenges (e.g. English and French nationalism); *traumatic* nationalism, in which popular mythology stresses defeats in the struggle against external challenges and threats (e.g. Czech, Serbian, Hungarian and Armenian nationalism); *defiant* nationalism, which stresses uncertainty in struggles and the continued existence of external threats (e.g. Polish, Lithuanian, Albanian, Croatian, German and, possibly, Romanian nationalism); *muted* nationalism, in which there is less stress on struggle, more stress on cultural achievements or economic productivity or simply the community's way of life (e.g. Austrian, Belorussian, Slovak and Slovenian nationalism); and *problematic* nationalism, in which group members do not share a consensus about their collective identity, so that some members identify themselves one way, others another way, with still others changing their self-identification from one group to another (e.g. Macedonians, Moldavians[3] and Bosnia's 'ethnic Muslims'[4]).

To these one may add *messianic* nationalism, with Russian nationalism being the only example from the region under discussion (although the fifteenth-century Hussites in Bohemia also displayed messianic convictions). Messianic nationalism is probably a subset of heroic nationalism, in so far as both orientations are inspired by visions of victory over external enemies. But there is a difference. Heroic nationalism is oriented primarily towards past or present victories, while messianic nationalism (which, in the Russian case, may draw energy from contemplation of past trauma) is riveted on visions of the future. Moreover, while heroic nationalism is apt to nurture feelings of collective superiority over outsiders, messianic nationalism *necessarily* portrays the nation as superior and dreams of exporting its culture to its 'inferior' neighbours.[5]

Any of these types of nationalism may be declared 'taboo' by the given regime. To the extent that this is done explicitly and forcefully, the population inevitably grasps that its nationalism is not 'legitimate', not on a par with other nationalisms. This in turn may lead to a change in consciousness and behaviour, especially towards such nationality groups as may be identified with the regime in question. In this sense, *taboo* nationalism may appear in some ways to be a distinct category; it is, however, important to keep in mind that *any* nationalism may become taboo. Examples include German, Croatian and Ukrainian nationalism, all of which were taboo for many years after the Second World War.

Obviously, Churches will relate very differently to different types of nationalism. In communities animated by defiant nationalism, the Church is apt to find itself investing more of itself in nurturing and supporting the national culture than would be the case in communities characterized by muted nationalism. Where national identity is problematic, the religious organization can be expected to take a low profile, even if it has sympathies one way or the other. And in instances characterized by traumatic nationalism, the essential question is whether the Church is identified with the nation-as-victim (e.g. the Serbian Orthodox Church in the centuries following the 1389 Battle of Kosovo polje) or with the nation's oppressors (e.g. the Catholic Church in Bohemia and Moravia in the centuries following the 1620 Battle of White Mountain).

The communist regimes of Eastern Europe and the Soviet Union have made it abundantly clear, both through their statements and through their behaviour, that in framing their policies towards religious organizations, they are concerned, among other things, with the latter's orientation towards nationalism. Accordingly, the nature of the given nationalism can be expected to enter into the calculus of religious policy.

HOW MARXISTS VIEW RELIGION

The specific charges levelled by Marx and early Marxists against religion – for example, that it is a source of solace for the weak (an 'opium') and a buttress of reactionary ideology – are well known and do not require any elaboration here. There are, however, three points about the Marxist view of religion which I would like to explore briefly.

First, leaving aside Albania, where all religion was illegal until 1990, the regimes in the other countries of the region have repeatedly described religion as the 'private' concern of the individual. On the one hand, this constitutes a kind of promise (not always kept) that the excesses of the Stalin era will not be repeated and a pledge that the authorities will respect the privacy of people's religious faith and practice. On the other hand, clergy have from time to time protested that this formula is the fig leaf for a policy of 'privatization' of religion, meaning that religious organizations shall not have the right to be actively engaged with matters of public concern or to play a role in public life.[6] Churches, in the long-prevailing Marxist viewpoint, were to be reduced to liturgical institutions, with no other task than the holding of divine services. This view best characterized the Soviet regime, although it also coloured the thinking of most of the East European regimes, especially in the 1950s. By the late 1980s, however, this had at least begun to be eroded almost everywhere.

The second point is almost at cross purposes with the first, for in so far as the Churches are riven by internal tensions, the authorities often exploited these tensions, typically with an eye to undermining the position of the bishop or priest. Hence, in most of the countries of Eastern Europe, the early postwar years saw active communist encouragement of priests' associations independent of hierarchical control – associations which the communists hoped would weaken the authority of the hierarchy. The same strategy was played with different tactics in the USSR, where in the 1920s, reformist lower clergy were encouraged to set up an anti-hierarchical 'Living Church' which was, in turn, condemned by the patriarch.[7] The Yugoslav newspaper *Vjesnik* explained this strategy in 1982, noting the desirability of creating 'social conditions in which both believers and priests will be as little dependent on the hierarchy as possible'.[8]

In the USSR,

> the day-to-day affairs of the parish are in the hands of an executive committee (*ispolnitelny komitet*), whose members are elected by the general assembly of the religious society, but whose election is subject to a veto by the state registration agencies.[9]

This system, designed to diminish the role and stature of the parish priest, is now, however, subject to change under a 1990 Law on Freedom of Conscience and Religion. If fully implemented, this law would effectively move state policy in the Soviet Union away from an anti-religion posture and towards a more neutral stance.

And finally, there is the more general question of the place of religion in communist society. This question has various aspects. To begin with, some regime spokesmen, e.g. in the former GDR, argued that the Church could play a 'necessary' role under socialism.[10] Certain prelates (such as Hungary's Bishops Cserháti and Káldy[11]) tried to exploit this opening and offered at one time to put Church ethical teachings to work in the service of the state. Then there is the further question as to whether religion was seen as being doomed to extinction or whether it can survive indefinitely. The latter opinion gained ground among East European Marxists, before the events of 1989–90 overwhelmed their cause.[12] And this in turn related to the question as to whether believers should be admitted into the Communist party. Party regulation proscribed the admission of believers, but in practice believers quietly obtained admission to at least half of the parties in the region, including those of East Germany, Poland and Czechoslovakia. The traditional communist view was, as Klaus Gysi, the one-time East German Secretary for Church Affairs, put it in 1981, that the Church could 'never be fully integrated in our society as a social force.'[13] But the consensus on that prescription gradually broke down and then, of course, became largely irrelevant in the light of the new circumstances which arose in 1989.

THE CONFRONTATIONAL MODE

I shall distinguish, in discussing the East European pattern as it existed until 1989–90, between accommodative and confrontational relations between Church and state, and again between a regime strategy of co-opting the national heritage and of repressing it. There are other conceivable relationships which a regime may nurture where religion and nationalism are concerned respectively,

Figure 3.1   Permutations of regime religious policy

	ACCOMMODATIVE RELIGIOUS CLIMATE	CONFRONTATIONAL RELIGIOUS CLIMATE
REGIME POLICY CO-OPTIVE TOWARD NATIONALISM	Evangelical–Lutheran Church in the GDR since the 1970s Serbian Orthodox Church since 1984 Macedonian Orthodox Church since 1967 Armenian Apostolic Church Major Churches in Hungary Bulgarian Orthodox Romanian Orthodox Russian Orthodox Church under Gorbachev	Albania Uniates in Romania
REGIME POLICY HOSTILE TOWARD NATIONALISM	Muslims in Yugoslavia	Evangelical–Lutheran Church in the GDR up to the 1970s Catholic Church in Poland Catholic Church in Croatia Uniates in the Ukraine Soviet Jews Lutheran Church in Latvia Catholic Church in Lithuania Muslims in Central Asia

but in practice, as Bohdan Bociurkiw has noted,[14] these are the dominant modes. This in turn suggests four possible permutations for regime policy: accommodative towards religion and co-optive of nationalism, accommodative towards religion and hostile to nationalism confrontational towards religion and hostile to nationalism, and confrontational towards religion but co-optive of nationalism. These alternative patterns, together with religious organizations illustrative of each, are mapped out in Figure 3.1.

Two things are immediately striking about this diagram. First, there is obviously a high correlation between regime policy towards religion and regime policy towards nationalism. And second, matching these cases against the cases identified in the typology of nationalisms, one finds that cases of traumatic and problematic nationalism are consistently associated with accommodative relations between Church and state, while cases of defiant nationalism are, with one exception (the Romanian Orthodox Church), associated with confrontational relations between Church and state.

I propose to discuss these alternative modes, drawing upon several examples, but with a special focus on the experiences of the Evangelical–Lutheran Church in East Germany.

When Church and state disagree on the premiss for their mutual relations and operate in the absence of a *modus vivendi*, that Church and state are in a *confrontational mode*. Within this broad category there is room for considerable variation. At one extreme, the Greek-Rite Catholic (Uniate) Church in the Ukraine was made illegal in 1946. Its churches and other facilities were either turned over to the Russian Orthodox Church or closed down. Its bishops and priests were either absorbed into the Russian Orthodox Church or jailed. Its believers were told their Church had been flirting with Ukrainian 'bourgeois nationalism' and that it had compromised itself with the Nazis. Repeated petitions by believers in the course of the 1970s produced nothing, and even in the Gorbachev era, despite hints that the secular authorities (as opposed to the Russian Orthodox Church) had no interest in the matter, the Uniates made only very slow headway towards regaining legal status. Not until the November 1990 Law on Freedom of Conscience and Religion did the situation change. If implemented, this will give all churches official recognition, enabling them to own property and function as legally recognized entities.[15]

At the other extreme one might list the Catholic Church in Poland, against which the authorities had to proceed with considerable caution. In fact, in Poland, the launching of the anti-religious drive was delayed by several years and when it did come, the Church was able to retain its Catholic University at Lublin, its seminaries and its churches. On the other hand, the authorities seized Church hospitals, nursing homes and orphanages, imprisoned several bishops in the mid-1950s and, in 1953, passed a decree requiring government approval of all Church appointments, transfers and even changes in pastoral jurisdiction.[16] The Gierek era (1970–80) brought some improvements for the Church, especially in the latter years; in these years it became easier for the Church, for example, to construct new churches and to develop its publishing activity. But even then, the regime held the Church at arm's length, and there were new difficulties in the 1980s.[17]

Suppressing the Polish Church was never a realistic option, but the communists did try, in the early years, to persuade local bishops to break their ties with the Vatican and set themselves up as an autocephalous National Church.[18] The authorities also tried to rewrite Polish history in such a way as to minimize the role of the Church in the sustenance and defence of the national culture. The Church responded in the spirit of defiance, criticizing the party's distortion of history and organizing cultural events and educational forums through which to disseminate its own views.[19]

And again, in Croatia, one found the Church on the defensive – often with a sense of being embattled, welcoming dialogue with the authorities, but simultaneously speaking out in defence of Croatian history and culture, human rights and the rights of believers. Regime spokesmen repeatedly tried to tarnish the Catholic Church with the brush of fascism, alleging that its earlier bishops (Stepinac, Rožman, Šarić, Bonefačić) were supporters of the wartime *Ustaše* regime, and occasionally that its current bishops were admirers of fascist ideas.[20]

These examples have several things in common. First, the local nationalism was and in some respects remains, in each case, an unwelcome 'opposition' nationalism: Ukrainian and Polish nationalisms are traditionally anti-Russian, while Croatian nationalism is above all anti-Serbian and, in the Yugoslav context, potentially secessionist. Second, in none of these countries were the authorities able to subvert the Church from within or to co-opt the Church into accommodative co-operation: in the Ukraine, with the exception of a few quiet approaches to Father Iosyf Terelya, suggesting that he organize an autocephalous Catholic Church, the authorities did not really try, and in the other countries, regime efforts proved unavailing. Third, in each case, prelates and clerics alike had had long experience in opposition politics – especially in Croatia.[21]

These same themes re-emerge in East Germany, although with a particular twist, mainly because there was no such thing as 'East German nationalism' or 'East German culture'. When the GDR was established in 1949, it was a severely truncated state. In order to justify its refusal to unite with West Germany in a single German state, and hoping to attenuate the population's ties with

West Germany, the regime tried to perpetrate the notion that a new 'socialist German' nation had arisen, which was culturally distinct from the 'bourgeois German' nation in the west.[22] This new socialist German nation could be dated from 1949. Prior to that, there was little positive to be found in German history, though Beethoven and Goethe were appropriately appreciated. East German historian Alexander Abusch, in his 1946 book, *Der Irrweg einer Nation*, described the German people as 'corrupted by chauvinistic nationalism' and found nothing of lasting value in German history. He described Luther as 'the greatest spiritual figure of German counterrevolution for centuries.'[23] Abusch's contemporary, Wolfram von Hanstein, tried to trace Nazism to a spiritual ancestry deeply imbedded in German history. For von Hanstein, the ultimate source of Nazism was Martin Luther, because he had opposed popular revolution and in particular the rebellion being stirred up by the radical clergyman, Thomas Müntzer.[24]

The SED, or Sozialistische Einheitspartei Deutschlands, the ruling party of the GDR (now renamed the Party of Democratic Socialism in the post-unification period), wanted not only to split the German nation, but also to split the Evangelical Church which, for the first twenty years, maintained its organizational unity across the two Germanys. The Church resisted state pressures until 1968, finally coming to the conclusion that there was no alternative to accommodation.[25]

The state tried actively to draw citizens away from religion. Even before the GDR was formally established, Soviet occupation authorities ordered villagers and citizens in many towns to report for work on farms and in factories on Sundays, in order to prevent them from attending church. The authorities also interfered in religious instruction in some communities, banned most Bible study groups and, in 1954, introduced a youth dedication ceremony (*Jugendweihe*) in which young people were pressed to take a pledge of loyalty to atheism.[26] The SED also directed its press to slander Berlin's Bishop Dibelius as 'an agent of western militarism and imperialism'.[27] Later, in January 1953, *Junge Welt*, the official organ of the East German youth organization, spearheaded a press campaign aimed at portraying Christian young people as saboteurs and traitors.[28] A few clergymen were tried on trumped up charges and imprisoned.

In 1956, *Neue Zeit*, the official newspaper of the east wing of the Christian Democratic Union (hereafter, CDU–East), published an article which included a telling warning:

In the light of the two-state division of Germany it is unendurable that the loyalty of the Church in the German Democratic Republic remains constantly under a shadow. It would be in order for Church leaders to declare that they respect our laws and that they separate themselves from the NATO policies which seek to involve the EKD [the Church union] in the cold war.[29]

Despite certain amicable contacts between Bishop Moritz Mitzenheim of Thuringia and the regime (symbolized in a joint communique issued on 21 July 1958), and despite the Church's eventual agreement to sever organizational ties with the West German Church and to establish a separate organizational structure within the GDR, relations between the Evangelical–Lutheran Church and the state remained tense into the 1970s. Church and state enjoyed some co-operative links, for example, in pooling resources in psychiatric care and in state support of six theological faculties, but the regime continued to think of the Church as an institution doomed to die out – a view clearly embodied in the regime's refusal, until 1976, to authorize the construction of churches in any of the 'new communities' built after the war.

All in all the SED repudiated the national memory, rejected the Church's past (most tellingly, Martin Luther, the central unifying symbol for the Evangelical–Lutheran Church), and aspired to strangle religion out of GDR society – through the constriction of church construction, the establishment of ceilings for seminary enrolments, the disparagement of religion in the schools and media and systematic discrimination against believers in education and career advancement.

THE ACCOMMODATIVE MODE

When Church and state are in a confrontational mode, neither side makes serious compromises. State hostility towards religion is overt and scarcely disguised and the Church is thrown into a posture of defensive defiance. The accommodative mode, by contrast, involves compromise on both sides – sometimes mostly on the Church's side (as in the case of the Romanian and Bulgarian Orthodox Churches), but sometimes more clearly on the part of both Church and state (as in the case of the Serbian and Macedonian Churches and the Churches in Hungary generally). More fundamentally, it entails a consensus on the premises for their mutual relations, the achievement of an agreement on the 'rules of the game'. Church and state can move from a confrontational mode to an accommodative mode when they become convinced that the confrontational mode is unduly costly and that they may be able to realize certain advantages through mutual accommodation. In the GDR, Evangelical Bishop Albrecht Schönherr, first chair of the Evangelical Federation, sent a very clear conciliatory message at a synodal meeting in Eisenach in 1971, when he declared the Church's interest in being 'not ... the Church *against* socialism, nor the Church *beside* socialism, [but] ... the Church *in* socialism'.[30] Earlier the SED had complained that the Church would not avow its political loyalty to the state. Now Schönherr offered this too, promising that 'the Church will oppose all attempts to militate against the state'.[31]

Church and state began to explore the possibility of reaching a *modus vivendi*. As Robert Goeckel has noted, the SED was starting to appreciate that the Evangelical Church's western ties could play a certain role in buttressing the incipient inter-German detente, and in consequence, Church–state relations became tangibly less conflictual in the years 1973–74.[32] Meanwhile, the SED was also reviewing its entire posture towards German history. These two processes – re-examination of religious policy and re-examination of the posture towards the national heritage – came to a head at almost exactly the same time in early 1978, when the GDR began to reclaim its German heritage (beginning with an ostentatious rehabilitation of Friedrich the Great and Otto von Bismarck) and agreed to hold a summit meeting with Church leaders. On 6 March 1978, SED General Secretary Erich Honecker received Bishop Schönherr and other Church dignitaries for a formal working meeting. As a result of this meeting, the Church was able to extend its publishing activity, to construct and renovate church buildings more or less without difficulty and to broadcast monthly radio programmes with Church news and information. Clergymen were also now made eligible for state pensions.[33]

By this point, Marxist historiography of Luther had already undergone considerable transformation. Luther was now credited with having contributed to the 'early bourgeois revolution' in Europe and his opposition to the 'feudal' Roman Catholic Church was especially praised.[34] The party theoretical journal, *Einheit*, published '15 Theses on Martin Luther' in 1981, noting now that 'Luther's progressive legacy has been absorbed into the socialist culture of the [East] German nation'.[35] The SED was clearly looking towards the quincentenary celebration of Martin Luther in 1983, which would now fit in very well with its new, embracive approach towards German history. On 13 June 1980, the Martin Luther Committee of the GDR was established, with Erich Honecker as its president. Various Church dignitaries participated as members of the committee, and during the year-long celebrations in 1983, Church and state co-operated in many ways. The state financed the reconstruction and repair of various churches and other sites of importance for Luther, and provided transportation to certain Church events. Church and state dignitaries also participated in various ceremonies to honour Luther. Martin Luther, once scorned as a 'counter-revolutionary', was now hailed by the East German press as 'one of the greatest sons of the German people'.[36] Honecker himself would say, 'In the battles of his times, Martin Luther exerted great influence upon the development of history. He was one of the most prominent humanists, whose efforts were of value to a more just world'.[37]

Luther's teachings were now found to be compatible with 'socialist foreign policy', and due attention was paid to Luther's exhortations to Christians to be socially active and loyal to their secular authorities. *Neue Zeit* even praised Luther's work ethic which, it said, 'has the same consequences as the political economics of socialism, i.e., the readiness to put talents and knowledge in the service of continued economic and social progress of our society'.[38]

In the wake of the 'Luther Year', Dresden's Bishop Johannes Hempel, then chair of the Evangelical Federation, noted that there was a new warmth in Church–state relations, despite the persistence of certain unresolved problems. It is true, of course, that there have been frictions in Church–state relations both before and since the Luther Year, in connection with the Church's involvement in pacifist and environmentalist concerns. The Church's willingness to allow hundreds of grass roots pacifist groups to use its premises has not gone unnoticed by the state. Moreover, beginning in early 1988 there were a series of occasions of state censorship of Church newspapers which led to outcry and protest from Church circles.[39] But the Church remained committed to its loyalist posture, embodied in the concept of 'Church in socialism'[40] and the state, for its part, has clearly wanted to preserve a basic working relationship. Moreover, the SED continued to look to early religious figures as sources of legitimation of German socialism, forming a committee, in March

1988, to celebrate the quincentenary (in 1989) of utopian theologian Thomas Müntzer.[41]

It is worth emphasizing that the degree of compromise necessary to achieve an accommodative relationship, in which Church and state derive certain benefits from forms of co-operation, is variable. The East German Church, surely, compromised much less than, for example, the Bulgarian, Romanian, or Russian Orthodox Churches. Indeed, the speed and totality with which the Bulgarian and Romanian Churches submitted (or succumbed) to communist dominance inevitably coloured the relationships which they developed, respectively. Hence, one may speak of the Bulgarian, Romanian and Russian Orthodox Churches as having been co-opted by the regime,[42] but one could not speak of the Church in the GDR as having been co-opted. The typical price that the Churches had to pay for an accommodative relationship (though *not* in East Germany) was self-censorship in public statements regarding the regime or its policies. Hungary's Catholic Bishop Endre Gyulay of Szeged alluded to this in an interview with the Budapest magazine *Nök Lapja* in early 1989. 'Even a year ago', he said, 'it would have been unthinkable that a bishop's statement could appear without prior approval.' He added that any article written by a priest or bishop had had to be 'full of praise' for the regime or it would not have been published.[43]

In Bulgaria, the communists recruited uncooperative priests for hard labour, encouraged a left-wing League of Orthodox Priests of Bulgaria to assert itself within the Church, stripped the Church of its lands, placed the clergy on state salaries, and all the while praised the Bulgarian Church for its past and present patriotism and defence of national culture.[44] The Bulgarian Orthodox Church was quickly reduced to a timid spokesman of Bulgarian foreign policy interests, and it came to be supervised by an office within the Ministry of Foreign Affairs.[45]

The pattern in Romania was similar. Again certain clergy had to be removed from office and many were consigned to hard labour. The more 'co-operative' clergy were supported and advanced. The Church press was cut back and tamed. The borders of ecclesiastical provinces were redrawn to accord with the administrative convenience of the secular authorities. Hundreds of monasteries and convents were shut down, with 4,000 monks and nuns, mostly younger ones, being abruptly suspended from their duties after a state order in 1958. At the same time, the Department of Cults forced the Church, henceforth, to allow only persons aged sixty and above to enter the monastery.[46] The Church's nationalism did not seem politically relevant in the early postwar years.

When the Romanian regime decided in the early 1960s to defy Moscow in economic and foreign policy matters, it wanted to appeal to Romanian nationalism and turned to the Church for support. Party Secretary Nicolae Ceausescu announced, soon after his accession to power in early 1965, that the Church would be 'rehabilitated' and that the leading figures of Romanian Church history would once again be extolled for their contributions to Romanian culture or independence.[47] The result was a 'thaw', in which the state subsidized the reconstruction of dilapidated Church edifices, allowed the publication of impressive theological journals and books and encouraged the Orthodox Church to engage in ecumenical activities, including the hosting of lavish interdenominational conferences, provided that the Church keep in mind its state-supportive role. The resultant relationship is a classic example of ecclesiastical co-optation of an extreme kind. It also provides further evidence of the role of nationalism in encouraging Church–state accommodation.

Finally, a few words should be said about the Russian Orthodox Church. Subjugated in the course of the 1920s, decimated in the years up to the Second World War, and partly rehabilitated during the war, only to be subjected to renewed pressure in the Khrushchev and Brezhnev eras, the Russian Orthodox Church has more recently become a beneficiary of Gorbachev's *perestroika* in the religious sphere. Hundreds of churches were returned to the Orthodox Church between 1987 and 1988, along with at least seven monasteries. It was able to publish a jubilee edition of the Bible in 100,000 copies and to arrange for the import of another 150,000 Bibles. Then, in November 1990, new religious legislation, which had been in preparation since summer 1986, finally gave hope that certain rights would be restored to the Church. As already noted, these include the right to own property and the right to engage in charitable and proselytizing activities. It has not, however, been restored to any position of special standing or preferment in the Russian Republic. However, the Church can, in good faith, write that:

the process of restructuring life in our country on the principles of democratization and *glasnost* with an emphasis on problems of spirituality and morality, is of cardinal importance for the destinies of our nation as a whole. The children of the Church, as Soviet citizens, welcome this process of renewal and take an active part in it. This beneficial process is telling favourably on the life of the Church too, promoting its further improvement.[48]

After coming to power in March 1985, Soviet General Secretary Mikhail Gorbachev gave the Russian Orthodox Church a new role, gradually redefining the nature of the co-optive relationship. In April 1988, in a highly symbolic gesture, Gorbachev received Patriarch Pimen at the Kremlin – the first time that any patriarch had been received by the general secretary since 1943.[49] More particularly, the massive commemoration of the millennium of Christianity in Russia was simultaneously a legitimation of the Church as a historical institution and a celebration of *Russian* national culture.[50] Indeed, this confluence of Orthodoxy and Russian nationalism was explicitly highlighted by Metropolitan Filaret of Kiev and Galich in an interview published in the Soviet newspaper, *Trud*, on 5 June 1988. Appearing under the headline, 'One History, One Motherland', the interview sketched the positive role played by the Russian Orthodox Church over the centuries, noting in particular the contributions of St Sergii of Radonezh and Prince St Dimitrii Donskoi.[51]

It would be too much to argue that Gorbachev's rehabilitation of the Russian Orthodox Church is designed to fit in with a larger project of reclaiming Russian history. On the contrary, it is part of a larger policy of liberalizing religion in general and easing conditions for believers of all faiths. Underlying that strategic shift seems to be a conviction that the old policy of confrontation and repression backfired and that a more conciliatory approach is therefore to be preferred. Simultaneously, Gorbachev has also opened the floodgates to a broad re-examination of the past. Within that context, it becomes possible for the Church to reclaim some of its historic heritage.

DEVIANT CASES

There seems to be a strong tendency for accommodative Church–state relations to be associated with co-optive policies *vis-à-vis* nationalism, and for confrontational Church–state relations to be associated with repressive policies *vis-à-vis* nationalism. There are no doubt many reasons for this association, some of them organic and some having perhaps more to do with larger questions of system building or leadership style.

There are also a few cases in which confrontational policies in one sphere are associated with some form of accommodation in the other sphere, with accommodative relations in one sphere existing side-by-side with confrontational relations in the other sphere. These deviant cases stand in need of explanation.

The Albanian case is the easiest to explain. Albania's hard-line Stalinists wanted to accomplish a complete and total break with the past. The complete suppression of all religion in late 1967 was a part of this broader programme. At the same time, after breaking first with Yugoslavia in 1948 and then with the Soviet Union in 1961, Albania's rulers looked to Albanian nationalism as a source of legitimation and inspiration. Hence, instead of accusing the Churches of 'bourgeois nationalism', as authorities had done in the Ukraine, Lithuania, Croatia, Serbia and Czechoslovakia, Albania's Marxist–Leninists denied that any of Albania's three major religions (Islam, Catholicism and Orthodoxy) could claim to be genuinely 'national'.

Albania's long-time ruler, Enver Hoxha (1944–85), explained:

All the religious sects existing in our country were brought to Albania by foreign invaders, and served them and the ruling classes of the country. Under the cloak of religion, god, and the prophets, there operated the brutal law of the invaders and their domestic lackeys. The history of our people demonstrates . . . how [religion] engendered discord and fratricide in order to oppress us more cruelly, enslave us more easily, and suck our blood.[52]

On the contrary, in 1967, Hoxha declared that the authentic religion of the Albanian people is 'Albanianism'.[53] In essence, the Albanian regime completely divorced religion from nationalism, even inverted the relationship, making a repressive policy towards religion thus compatible with a programme of Albanian nationalism.

The Romanian regime's policy towards the Uniates likewise combined a repressive religious policy with a co-optive nationalist policy. But it is somewhat more complicated to explain why this policy combination has been retained. Indeed, the Romanian Uniates felt encouraged, at one point, by Ceausescu's rehabilitation of the Romanian past and hoped that their own close association with Romanian culture and heritage might encourage Ceausescu to reverse his policy and relegalize that Church. But their repeated appeals fell on deaf ears. The Romanian regime already had the docile and equally nationalist Romanian Orthodox Church at its service; it did not need to rehabilitate a second nationalist Church, and, at that, one which would surely prove far less docile.

On the other hand, Yugoslav policy towards its Muslim population offered the rare combination of a supportive religious policy and a policy distrustful of nationalism. In Yugoslavia, the authorities permitted a very extensive programme of mosque construction, allowed the establishment of an Islamic monthly (*Islamska misao*) in 1979, authorized the establishment of an Islamic theological faculty in Sarajevo in 1977, and approved the development of a newspaper (*Preporod*) for the Islamic community. All the same, there were signs of an Islamic revival in Yugoslavia in the late 1970s and early 1980s and some prominent Yugoslavs expressed concern lest pan-Islamic ideas should, under the influence of Iranian Ayatollah Khomeini, acquire a following in Bosnia.[54]

Oddly enough, although Yugoslav authorities repeatedly expressed hostility towards what they read as signs of Muslim nationalism, they had themselves been enthusiastic about encouraging the development of Muslim national identity, which they had considered useful in syphoning away potential adherents to either the Serbian or the Croatian nation. In 1968, thus, the party explicitly endorsed the concept of Muslim ethnicity, placing the Muslims on a par with Serbs, Croats, Slovenes and other nationalities in Yugoslavia. Yugoslav policy was thus ambivalent towards the Muslims both in the religious dimension and in the ethnic dimension. Even compared with the 'deviant' cases, the Yugoslav policy towards the Muslims looked deviant.

CONCLUSIONS

The central argument of this chapter has been that in the Soviet Union and Eastern Europe, Church–state relations were, and in many cases remain, very much affected by the regime's orientation towards the national heritage. This is true both because the choice between an anti-nationalist and a pro-nationalist posture is apt to affect the way a regime looks at the Church, and because the Church necessarily finds its orientation towards the national heritage affected by the climate created by the regime.

Neither in East Germany nor in any other country in the region can one speak of a mechanical relationship between the two policies. The SED did *not*, for instance, seek to improve its relations with the Church *in order* to exploit the Church and Church history for nationalist purposes. But there was clearly a natural symbiosis between the state's project of reclaiming the German past and its decision to work for a *rapprochement* with the Church. In this sense, nationalism emerges as an important factor in Church–state relations.

However, there are other factors involved, as has been noted above. Foreign policy considerations figured prominently (as in the examples of the Bulgarian, Romanian and Russian Orthodox Churches, and in the case of the Evangelical Church in the GDR). Leadership style played a role. Then there were the traditional Marxist views about religion, which were neither monolithic nor homogeneous, and which were, in any event, filtered through factional politics at the elite level. The rough consensus within political elites of the area as to how to deal with the Churches (privatization, social isolation, atheization of the youth, gradual strangulation of religion) broke down. In Poland, new religious legislation was passed into law in May 1989. The new legislation recognized, for the first time, the juridical rights of the Catholic Church and made explicit guarantees of the legality of activities of the Church which up to then had lacked explicit legal sanction.[55]

The same has also been achieved in Hungary where, in January 1990, prior to multi-party elections, a law guaranteeing freedom of religion was adopted. In the previous year, official ties with the Vatican were re-established and the State Office for Church Affairs, which controlled ecclesiastical activity, was abolished. In Yugoslavia, there have been signs of a thaw within the political establishment regarding policy toward the Churches. In June 1989, for example, a newly built Serbian Orthodox cathedral was opened in Belgrade, a ceremony reportedly attended by over 150,000.

In Czechoslovakia too, a transformation occurred with the collapse of the old regime in November 1989. Vaclav Havel, the former dissident playwright, was elected President a month after the resignation of Gustav Husak. Finally, in June 1990 national elections were won by Civic Forum, the protest group founded by Havel, who then formed a government. The result will undoubtedly be a normalization of relations between the state and the various religious bodies.

Finally, in East Germany, the Communist regime led by Erich Honecker also fell apart during 1989. To this, the Churches made a considerable contribution by providing organizational support to an otherwise relatively inchoate opposition. The longer term result, however, has been a process of gradual unification with, or more accurately absorption by, West Germany. This too has transformed Church–state relations – reflected in the reuniting, after a twenty-year break, of the East and West German Evangelical Churches. It is also indirectly reflected in the success of the East German Christian Democratic Union in the national elections of March 1990, and the five state-level elections which followed re-unification with the Federal Republic in October 1990. In the all-German elections held two months later, the old ruling Socialist Unity Party (SED), now renamed the Party of Democratic Socialism (PDS), only achieved double figures in two former East German states – Brandenburg (11 per cent) and Mecklenburg-Pomerania (14.2 per cent). In that context, Church–state relations will no doubt come to approximate those in the rest of Germany, as discussed in the previous chapter of this volume.

There was a time when the countries of Eastern Europe looked remarkably alike. Designed as carbon copies of the Soviet Union, the East European communist states showed some important common-alities of purpose in the early 1950s and, in some ways, even into the 1960s and 1970s. This holds true for the religious sphere as well as for other policy spheres. Yet even in the 1950s, there were differences. The GDR, for instance, put very few clergy on trial and did not confiscate Church hospitals and old-age homes, as happened elsewhere in Eastern Europe. In the 1980s, these differences were magnified, resulting in what Joseph Rothschild has called a 'return to diversity'.[56] And hence, even within these broad categories of 'co-optive' and 'repressive' policy, there was always considerable variation from country to country. But, since the 'Democratic Revolution' of 1989, in most of Eastern Europe these categories have become irrelevant. They perhaps only continue to apply in relatively unmodified form in Albania, but even there clear signs have appeared that change is on the horizon.

NOTES

1   For discussion, see Z.T. Irwin (1989), 'The fate of Islam in the Balkans: A comparison of four state policies', in P. Ramet (ed.), *Religion and Nationalism in Soviet and East European Politics*, rev. edn, Durham NC: Duke University Press, Ch. 16.

2   This typology is based on an earlier version in my chapter, 'Christianity and national heritage among the Czechs and Slovaks', in Ramet, op.cit.,

Ch. 11.

3 Irina Levezeanu has argued that, despite the common Romanian lanuage, Moldavians have developed a sense of regional distinctiveness from (other) Romanians. See her two-part article, 'Urbanization in a low key and linguistic change in Soviet Moldavia', (1981), *Soviet Studies*, vol. 33, no. 3, pp.327–51 and vol. 33, no. 4, 1981, pp.573–92.

4 M. Hadžijahié (1974), *Od tradicije do identiteta: Geneza nacionalnog pitanja bosanskih muslimana*, Sarajevo; Svjetlost, pp.39, 144, 164, 207–9, 219.

5 See V. Gorskii (1977), 'Russian messianism and the new national consciousness', in M. Meerson-Aksenov and B. Shragin (eds), *The Political, Social and Religious Thought of Russian 'Samizdat' – An Anthology*, Belmont, MA: Nordland Publishing Co., pp.353–93.

6 See I. Cvitkovic (1978), 'Stavovi suvremenih teologa o odnosu religije i religijskih zajednica prema politici u socijalizmu', *Politicka misao*, vol. 15, no. 4, p.653.

7 See the discussion in D. Pospielovsky (1984), *The Russian Church under the Soviet Regime, 1917–1982*, 2 vols, Crestwood, New York: St Vladimir's Seminary Press, vol. 1.

8 *Vjesnik: Sedam dana*, Zagreb, 16 January 1982, p.19.

9 J. Ellis (1986), *The Russian Orthodox Church: A Contemporary History*, Bloomington, IN: Indiana University Press, p.45.

10 O. Luchterhandt (1982), *Die Gegenwartslage der Evangelischen Kirche in der DDR*, Tübingen: J.C.B. Mohr, p.50; also F. Ehlert (1988), 'Suchet der Stadt Bestes!': Bischof Mitzenheims Bemühungen um Einvernehmen mit dem Staat', *Kirche im Sozialismus*, vol. 14, no. 3, p.99.

11 *Kritika* (1983), Budapest, September, trans. in Joint Publications Research Service (JPRS) (1983), *East Europe Report*, no. 84830, 28 November, p.119; and J.V. Eibner (1985), 'Zoltán Káldy: A new way for the Church in socialism?', *Religion in Communist Lands*, vol. 13, no. 1, pp.13–47.

12 An early convert to this idea is I. Cvitković. See his *Marksistička misao i religija* (1980), Sarajevo: Svjetlost.

13 Quoted in R. Henkys (1983), 'Kirche in der Deutschen Demokratischen Republic', in P. Lendvai (ed.), *Religionsfreiheit und Menschenrechte*, Graz: Verlag Styria, p.176.

14 B. Bociurkiw (1988), 'Religion and the law in communist Eastern and Central Europe', *Cross Currents*, vol. 7, pp.75–86.

15 On 1 December 1989, on the occasion of President Gorbachev's visit to the Vatican, an agreement was reached to establish official relations between the Soviet Union and the Holy See. At the same time, Ukrainian authorities announced a decision to grant Uniate congregations the legal right to register for public worship. But this will fall short of full legalization which, as noted, is now finally promised under the 1990 legislation. The Uniate Church is not the only Ukrainian Church affected by the legalization issue. In early 1989, an Initiative Committee for the Restoration of the Ukrainian Autocephalous Orthodox Church was established in Kiev by Fr Bohdan Mykhailenko, together with Taras Antonium, Anatoli Bytchenko, and Lyrysa Lokhvytska. See *Keston News Service* (1989), no. 320, p.8.

16   J. Nowak (1982), 'The Church in Poland', *Problems of Communism*, vol. 31, no. 1, January–February, pp.6–7.

17   Detailed in J. Bugajski (1985), 'Poland's anti-clergy campaign', *The Washington Quarterly*, vol. 8, no. 4, pp.157–68.

18   G. Simon (1975), 'The Catholic Church and the communist state in the Soviet Union and Eastern Europe', in B. Bociurkiw and J.W. Strong (eds), *Religion and Atheism in the USSR and Eastern Europe*, London: Macmillan, p.205; and S. Rosada and J. Gwozdz (1955), 'Church and state in Poland', in V. Gsovski (ed.), *Church and State behind the Iron Curtain*, New York: Praeger, p.198.

19   V. Chrypinski, 'Church and nationality in postwar Poland', in Ramet, op. cit., pp.247–50.

20   See *Politika*, 11 February 1981 and 13 April 1981; also I. Cvitković (1986), *Ko je bio Alojzije Stepinac*, 2nd edn, Sarajevo: NIŠRO Oslobodjenje.

21   See P. Ramet (1985), 'From Strossmayer to Stepinac: Croatian national ideology and Catholicism', *Canadian Review of Studies in Nationalism*, vol.12, no. 1, pp.123–39.

22   W. Volkmer (1979), 'East Germany: Dissenting views during the last decade', in R.L. Tokes (ed.), *Opposition in Eastern Europe*, London: Macmillan, pp.116–17.

23   S. Brauer (1983), *Martin Luther in marxistischer Sicht von 1945 bis zum Beginn der achtziger Jahre*, East Berlin: Evangelische Verlagsanstalt, p.5.

24   P. Hoffman (1986), 'The GDR, Luther, and the German question', *The Review of Politics*, vol. 48, no. 2, pp.250–1.

25   P. Fischer (1987), *Kirche und Christen in der DDR*, East Berlin: Verlag Gebr. Holzapfel, p.87.

26   R.W. Solberg (1961), *God and Caesar in East Germany: The Conflict of Church and State in East Germany since 1945*, New York: Macmillan, pp.74–5; and H. Dahn (1982), *Konfrontation oder Kooperation? Das Verhältnis von Staat und Kirche in der SBZ/DDR 1945–1980*, Opladen: Westdeutscher Verlag, p.44.

27   Solberg; op. cit., p.107.

28   ibid., pp.142–3.

29   *Neue Zeit* (1956), East Berlin, March, as quoted in Solberg, op.cit., p.213.

30   Quoted in Schönherr (1982), 'Opportunities and problems of being a Christian in a socialist society', in N. Greinacher and V. Elizondo (eds), *Churches in Socialist Societies of Eastern Europe, Concilium: Religion in the Eighties*, New York: Seabury Press, pp.47–8.

31   Quoted in K. Sontheimer and W. Bleek (1975), *The Government and Politics of East Germany*, trans. by U. Price, London: Hutchinson University Library, p.124.

32   R.F. Goeckel (1990), *The Lutheran Church and the East German State: Political Conflict and Change under Ulbricht and Honecker*, Ithaca, NY: Cornell University Press, Ch. 7.

33   For details, see P. Ramet (1987), *Cross and Commissar: The Politics of Religion in Eastern Europe and the USSR*, Bloomington, IN: Indiana University Press, pp.82–3; also A. Schönherr (1988), 'Ten Years on:

The Church–State Discussions of 6 March 1978 in the GDR', *Religion in Communist Lands*, vol. 16, no. 2, pp.126–34.

34 Brauer, op.cit., pp.12–23.

35 See R. Kuster (1983), 'Luther in East Germany', *Swiss Review of World Affairs*, vol. 33, no. 4, p.8.

36 Honecker, in a speech (June 1980), quoted in Hoffmann, op.cit., p.257.

37 *Neue Heimat* (1983), May, p.28, quoted in Dan Beck, 'The Luther revival: Aspects of national *Abgrenzung* and confessional *Gemeinschaft* in the German Democratic Republic', in Ramet (ed.) (1989), *Religion and Nationalism in Soviet and East European Politics*, Durham NC: Duke University Press, pp.228–9.

38 *Neue Zeit*, 5 October 1982, p.3, trans. in JPRS (1982), *East Europe Report*, no. 82346, p.10.

39 For details and discussion, see S. Ramet, 'Protestantism in East Germany', in S. Ramet (ed.) (forthcoming), *Protestantism and Politics in the Soviet Union and Eastern Europe*.

40 *Standpunkt*, East Berlin, February 1986, trans. in JPRS (1986), *East Europe Report*, no. EER–86–063; *Neues Deutschland* (1986), 11 February, pp.1–2; and *Neue Zeit*, 12 February 1986, p.3, trans. in JPRS (1986), *East Europe Report*, no. EER–86–053.

41 *Frankfurter Allgemeine*, 12 March 1988, p.4. See also F. Winterhager (1986), 'Thomas Müntzer und die Gegenwart in Beiden Deutschen Staaten' *Deutsche Studien*, vol. 24, no. 96.

42 For an explanation of the concept of co-optation, see P. Ramet, 'The interplay of religious policy and nationalities policy in the Soviet Union and Eastern Europe', in Ramet, op.cit., pp.16–24.

43 *The Guardian of Liberty (Nemzetör)* (1989), Munich, March–April, p.6.

44 D. Slijepcevic (1957), *Die bulgarische orthodoxe Kirche 1944–56*, Munich: R. Oldenbourg, pp.6–8; and S.T. Raikin, 'Nationalism and the Bulgarian Orthodox Church', in Ramet (1989), op. cit., pp.358–63.

45 For details, see Ramet (1987), *Cross and Commissar: The Politics of Religion in Eastern Europe and the USSR*, Bloomington, IN: Indiana University Press, Ch. 7.

46 D. Ghermani (1988), 'The Orthodox Church in Romania', *Religion in Communist Dominated Areas*, vol. 27, no. 1, pp.23–4.

47 Ibid., p.24.

48 'Communique of the Pre-Council Bishops' Conference' (1988), *Journal of the Moscow Patriarchate*, no. 6, p.7.

49 R. Ahlberg (1989), 'Die russisch-orthodoxe Kirche im Zeichen der Perestrojka', *Osteuropa*, vol. 39, no. 1, pp.3–4.

50 Ukrainians did not forget that, strictly speaking, it was the millennium of the introduction of Christianity in what is now the Ukraine. But most of the official celebrations gave it the character of a Russian event.

51 V. Chaplin (1988), 'Soviet mass media on the jubilee of the Russian Church', *Journal of the Moscow Patriarchate*, no. 10, p.63.

52 Quoted in P.R. Profti (1978), *Socialist Albania since 1944: Domestic and Foreign Developments*, Cambridge, MA: MIT Press, pp.157–8.

53 J. Kolsti (1981), 'Albanianism: From the humanists to Hoxha', in G. Klein and M.J. Reban (eds), *The Politics of Ethnicity in Eastern Europe*,

Boulder, Co: East European Monographs, p.15.
54   Z.T. Irwin (1984), 'The Islamic revival and the Muslims of Bosnia-Hercegovina' *East European Quarterly*, vol. 17, no. 4, pp.450–1.
55   *Frankfurter Allgemeine*, 18 May 1989, p.6.
56   J. Rothschild (1989), *Return to Diversity: A Political History of East Central Europe since World War II*, Oxford: Oxford University Press.

Chapter 4

The Islamic world: Egypt and Iran

Glenn E. Perry

Since the 1970s, if not earlier, the Islamic world has been caught up in a rising tide of movements to reverse the previously declining role of religion in political and social life. While such movements have taken on unique characteristics in each country, the examples of Iran and Egypt illustrate many of the important trends – all of which long predate the current phase of 'Islamic resurgence'.

THE MOVEMENTS: A BRIEF SURVEY

It was in these two countries that the best known movements for restoring Islam as the foundation of the state – usually known inexactly as 'fundamentalist' in the western world but which I shall call 'Islamist' – have centred.[1] The Society of the Muslim Brothers[2] originated in the late 1920s in Egypt under the leadership of the charismatic Hasan al-Banna and by the early post-1945 period had become one of the country's most powerful forces. While it advocated the peaceful transition of the Islamic world to a more truly Islamic society, at least some elements of the organization gave it a reputation for violence and evoked repeated attempts by Egyptian governments to repress it. While the regime led by Gamal Abdul Nasser after 1952 initially maintained amicable relations with the Brothers, they were crushed following an attempt on Nasser's life in 1954.

The movement surfaced again in 1965 as the government uncovered a plot allegedly led by a recently freed member of the organization, Sayyid Qutb.[3] This new spokesman for the Islamist movement, who died at the gallows the following year, represented a more extreme development; the books he wrote while in prison proclaimed that the world – and the Nasser regime in particular –

had returned to a state of *jahiliyyah* (that is, the pre-Islamic Arabian condition of 'ignorance' of God's revelation) and that a vanguard of true Muslims must 'withdraw' from society as a prelude to revolution.

While the Muslim Brothers remained technically banned, the regime of President Anwar al-Sadat after 1970 tolerated them and allowed them to grow increasingly influential as they stressed their moderation under a new leadership. More recently, under President Husni Mubarak, who succeeded Sadat in 1981, the Brothers have been able to form electoral alliances with various political parties and to enter the country's parliament in significant numbers, and capital accumulated by some of them in the petroleum-producing countries has allowed them to become a powerful economic force. Some observers believe that the goals of the Brothers are gradually being achieved.

The radical trend that goes to Qutb has manifested itself in diverse ways. As a way of combating leftists on university campuses, Sadat encouraged student Islamic societies, resulting in their complete takeover of the student movement by the late 1970s. Although the Islamic societies were themselves suppressed after they became a threat to Sadat, by this time they had spawned extreme offshoots. One of these groups came to public attention when its leader, Shukri Mustafa, and others were charged and later executed for kidnapping and killing the Minister of Awqaf (Endowments) in 1977. This group came to be known as *al-Takfir wa al-Hijrah*, an Arabic phrase that is nearly untranslatable but which sums up its ideas and strategy. The word '*al-takfir*' means the pronunciation of judgement against others that they are unbelievers, in this case, against the bulk of Egyptians and others from nominally Muslim societies in general. The word '*al-hijrah*' describes the group's strategy of withdrawal from the pseudo-Islamic society – either into the desert or to flats in Cairo to live in isolation prior to the time when they can overthrow the regime and create a larger society in their own likeness.

Others, like the Islamic Liberation Organization that tried to launch a coup d'état at the Technical Military Academy in 1974, rejected the claim that society as a whole was non-Islamic and strove only to overthrow the regime. The Jihad Organization, which came to prominence with its assassination of Sadat, did not share the idea of 'withdrawal' either but – as elucidated in a pamphlet written by one of its leaders, Abd al-Salam Faraj[4] – stressed the imperative nature of *jihad* (literally, striving; at least in this context connoting warfare) for true Muslims against their 'apostate' rulers.

The most dramatic events of all occurred in Iran, with the overthrow of Muhammad Riza Shah's dictatorship in 1979 and the establishment of an Islamic state under the leadership of a ranking Islamic religious scholar, Ayatollah Ruhollah Khomeini. An unprecedented pattern of revolutionary Islam seemed irretrievably to have reversed the previous trend, in which the religious scholars were losing their influence and in which Islam, at least in the form they understood it, was being undermined. A large-scale but abortive revolt led by religious scholars in 1963 amounted to a 'dress rehearsal'[5] for the successful attempt in 1979. And a movement in many ways analogous to the Muslim Brethren, founded by Isma'il Safavi in 1943 under the name Fida'iyan-i Islam (self-sacrificers of Islam), proved to be a powerful force in Iranian politics during the first decade following the Second World War – for a while aligned with the liberal, secular premier, Muhammad Musaddiq, in the early 1950s in his struggle against British petroleum interests and the Shah but then breaking with him and thus facilitating the return of the absolute monarchy.

Not only do the two countries exemplify opposite outcomes so far, but they also represent two main branches of Islam; Sunnism and Shi'ism. Egypt, aside from its significant Coptic Christian minority, is a Sunni country almost without exception, while Iran has been the main centre of Shi'ism since its conversion to that sect at the beginning of the sixteenth century, when the Safavid dynasty created the state in roughly its present boundaries, with perhaps only 10 per cent of its population adhering to Sunnism, apart from numerically insignificant Christians, Jews, Baha'is and Zoroastrians. Related to the sectarian distinction is the fact that the main Islamist movements in Iran have centred in the ranks of the religious scholars themselves, while analogous movements in Egypt – as in most other Islamic countries – have been made up and led primarily by lay people who blame their religions establishments for opportunistic alignments with un-Islamic rulers.

THE CONTENT OF ISLAMIST MOVEMENTS

While the movements under discussion share a commitment to restoring an Islamic society under an Islamic state, the actual contents of their visions differ a great deal from one another. All these movements are expressions of social forces which, if Islam did not provide an outlet, would tend to find expression in other ideologies. While some advocates of an Islamic state are conservative on economic issues, many others – especially the militant ones – tend to advocate policies that would normally be called socialist, though generally they are closer to the Fabian than to the Bolshevik variety. Such was the thinking of the early Muslim Brothers (but not those of today) and of the radical movements in contemporary Egypt, but while it was formerly commonplace to hear 'fundamentalists' argue that Islam advocates socialism, they decry such labels today as Eurocentric. Thus if they see similarities between their version of Islam and British socialism or Maoism, they insist that this is a matter of the latter resembling – even emulating – Islam rather than vice versa.[6] Similarly, the Islamic revolutionaries in Iran would never say that they are socialists, and in fact there is an economically conservative faction that continues to veto additional land reform and nationalization.

Khomeini and other Islamic radicals use a vocabulary that differs from that of socialism, speaking for example of the *mustad'afin* (the oppressed, literally 'weak') versus the *mustakbarin* (arrogant), words whose meanings, however, to a large extent parallel Marxist terms like 'proletariat' and 'bourgeoisie'. Such Muslim radicals also see the world in ways that closely resemble dependency theory, blaming the poverty of the Third World on imperialism and giving strong support to, say, Blacks in South Africa and the revolutionary government of Nicaragua (as well as to rebels against the communist regime in Afghanistan) – causes (aside from Afghanistan) that would be irrelevant from a 'traditional' Islamic worldview that distinguishes only between Muslims and others. Such Islamist movements indeed resemble the right-wing Moral Majority in the United States in their attitudes toward matters like family life (and call for the implementation of Islamic rules in such fields as criminal law that would generally be decried by everyone else as retrogressive), but on at least some broader social and political issues they represent something like a 'theology of liberation'.

In short, Islamic movements that are called 'fundamentalist' are often far from being generally conservative or 'traditional'. As revisionist writings on modernization have made clear, concepts like 'traditional' are highly misleading, as any society has diverse traditions that it can draw on, some of which – particularly the ideals of the remote past – are often congruent with modernity.[7] Or as a student of the pre-1954 Muslim Brothers concluded: 'In the very process of reaffirming the old, the old is newly conceived and formulated in a way which inevitably reflects the forces which helped to undermine it'.[8]

While arguably Islamist movements support some ideas which would interfere with modern technology, they do not oppose modernization as such – unless one arbitrarily defines secularism as an inherent facet of modernity. It would come closer to the truth to say that they represent resentment about the uneven spread of modernization in which the *mustad'afin* are left out. But an understanding of contemporary Islamist movements requires that we clarify some basic aspects of Islam and particularly of the theory of politics that it encompasses – and whose implementation is at the centre of the controversies with which we are concerned.

ISLAM AND THE STATE

In Islam there is no distinction between religion and politics, 'God and Caesar' or pope and emperor, for the sole purpose of the ideal state is religious. From an orthodox[9] Islamic point of view, the religion is missing an essential element in the absence of a state based on its principles. In the first place, Islam purports to create a community (*ummah*) that unites all of its members without regard to racial, national or other differences. The *ummah* is supposed to be under one government, although some medieval political theorists reluctantly recognized the legitimacy of separate governments in certain cases. The actual division of the Islamic world into many states is deplorable from the orthodox point of view, and a nationalism whose focus of loyalty is only part of the *ummah* or includes non-Muslims is even worse. Islamist movements totally reject nationalism, at least in principle, in favour of Islamic universalism.[10]

The Prophet himself was the ruler of the Islamic state from its founding in 622 AD in Medina until his death a decade later. Since to his followers he was the last ('seal') of a series of prophets, he could not be succeeded by a new prophet. The caliphs (literally, those who came after Muhammad) or imams (leaders) were his successors only in his non-prophetic capacity – that is, as the ruler of the *ummah* (and no equivalent of the Pope at all, since there is no Islamic 'Church' to have such a head).

The area controlled by the Islamic state is the Abode of Peace (*dar al-Islam*), which theoretically is in a permanent state of war with the Abode of War (*dar al-Harb*), that is, those areas that have not been incorporated so far. (The whole world eventually is to be included, either through peaceful conversion or in response to aggression against the Abode of Islam, as the Qur'an forbids aggression.) But this part of the classical theory is generally not invoked by contemporary Islamist movements. Today the focus is on the liberation of the Islamic world from what are perceived to be various forms of subjection by non-Islamic states such as the United States, the USSR and Israel, and on the establishment of what Iran's Islamic leaders call 'real independence',[11] not the extension of Islamic rule to non-Muslim countries. (Israel is a special case, since both Islamic and secular movements in the Islamic world and other parts of the Third World view it as a colonialist entity that has uprooted the indigenous population of an Arab/Islamic country.) The Islamist attitude towards the powers that dominate the Islamic world generally parallels that of Third World nationalists except perhaps for the Islamist perception of the two superpowers as equally imperialist.

The Abode of Islam is made up not only of Muslims but also of *dhimmi*s (protected people). The latter are 'Peoples of the Book' – Christians, Jews and others belonging to religions that have revealed scriptures and who are allowed to live autonomously, though in some ways unequally, under their own religious law and pay a special tax (*jizyah*) in lieu of the military services imposed on Muslims. While today's Islamist movements generally do not call – at least not explicitly – for the restoration of *dhimmi* status for religious minorities, the basis of solidarity for the people of an Islamic state leaves non-Muslims out, and few of them view the establishment of Islamic rule with alacrity. In Egypt in particular, the rise of revolutionary Islamist groups since the 1970s has been accompanied by a new kind of Muslim–Coptic tension. The tolerant attitude is totally lacking with regard to Baha'ism, since it has the distinction of appearing after the rise of Islam and is made up of ex-Muslims who see their faith as superseding Islam.

Islam has a body of revealed law, the *shari'ah*. Based on provisions of the Qur'an, the Sunnah (which in turn is based on reports of the Prophet's sayings and actions), the consensus of the *ummah* and analogy (for Sunnis) or reason (in the case of Shi'ites), the *shari'ah* provides detailed rules to guide the Muslim in all areas of life. It includes commercial and penal law, rules for marriage and divorce and the like, as well as provisions for purely devotional matters. These are God-given laws that cannot be changed. Even the right of religious scholars to reinterpret the *shari'ah* is severely limited in the thinking of conservative Sunni Muslims, who for about a millennium have accepted the idea that the gates of *ijtihad* (literally, striving; rethinking) are closed in favour of *taqlid* (imitation) of the interpretations of the early scholars. While Shi'ites allow greater leeway for *ijtihad*, this prerogative is limited to the most highly qualified scholars, with ordinary believers obligated to 'imitate' their interpretations. It may, however, come as a surprise to those who see 'fundamentalists' as 'traditional' that they share with 'modernists' an emphasis on the importance of *ijtihad*. Ayatollah Khomeini's proclamation at the beginning of 1988 that a true Islamic state has the authority to act without any limitations by previous 'divine statutes'[12] – particularly those that stand in the way of land reform and nationalization of businesses – would seem to be so far removed from the ideas of conservative Muslims as to subject him to accusations of heresy.

Aside from defending and expanding the borders of the Islamic state, the function of the ruler is the enforcement of divine law. In the classical Islamic conception, he has no legislative authority and all of his decisions must be within the limits of what the *shari'ah* permits. To use Majid Khadduri's term, Islam calls for a nomocracy,[13] the rule of (divine) law, rather than a theocracy. It is of course a theocracy in the most fundamental meaning of the term, that is, rule by God (through His vicegerent, the caliph or imam, who, however, is also bound by the law). It is the restoration of the *shari'ah* as the positive law of the state that constitutes the *sine qua non* of twentieth-century Islamist movements.

Islam, as is often pointed out, has no priests or priesthood. There is no religious function that only specially consecrated persons may perform. Any Muslim can be a preacher, prayer leader or whatever. But a category of learned people (ulama; singular, *'alim*) arose early, and eventually, as institutions of higher learning (*madrasahs*) came into being, the ulama became a relatively clear-cut category of people, that is, graduates of these *madrasahs*.

The ulama perform various functions in an Islamic society. Some of these functions are recognizably religious from a western point of view. Ulama are also teachers in the *madrasahs* and in the old-fashioned type of elementary schools (*kuttabs* or *maktabs*), for the learning of the ulama was nearly synonymous with learning in general in the Islamic world before the adoption of western-style education. Another province of the ulama in an Islamic state is the judiciary as judges and muftis (jurisconsults), for they are the specialists in the sacred law. At the centre of the learning that the *madrasahs* provide is *fiqh* (jurisprudence); thus while we usually think of ulama as theologians, they – or at least those whose studies emphasize *fiqh* – are jurists (*fuqaha*; singular: *faqih*). It was the ulama who shaped the *shari'ah*, for the 'consensus of the community' has usually been understood to mean that of the ulama. Of course, to the extent that *ijtihad* is deemed closed, the contemporary ulama are limited to repeating the interpretations of their predecessors.

It would be incorrect to think of the ulama as being analogous to a Church in their relationship with the state. There is no ecclesiastical structure other than the state itself. The ulama are a category of people, not an organization to which anyone belongs. Many of them occupy state offices, but the state itself is a religious organization. The office of the ruler of an Islamic state is no less a religious office than are those that are filled by ulama. A better analogy than the Christian concept of Church and state would be provided by the modern theory of separation of powers. In Islamic theory, God is the legislator, while the caliph or imam is the executive and is strictly limited by the law, which he cannot change, and the ulama, among other roles, staff the judiciary. In Donald Eugene Smith's terminology, the Islamic religio-political system is of the organic as opposed to the Church type,[14] for the state is the 'Church' and vice versa. This integration of political and religious structures has in fact tended to characterize Islamic societies even when they have deviated far from the Islamic model in other ways. Modern westernizing rulers have never strictly speaking tried to separate religion from the state but rather have asserted tighter control over religion at the expense of ulama prerogatives.

Sectarian differences arose in conjunction with issues relating primarily to rulership. One group – who came to be known as Sunnis – accepted a series of elected successors to Muhammad (although election soon became a fiction). The other main group – the Shi'ites – believe that the Prophet designated his son-in-law, Ali, as his successor and that the office (imamate) passed on to Ali's descendants. The Shi'ites are divided into several subsects, but the one that is relevant for our purposes – because it is the one that prevails in Iran and accounts for the bulk of Shi'ites today – is the Twelvers, who accept a series of twelve infallible imams, the last of whom disappeared in 874 AD. The Absent

Imam is supposed eventually to return as the Mahdi or Guided One, who will 'fill the earth with justice even as it is now filled with injustice'.

THE REALITY

Until the Islamic Revolution in Iran, the Islamic theory of politics seemed increasingly to be making way for 'modern' or westernized practices. Some of the states of the Arabian Peninsula, particularly Saudi Arabia, seemed at least superficially to correspond to the Islamic model (although many Muslims, pointing to corruption and social injustice, as well as to these regimes' dependence on western powers, considered them to be poor examples).[15] Everywhere else the *shari'ah*, beginning in the nineteenth century, had given way to law codes borrowed from Europe except in the field of personal status (marriage, divorce, inheritance and religious endowments) and Islamic law in this area also was slowly being eroded (and abolished in a few places, notably in Turkey and Tunisia) at the hands of 'modernizing' regimes.

With the Turkish Republic's abolition of the offices of caliph and sultan in the early 1920s, there was not even a nominal head of the *ummah* recognized by Sunnis, and the issue of reviving the caliphate was pretty much dead. Even the 'fundamentalists' have given little attention to the issue (which in any case is irrelevant from the point of view of the Shi'ites, whose political theory explains their imam's absence and whose *raison d'être* has always been the rejection of the Sunni caliph's legitimacy). In so far as states have remained Islamic, each has its own caliphs as it were, in the form of rulers whose titles usually have no specifically Islamic significance.

The political unity of the Abode of Islam disintegrated early in Islamic history. The ideal of Islamic universalism, together with the corollary notion of the separate nationhood of non-Muslim minorities, though still irritants to 'nation-builders', seemed slowly to be making way for nationalisms that united the people of each country – or in the case of the Arabs, of several countries that shared a common language, without regard to religion – and belied any special ties among the various Islamic peoples. But Islamic influence on the political systems of countries like Egypt and Iran, while not meeting the requirements of Islamists, was nevertheless always of great significance.

OFFICIAL ISLAM

Almost from the beginning the reality of government in the Islamic world saw the ideals of pious Muslims turned upside down, with regimes merely legitimating their rule in Islamic terms. In a purely personal sense, rulers have hardly been exemplars of Muslim behaviour. More to the point, the 'primitive democracy' of seventh-century Arabia, in which the Prophet Muhammad repaired his own clothing, one of the first caliphs milked his neighbour's sheep and the ruler was elected and engaged in consultation and even allowed himself to be reprimanded when he made a mistake, made way for despotism based on the model of the empires that the Muslims conquered. Proclaiming themselves the Shadows of God on Earth, rulers put themselves above the law that in theory they were bound to enforce. As God's agents on earth, they were answerable to no one, and to disobey them was to disobey God. While rulers allowed Islamic law to prevail in matters of marriage, divorce and the like and sometimes in other fields, they rarely if ever were inhibited about violating those rules pertaining to the exercise of power.[16] This began long before nineteenth-century rulers adopted western-style law codes.

While today's rulers in the countries under consideration are a far cry in many respects from their medieval predecessors, they continue – in a pattern that has recently been called 'official' or 'establishment' Islam as opposed to the 'populist' or 'activist' form – to base much of their legitimacy on religion. As Smith has pointed out, 'all traditional monarchs rule by virtue of some theory of the divine right or divinity of kings'.[17] While this applies to King Faruq of Egypt and to Muhammad Riza Shah Pahlavi of Iran, both of whom epitomized traditional monarchs in many respects, it also applies to a lesser degree to the presidents of republican Egypt.

The fact that the shah tried to destroy the influence of the religious scholars and in turn was overthrown by them may seem to contradict the above characterization of his rule. In fact, as will be shown, he was on good terms with the leading ulama for many years. Even when he turned against them, he was not attempting to separate religion from state but rather to assert his own religious leadership. He visited shrines, made religious appointments, financed religious activities and engaged in numerous other activities that belie any hostility to Shi'ite Islam, whatever his own personal beliefs may have been. He claimed that he was always guided by a supreme being, that he had been repeatedly saved by miracles and even that he once had literally met the Absent Imam on the street.[18] An admiring western interviewer concluded that the shah 'seemed to assert divine right'.[19]

Perhaps the shah's failure to secure legitimacy on this basis resulted in large part from his even greater reliance on pre-Islamic traditions of Persian monarchy that were basically at odds with Islamic legitimation, as was his espousal of an Iranian nationalism that stressed the continuity of a national community from pre-Islamic times rather than ties with the Islamic *ummah*. Also, the religious scholars that he tried to undermine were perceived much more as the true spokesmen for the faith than was the shah.

King Faruq, known best today for his corruption and lechery, relied heavily on religious legitimation. His reign began in 1936 amid the issue of whether he should be given the *bay'ah*, i.e. the pledge of alliegance in the form of a Muslim caliph, as the shaykh al-Azhar wanted. Indeed, Faruq aspired to be recognized as the new caliph of the Islamic world, and scholars at al-Azhar University went so far as to produce evidence that this scion of a dynasty of Balkan origin was a descendant of the Prophet Muhammad.[20]

The regime headed by Nasser between 1952 and 1970 arguably was a secularizing one in the sense that it imposed much change on Islamic institutions, weakening the ulama and even taking over judicial functions previously performed by them. This would seem to correspond to what Smith calls one form of secularism, namely 'the *expansion* of the polity' and even to what he calls 'a more radical form of secularization', involving 'the *dominance* of the polity over religious beliefs, practices, and ecclesiastical structures'.[21] Yet several students of the role of Islam in Nasser's Egypt have argued that this is not secularism at all and suggest that, instead of 'policy-expansion secularism', the appropriate term is 'policy-expansion sacralization', involving 'state expansion . . . in the name of religion, not against it . . . so that they [the leaders of the state] could propagate their new modern version of Islam'.[22] The regime indeed sought Islamic legitimization for its policies, arguing that its form of socialism was based on Islam, and sought rulings from religious authorities to that effect. While the pan-Arab nationalism of the Nasser regime was in principle in conflict with the idea of Islamic universalism, it was presented in such a way that it seemed congruent with Islam, since after all so much of Islamic history, especially for the early period, is also Arab history. Nasser's prominence in the struggle against Israel and more generally in anti-imperialist causes represented a thrust that was identical with that of the Islamists. Not only did the regime use the Friday sermon as a channel of communication for its version of Islam, but on at least one occasion Nasser himself spoke from the pulpit at al-Azhar.

Nasser's successor stepped up the use of religion to legitimize his rule, beginning to use his full name, *Muhammad* Anwar al-Sadat, taking pride in his description as the 'believer president' and sporting the marks on his forehead resulting from much prayer. Although he enacted a Personal Status Law in 1977 that limited polygamy and easy divorce for men, a constitutional amendment was adopted in 1971 that proclaimed the *shari'ah* to be a main source of Egptian law, while another amendment nine years later upgraded it to be the 'main source'.

While President Husni Mubarak, who succeeded Sadat, avoids the flamboyance of his predecessor, he has made no drastic changes and has seen the continuing growth of Islamic influence in the society. Especially in the context of countering populist, anti-regime religious trends, the state-supported Islamic establishment has continued to grow rapidly, controlling 10,000 mosques and having 'monopoly access to the state-controlled media', with radio and television time devoted to religion increasing four-fold in eleven years.[23]

SUNNI QUIETISM

Medieval political theorists readily provided the groundwork for the acceptance of the legitimacy of those rulers who were formally Muslims. One of the earliest theological debates related to whether a sinner – such as the typical tyrannical and impious rulers of the Umayyad dynasty (661–750 AD) – could be considered a Muslim. A negative answer would have meant that such a ruler lacked legitimacy. But the predominant view came to be that only God can decide, i.e. that such a person must be given the benefit of the doubt. Only the Kharijites, a radical sect that eventually nearly vanished, claimed the right to proclaim the inauthenticity of others' inclusion within the pale of believers, that is, *takfir*. Thus an evil ruler was nevertheless to be accepted as a Muslim, and members of the political and religious establishments of various Sunni countries are not entirely wrong when they now denounce their radical detractors as latterday 'Kharijites'.

As rulers came to power through force, Sunni writers eventually proclaimed that whoever takes power by any means and regardless of how evil he may be should be obeyed. Thus the great eleventh/ twelfth-century theologian, Abu-Hamid al-Ghazali, admitted that 'Government in these days is a consequence solely of military power', but, apparently seeing that the alternative would be chaos and reacting against Kharijite ideas, he added that 'whosoever he may be to whom the possessor of military powers gives his allegiance, that person is the caliph'.[24] According to al-Ghazali, even 'an evil-doing and barbarous sultan' must be obeyed if 'the attempt to depose him would create unendurable civil strife'.[25] A bad ruler, so various writers explained, is a punishment sent by God. Not to accept him would be to try to evade God's justice.

Had it not been a man of al-Ghazali's stature who made such statements, one might be inclined to treat them exclusively as the opportunistic attempt of establishment ulama to curry favour with the rulers on whom they depended for their livelihood, and indeed this has provided an additional motive over the centuries. Such quietism nevertheless predated the time when ulama 'became senior civil servants or lived off generous endowments funding the *madrasahs*', for, in their opinion, 'a bad Sunni ruler was still better than fitna [chaos]'.[26] Of course, there was no issue of accepting a ruler who explicitly rejected the *shari‘ah*, although most violated much of it in practice. By taking such a 'realistic' position, the theorists largely annulled the Islamic ideal of rule based strictly on immutable divine law and legitimized impiety in the name of piety. The Islamic organic religio-political system became one in which the imperatives of power predominated over the religious principles that originally were expected to provide the framework.

While this 'traditional' quietist view bolsters the position of existing regimes, recent Sunni activists in Egypt and elsewhere have found one important medieval theologian whose name and ideas they can invoke, that is, the fourteenth-century Ibn Taymiyyah. While Ibn Taymiyyah's writings are subject to other interpretations, he has become 'the spiritual father of the Islamic revolution, Sunni style'[27] by virtue of his ruling that Mongol rulers of his day who professed Islam and even prayed and fasted but violated other rules cannot be accepted as Muslims. These rulers had not merely neglected much of the *shari‘ah*, but had also applied the Yasa, the traditional Mongol legal system, instead. Ibn Taymiyyah proclaimed that 'he who forsakes the Law of Islam should be fought, though he may have once pronounced the two formulas of Faith'; one student of Islamic thought calls this 'the nearest any premodern theorist in Sunni Islam ever came to expounding the right of resistance to illegitimate power'.[28]

While most modern Muslim rulers have not replaced the *shari'ah* as a whole with another legal system, the parallel between the Mongols' Yasa and today's western-originated codes is compelling to contemporary Sunni militants. And Ibn Taymiyyah's writings are so revered that it would be unthinkable for any Muslim country to ban them; all the Egyptian government and its servile religious establishment can do is to explain that the militants have distorted his ideas.

It is true that Islamic states have theoretically possessed mechanisms for declaring acts of rulers *ultra vires*. Decrees of the Ottoman sultan required a ruling (*fatwa*) by the highest religious authority, the shaykh al-Islam, that they did not infringe on the *shari'ah*, and the shaykh al-Islam could even depose the sultan. That was the way the Ottoman state worked in principle, but the reality was that the shaykh al-Islam was chosen by the sultan and was utterly dependent on him. When such an official declared a sultan unfit to rule, that was merely a matter of legalizing what others in the power structure had decided. Similarly, in Saudi Arabia, one Sunni state in which Islam is still officially supreme, the leading ulama required a king, Sa'ud, to step down as late as 1964. For some observers, the Saudi ulama thus seem to represent a central part of the political system. But another analyst shows that they are hardly 'more than a rubber stamp' for decisions reached by the royal family'.[29] In a country like Egypt, there is no such formal role for the ulama, although the religious legitimacy of what the rulers do remains of great significance in practice – and is readily confirmed by top ulama dependent on the state.

THE EGYPTIAN ULAMA AND THE STATE

The Egptian Muslim religious establishment is centred in the famous al-Azhar University. It has long been the unrivalled seat of scholarship of the indigenous type (as opposed to the universities established on the western model) for the whole Sunni world. The shaykh al-Azhar (rector), a government appointee, may be regarded as the head of Egypt's Islamic religious establishment. There is also an al-Azhar Fatwa [Rulings] Committee and a Grand Mufti, whose rulings, however, do not bind the government.[30]

Much of the religious life of the country is administered by the Ministry of Awqaf (religious endowments). While voluntary benevolent societies are now left to the Ministry of Social Affairs, the Ministry of Awqaf includes two divisions that are responsible for administering mosques and Sufi orders respectively, and mosques cannot 'function in any formal sense apart from a defined relationship to the state', while Friday sermons require 'an implied form of political as well as religious authorization'.[31] This is particularly true of the government mosques, whose officials are simply employees of the Ministry of Awqaf. However, the majority of mosques are still of the 'popular' type, which are supported by benevolent societies. Despite attempts to do so, the Ministry has not been financially able to take control of these popular mosques. But while the preachers in such mosques are not simply government 'mouthpieces', they also lack complete independence, 'for both money and goods originating directly or otherwise in several official agencies ... are sought after and accepted by the benevolent society'.[32] Popular as well as government mosques are subject to the Ministry of Awqaf's authority to inspect the way they are administered.

In light of their role as government employees, the Egyptian ulama – at least those in top positions – have been unable to challenge the state. Instead, they have readily legitimized the acts of successive regimes. The Egyptian ulama historically, until the early part of the nineteenth century, were not without influence. Rulers seriously consulted them, and they acted as spokesmen of the indigenous population *vis-à-vis*, the foreign rulers, although even then the ulama were dependent on the latter for funds and tended to act as their spokesmen too. But they led popular opposition to particular policies and forced the Mamluk ruler to give in on at least one occasion in 1794.[33] They enjoyed their 'Golden Age' after 1798 as they led popular resistance to General Bonaparte's forces and, following his departure five years later, played a leading role in the rise to power of Muhammad Ali Pasha, who, however, proceeded to break 'the independent power of the religious establishment' by removing their independent sources of income, making them instead into 'propagandists for his regime' in return for 'high positions'.[34] Such has been the pattern ever since, particularly in the case of the high-ranking ulama.

The post-1945 period has clearly demonstrated this pattern of ulama subservience, of sometimes dragging their feet behind the scenes but acting as virtually a rubber stamp for official policies. Before 1952, the situation was complicated by the struggle between the king and the Wafd Party, which dominated the parliament whenever elections were free. In this situation, al-Azhar was allied with the king, who financed this institution from his own funds from 1927 onwards.[35]

Since the 1952 Revolution, the establishment ulama have been notorious as 'yes-men' for the government, reversing themselves seemingly without hesitation whenever the regime has changed its direction. At least, under Nasser preachers got weekly direction from the government on the topic of the Friday sermon and the option of a sermon actually prepared by the government.[36] When Nasser established a highly statist economy under the rubric of Arab socialism, he had no trouble obtaining a plethora of statements from the religious establishment that Islam, correctly understood, has always called for socialism. The post-Nasser opening of the economy to private enterprise has found ulama backing equally forthcoming. Similarly, the top ulama long supported the country's struggle against Israel but readily – even predictably – found the Prophet's peace treaty with the Meccans to be the guiding precedent for Sadat's peace with the Jewish state.

On such an issue as birth control, many western writers conclude that Islam does not oppose it, citing the top ulama's endorsement of government policies in this area in Egypt and elsewhere. While indeed there is some basis in Islamic jurisprudence for allowing birth control, it is doubtful that many truly independent traditionalist ulama would uphold it. It is said that local preachers who convey the rulings of the establishment ulama on this matter sometimes privately tell their listeners to pay no mind. Supposedly, when one religious scholar was asked to participate in a debate on family planning, he agreed and then asked whether he should present the pros or the cons.[37] As for a broader issue, when the personal status law was passed in 1979, the religious leadership that had so many 'reservations, open and tacit', nevertheless 'gave it official support'.[38]

It has been the acquiescence of the establishment ulama in Egypt to government policies detrimental to their own group interests that has perhaps been most telling. Notably, although the Nasser regime did not dare push for the abolition of *shari'ah* courts until 1956, this action – which took away the ulama's important judicial functions and gave them to secular judges – evoked no open opposition but rather 'congratulatory statements from various highly respected shaykhs'.[39] Similarly, the government imposed a stringent reorganization of al-Azhar – establishing new modern faculties alongside the traditional religious studies – about which the shaykhs were quite 'unhappy. . ., for they knew it meant the end of al-Azhar's quasi-independent existence'. And yet the religious establishment 'quickly fell in line' in support of the reorganization.[40]

NON-ULAMA EGYPTIAN ACTIVISTS

The co-optation of the ulama, particularly their upper strata, by the state has largely left Islamist movements in the hands of laymen. Such leaders as al-Banna and Qutb were not from the ulama. They were graduates of a modern institution, Dar-al-Ulum, not of al-Azhar, although, at least in the movement's early phases, the Muslim Brothers had an 'active core of' members who were al-Azhar students.[41] As for the more recent ultra-militant organizations, Shukri Mustafa of *al-Takfir wa al-Hijrah* was an agronomist, while Abd al-Salam Faraj of the Jihad Organization was an electrician. However, the latter group was able to recruit one al-Azhar shaykh as its mufti. A disproportionate percentage of those who were accused of involvement in Sadat's assassination were students, particularly from 'the elite faculties of medicine and engineering',[42] and the prevalence of people with modern university education is a striking characteristic of other such Egyptian groups.

Only recently have some independent-minded ulama become outspoken critics of the regime. These include Shaykh Abd al-Hamid Kishk, whose fiery sermons made him famous in the 1970s, with cassette recordings of them widely distributed. This led to his arrest in 1981, followed by several months in prison. He was not associated with the extreme groups, whom he dismissed as 'pubescent thinkers'.[43] But he also attacked the religious establishment, blaming al-Azhar for failing to perform its proper role. He called for a number of reforms that would, *inter alia*, allow election of the shaykh al-Azhar and payment of his salary from endowments rather than by the government, sarcastically suggesting that, for all he knew, the government would appoint a general to this position.[44] Other prominent figures of this sort have been Shaykh Ahmad al-Mahallawi, who preaches against social injustice, and Shaykh Hafiz Salama, who has concentrated on the issue of Israel. Shaykh Salama planned a march in Cairo in 1985 demanding immediate implementation of the *shari'ah*, but this action was banned. A subsequent attempt to organize a large demonstration against government attempts to impose tighter controls over private mosques resulted in his temporary imprisonment and the closing, for a while, of his mosque.

The lay activists and the ulama establishment have generally held each other in low regard. This was true at the time of al-Banna, although his relationship with al-Azhar was not consistently unfriendly, and he was restrained in his expression of hostility to that institution.[45] It was with some irony that in his reply to the then-secularist Khalid Muhammad Khalid's influential book, *From Here We Start*, in the late 1940s (during the 1980s, Khalid has repudiated his earlier position and joined the ranks of the Islamists), the prominent Muslim Brother, Shaykh Muhammad al-Ghazzali, expressed much agreement, especially in putting blame on the establishment ulama. Ghazzali declared that 'Those 'ulama who befriend the tyrants in order to obtain office, power or wealth . . . are the most evil and God-accused people' and that Egypt's 'afflict[ion] with a large number of such false 'ulama' was 'a calamity'. While the establishment ulama rejected more recent Islamic militants as 'alien to Islam' and even 'joined the lengthy "deprogramming" sessions . . . held in prison camps',[46] interviewers found that imprisoned militants in the late 1970s reciprocated with a highly negative view of the ulama in general – at best as pathetic bureaucrats and 'pulpit parrots'.[47]

PRE-REVOLUTIONARY IRAN: THE 'CHURCH' MODEL

The relationship between the ulama and the state in modern Iran took on characteristics that were radically different from that in Egypt or any other country in the Islamic world. Unlike their Egyptian counterparts, the Iranian ulama enjoyed – and were able to defend against state encroachment – a special kind of state – 'Church' dualism and thus recurrently posed challenges to state power. Although this phenomenon was closely related to modern developments in Shi'ite theology, it was not the result of anything inherent in Shi'ism. In the Safavid state, in fact, the shah appointed a top religious official, the Sadr, whose position closely paralleled that of the Ottoman shaykh al-Islam, particularly in terms of subservience to the ruler. The ulama were '"wards" of the state, or at least its dependents'.[48] In fact, the Safavids, who were originally dependent on radical, heterodox tribesmen, imported Shi'ite ulama from Iraq and Lebanon precisely with the idea of having a servile religious establishment.[49]

However, the new predominance of the Usuli school of thought among the Iranian ulama in the eighteenth century – at the time of the disintegration of the Safavid dynasty – created a kind of religious authority that was independent of the state. This made Iran conform in many ways to the 'Church' rather than the 'organic' model of religio-political systems. Indeed, a prominent historian of modern Iran has compared the relationship between shahs and top Iranian ulama to that between emperors and popes in medieval Catholicism[50] – contrary to all that we have previously said about both the Islamic norm for the religio-political order and the actual practice in other Islamic countries.

Unlike the rival Akhbari school, the Usulis emphasize the importance of *ijtihad* and the role of those – the *mujtahids* – whose exceptional learning qualifies them for this role. The bulk of the people, including the lower-level ulama (*mulla*s) are *muqallid*s, that is, practicioners of *taqlid*. As in the case of Sunni Muslims, *taqlid* means being bound by the views of others, as opposed to being qualified to exercise *ijtihad*. But whereas Sunnis – at least the traditionalists, as opposed to both modernists and 'fundamentalists' – are *muqallid*s of authorities who have been dead for over a millennium, the Usuli Shi'ite *muqallid* must defer to the rulings of a living *mujtahid*, who is termed his or her *marja al-taqlid* (source of imitation).

During certain periods, a universally accepted, sole Marja has emerged. At other times, there are several of more-or-less equal prestige from among whom one can pick the Marja of his or her choice. The best known recent Marja was of course Ayatollah Khomeini (the title '*ayatollah*', meaning 'sign of God', is borne by all Marjas and many others of somewhat lesser status), who – his eventual preponderant role as a political leader notwithstanding – was only one of five top rank Marjas. This represents a kind of religio-political pluralism that is lacking in any Sunni country. One recent western observer has gone so far as to proclaim the pattern to be 'one of the most democratic and populist [institutions] in the comparative history of religion', constituting 'democracy at the very grassroots of society'.[51] This practice allows a unique kind of influence from below, for a Marja whose ideas are rejected by his followers may see them slip away and accept another Marja.

The appellation 'democratic' requires some qualification. In practice, there is an informal hierarchy in which the typical person defers to the local *mulla*'s choice of Marja,[52] presumably in most cases one under whom he (or his teacher) has studied. Also, while this provides an opportunity for social mobility, the top ulama tend in practice to form a hereditary intellectual elite, with important *mujtahid*s often coming from families of *mujtahid*s and disproportionately, as in Khomeini's case, from among the *sayyid*s or putative descendants of the Prophet. But the crux of the matter is the fact that, at least before some of them became the rulers, they were organized in such a way that their leadership was not decided by the ruler and thus were in a position to challenge him.

Events following the death of the sole Marja, Ayatollah Sayyid Muhammad Burujirdi, in 1961 confirmed the inability of the shah to interfere in the heirarchy of ulama. In an attempt to overshadow the influence of the ulama in the holy city of Qum, site of the important Fayziyyah Madrasah, Iran's most important such institution, and to get someone who, besides being apolitical, would, as a non-Iranian, be less able to interfere in Iranian politics, the shah strove to gain the acceptance of Ayatollah Shaykh Muhsin al-Hakim of Najaf, in Iraq, as the new sole Marja. Hakim, however, was able to gain 'only a limited following'.[53] The shah was equally unsuccessful in his apparent choice of a sole Marja after Ayatollah Hakim's death in 1970, that is, the quietist Iranian scholar, Ayatollah Sayyid Muhammad Kazim Shari 'atmadari.[54]

FACTORS REINFORCING ULAMA INDEPENDENCE

In addition to the way in which each believer is able to choose his or her own Marja, several other factors reinforced the Iranian ulama's ability to resist government control. Unlike Egyptian ulama, they were not dependent on the state for funds. Instead, their followers contribute alms (*zakat*) and the *khums* (literally, fifth) tax directly to the Marjas. This makes the Marjas dependent on the people – or rather on the wealthy bazaar merchants, whose large contributions have always been crucial – rather than on the government. At least in the past, those who made these payments could threaten to stop. As a result of such contributions, the ulama controlled vast properties in the form of endowments, which provided further income.[55] The wealth was not for the personal use of the ulama. Their reputations would have been ruined had they kept it for themselves, and the chief ulama have been 'men of personal integrity who led simple and ascetic lives while in the process serving the people among whom they have lived'.[56] The money goes to maintain mosques, *madrasah*s, and the like, as well as for social welfare. And the dependence of the poor on the ulama creates an important kind of patron–client relationship that is another foundation of ulama influence.

Add to all this the fact that while the Ottoman Empire was centralizing its control in the nineteenth century, Iran during the same period had a government whose effectiveness was only sporadic. It should then come as no surprise that the eclipse of ulama influence in the Ottoman Empire and Egypt was matched by a growing importance in Iran that neither of the two Pahlavi shahs of the twentieth century was able ever totally to reverse. In fact, some ulama in Iran during the rule of the last shah were able to push for reforms that strengthened their own organization. While some of the proposed reforms, such as one for replacing individual Marjas with a commission of *mujtahid*s to reach collective decisions, were not realized, Ayatollah Burujirdi did much to modernize financial practices, by, for example, the introduction of modern bookkeeping practices.[57]

The position of Shi'ite southern Iraq, particularly the holy cities of Najaf and Karbala, has been of great significance for religious opposition to Iranian rulers. Shi'ite ulama are at home in a religious sense on both sides of the border, and there has been much movement from one side to the other. During the nineteenth century, Iranian critics of the Qajar shahs often took refuge in Iraq, outside the reach of their own government. Such an activist religious scholar as Ayatollah Sayyid Abu al-Qasim Kashani – about whom we shall hear more later – lived in Iraq in the early part of the century and, along with other Iranian ulama, even became a leader of the anti-British revolt in 1920 that led to Iraqi independence.[58] Ayatollah Khomeini's exile in Najaf for the thirteen years ending in 1978 provides a more recent example. And in the 1980s Najaf was the setting for the closely restrained activity of a conservative, quietist Iraqi Shi'ite Marja, Ayatollah Abu al-Qasim al-Khu'i, possibly the senior scholar of the Shi'ite world, who though he refrained from endorsing the war against Iran, remains clearly an opponent of Ayatollah Khomeini's revolutionary Shi'ism and demonstrates that Shi'ite ulama are not a monolithic force.[59]

THE TRADITION OF OPPOSITION

The Iranian ulama's independent position allowed them to spear-head important opposition movements on several occasions from the nineteenth century onwards. With the shah in each case seeming to be in cahoots with European imperialism, ulama-led opposition in 1873 and again in 1890 forced the cancellation of concessions to British nationals that threatened the country's independence. The Constitutional Revolution of 1905–6 is particularly notable, for the ulama were perhaps the core of a movement that sought limits on royal authority, resulting in the adoption of the country's first constitution, which lasted, though with little effect most of the time, until the Islamic Revolution of 1979. One historian comments that 'perhaps uniquely in world history was the power of the leaders of the official, traditional religion exercised in favor of a popular modernizing constitutional revolution'.[60]

It is true that, despite the 1906 constitution's provision for a committee of *mujtahids* with authority to declare legislation contrary to Islamic law *ultra vires* (a consistently inoperative part of the document, as it turned out), a major sector of the ulama, led by the eminent Ayatollah Fadlullah Nuri, eventually broke with the constitutional movement. Yet this does not belie the oppositional role of much of the ulama that in some ways foreshadowed the ulama-led revolts of the 1960s and the 1970s. One can hardly see the contemporary role of the Iranian ulama in its proper perspective without taking these precedents into account even if, as has been argued, ulama 'participation [in the Islamic Revolution of 1979], given the centuries of. . .quietism and aversion to overthrowing regimes, was an unprecedented action in Iranian history'.[61]

THE SHI'ITE QUIETIST TRADITION

Even with its greater potential for opposition, the Iranian religious establishment has typically followed the quietist approach. The ulama have clearly not been a revolutionary force generally,[62] and for that matter it was only a minority of the ulama under Ayatollah Khomeini's leadership that were truly revolutionary in 1978 and subsequently. The top ulama have historically formed one section of the ruling class, and if they enjoyed more autonomy from monarchs than did their counterparts in other states, this hardly made them representatives of the masses *vis-à-vis* the rulers. Their oppositional role was generally in circumstances in which shahs were succumbing to imperialist penetration or were assaulting ulama prerogatives. Such grievances provided the broad base for ulama opposition to the shah in the 1970s on which Ayatollah Khomeini's less typical outright revolutionary stance was able to win out.

The immediate post-1945 period clearly exemplified the quietist stance of the Iranian religious establishment that paralleled that of its Egyptian counterpart. This was the period when Ayatollah Burujirdi was the sole Marja. A meeting of about two thousand ulama in Qum under Burujirdi's auspices in 1949 went so far as to call for total non-involvement in politics and for withdrawal of the professional status of those who violated this rule.[63] In the confrontation between the shah and Premier Musaddiq in the early 1950s, this dominant group of ulama – including Ayatollah Burujirdi and his close associate, Ayatollah Sayyid Muhammad Bihbihani – at first tried to reconcile them but ultimately sided with the royalist forces, providing crucial help in mobilizing crowds against Musaddiq by distributing so-called 'Bihbihani dollars' of CIA origin.

Following his return to power in 1953, the shah and the Burujirdi faction remained closely allied for a long time. A government campaign against the Baha'i minority in 1955 represented the shah's need to keep on good terms with the conservative ulama, who were in a position tacitly to legitimate him and his pro-western policies, if only by withdrawing from politics, with political leaders regularly making their way to Qum to court them.[64]

Activism at this time was limited to independent-minded lower-echelon ulama of modest social background who made up the militant Fida'iyan-i Islam. To the religious establishment, these activists were 'undisciplined agitators' of low status and a threat to 'the clergy's stewardship over religious affairs'.[65] Only one prominent religious scholar, the activist Ayatollah Kashani (not of Marja status and not well thought of by the top ulama) had ties with the Fida'iyan.[66] Even he was not a member of the organization and broke with it in 1951.

Perhaps surprisingly, the future leader of Islamic activism, Ayatollah Khomeini, found it necessary to work 'in the shadow of his teacher [Ayatollah Burujirdi]' during the latter's lifetime and seems not to have been involved with either Kashani or the

Fida'iyan,[67] although the revived Fida'iyan were to provide some key members of the leadership of the future Islamic Republic. Khomeini is even said to have worked to get his quietist colleague accepted as the sole Marja and to have remained 'his close confidant'.[68]

It would thus seem to have been the absence of any sole Marja after Burujirdi's death that permitted one among several such Sources of Imitation, Ayatollah Khomeini, to lead an activist movement of unprecedented proportions. However, even during the period of establishment ulama quietism, the centrality of ulama in the activist ranks provides quite a contrast to the relative absence of ulama in such movements in Egypt and elsewhere. Also, one should not suppose that even Burujirdi and his associates were pawns in the hands of the regime, for unlike the top Egyptian ulama, Burujirdi's group did not let their basic quietism prevent them from clearly opposing certain government policies and from gaining concessions on various matters – not to mention their eventual challenge to the shah when he became powerful enough to threaten their basic interests.

THE RATIONALE FOR SHI'ITE QUIETISM

While Shi'ism, which emerged as a rebellion against rulers whose legitimacy the majority of the Islamic community accepted, has a built-in activist thrust *vis à vis* the Sunni regimes that have tended to predominate, that thrust has also been deflected in a quietist direction. Of course, Iran has had Shi'ite rulers since 1501, and while they did not tend to be any more devout than their Sunni counterparts, this was not necessarily more detrimental to the legitimacy of the former than to that of the latter. The members of the Safavid dynasty claimed to be representatives of the Absent Imam – and the descendants of one of the twelve imams. Subsequent dynasties could not make such claims, but like other traditional monarchs, they presented themselves as just rulers and protectors of their faith.[69]

Certain Shi'ite doctrines, despite potential revolutionary connotations, were particularly conducive to bolstering the status quo, even under non-Shi'ite dynasties. It is notable that when the Twelver Shi'ite Buwayhid dynasty conquered Baghdad in the tenth century, it left the Sunni Abbasid caliphs as nominal heads of the state, the implication being that a truly legitimate government from a

Shi'ite point of view had to await the coming of the Mahdi.[70] The impossibility of legitimate government for the time being thus provides a rationale for not trying to create one.

At least three parts of the Shi'ite tradition that have formed the basis for quietism have recently lent themselves to opposite implications or else have been partially rejected at the hands of Shi'ite proponents of Islamic Revolution. First was the lesson drawn from the Battle of Karbala (680 AD), a central formative event for Shi'ism and, with its celebration in the annual Ashura festival and its portrayal in passion plays over the centuries, comparable to the Crucifixion for Christians. At Karbala, in Iraq, following the death of his quietist brother Hasan (the second Shi'ite imam), the Prophet's grandson and third imam, Husayn, led a small group of people from Medina to claim his birthright, but the army of the evil Umayyad caliph, Yazid (for Shi'ites, the subsequent symbol of tyranny) massacred them while the people of the nearby city of Kufah who had invited Husayn to lead a revolt were too terrified to come to their assistance.

Until recently, the lesson learnt from Karbala was that it is futile to resist tyranny. One was to weep for Husayn, not to see him as an example of a rebel to be emulated.[71] But for Khomeini and his followers Husayn had provided a model for fearless revolt and during the 1960s the Ayatollah called on students in the Shi'ite seminaries to present new versions of the story for enactment as dramas to 'stimulate the masses'.[72] Numerous Sunni Muslim writers have in recent decades also found the revolutionary implications of the Karbala story, ironically with fewer obstacles in their way than those presented to Shi'ites by quietist accretions that had taken on the qualities of orthodoxy. The activist version was expounded by Ni'matullah Salihi Najaf-abadi, a former student of Khomeini (the introduction was written by Ayatollah Husayn Ali Montazari, whom Khomeini later picked – and eventually rejected – as his successor as the leader of the Islamic Republic). Najaf-abadi's book, published in 1968, presented Husayn's defiance of the Umayyads as a rationally calculated attempt to overthrow a despotic regime whose weaknesses were apparent, while Khomeini presented Husayn as having fought against the establishment of monarchy and called on Iranians likewise 'to create an "Ashura" in their struggle'.[73] An American anthropologist who lived in an Iranian village during the months leading up to the fall of the shah's regime recounted the shift she

witnessed in the way the people viewed Husayn – from being an
'Intercessor, the quietist ideology of adaptation to the existing
relations of power' to one of 'Example – the revolutionary ideology
of struggle against tyranny'.[74]

Second, Shi'ism has always permitted *taqiyyah* (dissimulation) to
avoid persecution, a response to a heritage of minority status during
many periods. Khomeini, however, has largely broken with this
distinctive Shi'ite practice, limiting it to such matters as 'performing
ablution in different ways' and excluding situations where 'the chief
principles of Islam and its welfare are endangered'. He furthermore
specifies that the *fuqaha* (ulama; specifically Islamic jurists) cannot
practise *taqiyyah* at all.[75] It has been argued that in taking these
positions, Khomeini is 'in effect putting an end to Ja'fari Shi'ism,
which had accomodated the temporal state'.[76]

Finally, the doctrine of the Absent Imam has in the past been
used as a sort of 'opiate of the masses'. Though it has always been 'a
potential tool of radical activism', in practice it historically provided
'a sanctifying tenet for the submissive acceptance of the *status quo*'.[77]
Truly legitimate and just government can, in the logic of quietism,
only emerge when the Mahdi comes, and there is no use in struggling
against tyranny now. Indeed, it is wrong to revolt against unjust
government before his coming. There seems even to have been an
idea that the worst is best, that is, that it might induce the Return, for
Khomeini adamantly rejects the idea 'that the Imam will not come
until the earth is full of corruption'.[78]

One western scholar has produced historical evidence that the
doctrine of the Absent Imam was purposely invented by a member
of 'a powerful and wealthy [Shi'ite] family' in the ninth century to
justify accomodation with the rulers of his day and to free members
of his sect from suspicion. He concludes that as a result of this
transformation in doctrine Twelver Shi'ism became 'depoliticized'
and was to remain only 'a "personal" religion' until the fifteenth
century. There was, however, a quietist trend that preceded the
Absence, for the sixth imam, Ja'far al-Sadiq – the jurist for whom the
Twelver legal system is named – recommended complete abstention
from political disputes.[79]

In contrast, the activist interpretation of the Absence and Return
is that of seeking 'social justice and the relief of the downtrodden'.
Unlike traditionalistic, quietist ideas, the activist concept allows the
conditions for the Return to 'be partially achieved by those who
desire his [the Mahdi's] coming'.[80]

DEFENCE OF SELF-INTEREST BY IRANIAN ULAMA

However much the quietist trend generally dominated the thinking of Shi'ite ulama in the past, they still tended to defend their own group interests much more effectively than have those in Sunni countries like Egypt. When the well-being of the Islamic institution has been severely threatened, they have rallied to the defence. Such was the case in the early 1960s and again in the 1970s. Conservative ulama thus joined forces with their revolutionary colleagues, notably Ayatollah Khomeini.

The first clash began in 1959, ending the period of amity between the shah and the religious establishment. The key issue apparently was the recently proposed bill providing for land reform. Many lower ulama, as well as higher-ranking ones like Ayatollah Sayyid Mahmud Taliqani, seem actually to have favoured radical social change.[81] In light of his rhetoric about the *mustad'afin*, it also seems unlikely that Ayatollah Khomeini was opposed to land reform, and a researcher who stressed the unrevolutionary character of the ulama nevertheless concedes that he has been unable to find 'any statement or speech in which he [Khomeini] declared himself against land reform'.[82] Khomeini was then still not in the forefront of ulama activity, apparently biding his time as long as Ayatollah Burujirdi lived. This may have been only one of several issues related to the broader 'unhappiness about the growing power of the state'.[83] But considering that many leading ulama were large landowners,[84] it should come as no surprise that Ayatollah Burujirdi criticized the land reform bill.

Khomeini, who gained prominence in the years immediately after Burujirdi's death, violently attacked the regime in June 1963. Following his arrest, a mass uprising nearly toppled the shah. Khomeini stressed mainly those issues relating to western domination.[85] Of special importance was the bill to grant immunity to United States military personnel, which he considered an insulting imposition on the country, much like the capitulations of earlier times. It was his ferocious attack on this bill in 1964 that got him arrested again and sent into exile.[86] He also attacked the shah's growing relationship with Israel.

Khomeini was the leader of a radical faction of ulama. Aside from being so untraditionalistic as to include philosophy (frowned on by his conservative colleagues) among the subjects he taught, he denounced corruption and exploitation of the poor. But though he attacked imperialism and dependence on foreign investment in general terms, he did not offer specific proposals for change in these areas.[87] Like other ulama, he opposed the shah's proposal for female suffrage at one point but later changed his mind.[88] (And when he eventually came to power, he made no attempt to deprive women of this right, the imposition of Islamic rules for dress and the like notwithstanding.)

With the ulama-led revolution of the early 1960s aborted, the shah's regime seemed secure for a long time. But again in the context of continuing attacks on the regime by Khomeini from abroad and the growing secular revolutionary ferment, it was the defence of their own interests in the face of attacks by the state that brought the clergy in general, including the conservative ones, into a broad coalition that toppled the monarchy in 1979.

The ulama role in the 1978–79 Revolution was induced by a renewed effort by the shah, starting at the beginning of the decade, to destroy their influence. With the Islamic system of education, represented by the *madrasah*s, suffering drastic decline in terms of income and numbers of students and with the ulama gradually losing control of what was left of the Endowments Department, they were increasingly becoming 'a *déclassé* stratum' and were 'on the defensive'.[89] As early as 1970, the authorities imprisoned, tortured and killed a prominent religious scholar, Ayatollah Muhammad Riza Sa'idi, because of his criticism of the shah's policies. In what was the beginning of a 'frontal attack' on the ulama, the regime, in 1971, shut down the Husayni Irshad, a popular centre for religious activities.[90]

The next year witnessed a memorandum sent by the director of Endowments to Prime Minister Amir Abbas Huvayda outlining 'a plan of action to destroy' Khomeini by such means as fabricating evidence of his collaboration with the Baghdad regime against Iran (noting the difficulty of doing this in light of his known dislike for that regime) and demanding the full involvement of all Marjas in discrediting him, as well as threatening those who refused to co-operate. Each preacher would be compelled to attack Khomeini's ideas, with prepared texts to be presented to *mulla*s in the countryside.[91] These and other actions evoked an ulama manifesto accusing the government of trying to destroy the religious institution and pointing to numerous arrests.[92]

At the same time, the state attempted to take over the religious functions of the ulama. A newly organized Religion Corps made up of young university graduates, not graduates of the *madrasahs*, and a Department of Religious Propaganda in the Endowments Organization represented an attempt by the state to encroach on the functions of the ulama,[93] and there was a plan to establish a state-run Islamic university in Mashhad, which threatened to undermine the *madrasahs*.[94]

It was such challenges to their own interests and the repression that ulama opposition evoked – secret police infiltration, closing publishing houses, putting shrines under military control, imprisonments and executions[95] – that brought normally quiescent, conservative ulama like Ayatollah Shari'atmadari to call for an end to the shah's dictatorship and to recognize Ayatollah Khomeini as the representative of the popular will.[96] Apparently a key event totally alienating Shari'atmadari from the regime was a forced entry into his home by the shah's forces in 1978, whereupon they proceeded to shoot one of his followers dead before learning that this was Shari'atmadari's house rather than that of Ayatollah Muhammad Riza Golpaygani.[97] However, Shari'atmadari continued to accept the possibility of a constitutional monarchy and failed to endorse Khomeini's more militant revolutionary rhetoric.[98] Had the royalist regime not engaged in such excesses, it is unthinkable that a conservative like Ayatollah Shari'atmadari would have joined in a broad-based ulama opposition movement.

THE GUARDIANSHIP OF THE JURIST

Under the rubric of the 'guardianship of the Jurist', a new kind of organic relationship between religion and state emerged under the aegis of Imam Khomeini after 1979.[99] What is new in contrast to the organic pattern that has always existed in other Muslim countries is that the religious scholars are in charge rather than subordinated to kings or soldiers. The oft-made suggestion that this reflects Plato's idea of a philosopher–ruler is not entirely far-fetched in light of the strain of Islamic neoplatonic philosophy that has survived only among Shi'ites (and which indeed influenced the Shi'ite doctrine of the imamate in its formation).

What may be surprising is that the guardianship of the Jurist is largely a new idea introduced by Ayatollah Khomeini. Admittedly, at least for some centuries the Shi'ite ulama have claimed the right to act in the name of the Absent Imam. But this ordinarily meant only the right to be consulted by the ruler, in addition of course to judicial, educational and other regular ulama functions. The position that the shah's rule was illegitimate and that a *mujtahid* should take his place surfaced in ulama circles during the seventeenth century, as the contemporary French writer and traveller, Jean Chardin, showed.[100] And the idea seems occasionally to have come up without being much stressed.[101] Khomeini himself did not go beyond calling for a 'supervisory role for the ulama' in his book published in 1943.[102] Only in the early 1970s did he openly declare that 'Islam is firmly opposed to the pillar of monarchy'.[103]

The doctrine of rule by a jurist arguably represents the logical culmination of the Islamic concept of nomocracy. In his book entitled *Islamic Government*, Khomeini stressed the imperative of having a state based on law run entirely by specialists in the law and pointed to the incongruity of anything else.[104] Such Islamic scholars as Shari'atmadari and Taliqani, however, opined that ulama involvement in politics should be 'exceptional'.[105] It may be worth noting that Khomeini's idea is in accord with the opinion of medieval Sunni political thinkers that being a *mujtahid* is a prerequisite for holding the office of caliph.[106] Perhaps this is what one analyst has in mind when he concludes that Khomeini's doctrine was 'derived from Sunni jurisprudence'.[107] It may be that the main problem with it from an orthodox Shi'ite perspective is the primacy it gives to one jurist, especially when there is no sole Marja.[108]

Even Khomeini's concept, in so far as it is implemented in the constitution of the Islamic Republic and particularly in his personal style of leadership, amounts to a sort of arbiter role rather than direct rulership. The constitution gives the Jurist vast powers that smack of potential absolutism, and yet Khomeini normally preferred to allow the parliament (Consultative Assembly), the cabinet headed by a prime minister and a president, to work things out themselves and to intervene only when necessary. And since it is unlikely that, following Khomeini's death in 1989, a person of his stature will ever fill the position of Jurist again (his immediate successor, Hojatolislam Ali Khamenei, is not even a Marja – the press now sometimes questioningly gives him Ayatollah rank – and of course lacks his predecessor's charismatic authority), the office will surely lose most of its significance. At times the Islamic Republic seems to a remarkable degree in some ways like a western-style democracy, with highly competitive (though apparently not totally free) elections and fierce debates in the parliament (and ministers given votes of no confidence) and a press that includes mutually hostile tendencies – at least within the limits of support for the revolution and Khomeini's leadership. And a Council of Guardians – ironically only half of whose members, unlike the analogous committee that previously existed on paper, are ulama – not only has the authority to declare legislation *ultra vires* (that is, contrary to the *shari'ah*) but regularly does so and continues to hinder the implementation of more radical land reform and more extensive nationalization.

But increasingly the ulama have come to occupy top offices. The president, the speaker of the parliament, and much of the body's membership are ulama.[109] Also, the Friday prayer leader appointed by the Jurist for each city is a key political figure. However broadly or narrowly we might define the country's political elite, it is heavily dominated by ulama.

One qualification to the organic nature of Iran's present system is in order. Until such a time that Khomeini's theory of the guardianship of the Jurist gains general acceptance among the Iranian ulama, his new order represents the organic fusion of only a part of the 'Church' with the state. Khomeini's occupation of the top state office notwithstanding, he remained only one of the Marjas. The other widely recognized Iranian Marjas – Ayatollahs Golpayegani, Najafi and Tabatabai-Qumi – as well as the Iraqi Ayatollah Khu'i are traditionalists who reject the guardianship of the Jurist and Khomeini's socio-economic radicalism. They have been subjected to house arrest or denied access to the media because of their criticism of the policies of the Islamic Republic.[110] Shari'atmadari, whose opposition to the guardianship principle inspired some of his followers in his native Azarbayjan to launch a revolt in 1980, subsequently faced house arrest, and the regime banned any publicity for his funeral when he died.[111]

Khomeini's being succeeded as Jurist by a non-Marja made it even more difficult to talk about an organic religio-political system unless the late Imam's 'imitators' accept the argument put forth by one faction that they need not choose another Marja to imitate but rather must follow the rulings of the new Jurist on matters not decided by his predecessor. Others – apparently radicals, using this as a tactic to undermine the regime's pragmatic direction – call on Khomeini's 'imitators' to accept the previously largely unknown Ayatollah Muhammad Ali Araki as their new Marja,[112] an option that would seem to provide the potential for a revived 'Church'–state dualism.

CONCLUSION

In Islamic theory, there is no distinction between religion and politics. The purpose of the ideal state is the enforcement of divine law, the *shari'ah*. The ruler merely administers this law, while the religious scholars – jurists – may overrule or even depose him if he deviates from the immutable rules. But the reality has usually seen this turned upside down, with rulers acting arbitrarily and the ulama too dependent on them to pose any limitation. However impious, rulers have made much use of Islam for purposes of legitimation even in the case of otherwise seemingly secularizing regimes in twentieth century Egypt and Iran.

Not only co-optation by the rulers but also a body of quietist political theory has inclined the religious scholars to refrain from opposing rulers and even actively to offer legitimation to almost any regime. This has been particularly true in Egypt, where the establishment ulama have long been ready to back whatever government is in power and whatever its policies. Islamist movements that reject this quietism and call for the restoration of Islamic government have been made up primarily of laymen.

In Iran, on the other hand, the emergence of a hierarchy of ulama whose leadership is popularly determined, not state-appointed, allowed them to display independence somewhat on the medieval Catholic model of Church–state dualism, at least until victory by a faction of ulama resulted in a new kind of organic relationship between ulama and state in which the former provided the leadership of the latter. Prior to 1979, the ulama had repeatedly clashed with rulers, but primarily in response to collaboration by shahs with European imperialism or to attempts to undermine the ulama's interests. Otherwise, a special Shi'ite brand of quietism generally safeguarded shahs from any threat from this quarter. It was the last shah's attempt in the 1970s to destroy their independence that rallied the ulama against him and, contrary to their intentions, allowed one religious scholar, whose radical insistence on an activist reinterpretation of Shi'ite symbols was out of tune with the thinking of his normally quietist colleagues, to lead a revolution. This scholar was thus able to implement his theory of the guardianship of the Jurist, not merely restoring the 'nomocratic' character of the state but – what is unique – actually putting a specialist in the sacred legal system – himself – in charge.

The Islamist struggle in Egypt continues in diverse forms. Its success is far from unthinkable if conditions unfavourable to the continuity of the existing regime further deteriorate. However, if this happens, we can be sure that the movement will not be centred in the religious establishment.

NOTES

1   If fundamentalism refers to the doctrine of inerrancy of scriptures, then all Muslims are fundamentalists, for the doctrine that the Qur'an is literally the Word of God – syllable by syllable Arabic – is a basic one in Islam. Western specialists on Islam increasingly recognize the inappropriateness of the term 'Islamic fundamentalism', which is unknown in the Islamic world.

2   The most thorough account of this movement through 1954 is R.P. Mitchell (1969), *The Society of the Muslim Brothers*, Middle Eastern Monographs 9, London: Oxford University Press. Also see I.M. Husaini (1956), *The Moslem Brethern*, translated by J. Brown *et al.*, Beirut: Khayat's.

3   On Islamist movements from this point on, see G. Kepel (1986), *Muslim Extremism in Egypt: The Prophet and the Pharaoh*, translated by Jon Rothschild, Berkeley and Los Angeles: University of California Press and E. Sivan (1985), *Radical Islam: Medieval Theology and Modern Politics*, New Haven and London: Yale University Press.

4   See J.J.G. Jansen (1986), *The Neglected Duty: The Creed of Sadat's Assassins and Islamic Resurgence in the Middle East*, New York: Macmillan; London: Collier Macmillian. The book's appendix (pp.159ff) is a translation of Faraj's text.

5   M.M. Milani (1988), *The Making of Iran's Islamic Revolution: From Monarchy to Islamic Republic*, Boulder, CO. and London: Westview Press, p.3. For another thorough study, not available when this chapter was written, see S.A. Arjomand (1988), *The Turban for the Crown: The Islamic Revolution in Iran*, Studies in Middle Eastern history, New York and Oxford: Oxford University Press.

6   S.E. Ibrahim (1980), 'Anatomy of Egypt's militant Islamic groups: Methodological note and preliminary findings', *International Journal of Middle East Studies*, vol. 12, no. 4, p.433.

7   See J.R. Gusfield (1971), 'Tradition and modernity: Misplaced polarities in the study of social change', in J.L. Finkle and R.W. Gable (eds), *Political Development and Social Change*, 2nd edn, New York and London: John Wiley & Sons, pp.15–26 and S. Huntington (1978), 'The change to change: Modernization, development, and politics', in N.W. Provizer (ed.), *Analyzing the Third World: Essays from Comparative Politics*, Cambridge, MA: Schenkman Publishing

Company, particularly pp.40–5.

8   Mitchell, op. cit., p.331.
9   As I use the word 'orthodox', it does not refer to a particular sect. Each
      sect can be considered to have its own orthodoxy.
10   For an argument that the Islamic world, including those movements
      I call 'Islamist', has in practice come to terms with the existence of
      'nation-states', see J.P. Piscatori (1986), *Islam in a World of Nation-states*,
      Cambridge: Cambridge University Press, in association with the Royal
      Institute of International Affairs.
11   This is the phrase used by spokesmen for the Islamic Republic of Iran.
      See R.K. Ramazani (1986), *Revolutionary Iran: Challenge and Response
      in the Middle East*, Baltimore and London: Johns Hopkins University
      Press, p.28.
12   *New York Times*, 8 January 1988.
13   M. Khadduri (1955), *War and Peace in the Law of Islam*, Baltimore and
      London: Johns Hopkins University Press, p.14.
14   D.E. Smith (1970), *Religion and Political Development*, Little, Brown Series
      in Comparative Politics, Boston: Little, Brown and Company, pp.7–8.
15   See, for example, M. al-Ghazzali (1975), *Our Beginning in Wisdom*,
      translated by I.R. el Faruqi, American Council of Learned Societies
      Near Eastern Translation Program Number Five, New York: Octagon
      Books, p.8.
16   J. Schacht (1955), 'The schools of law and later developments of
      jurisprudence', in M. Khadduri and H.J. Liebesny, *Law in the Middle
      East*, Washington DC: Middle East Institute, p.77.
17   Smith, op. cit., p.6.
18   Mohammed Reza Shah Pahlavi (1961), *Mission for My Country*, New
      York: McGraw Hill, pp.54–5. Also see J.A. Bill and C. Leiden (1974),
      The Middle East: Politics and Power, Boston: Allyn & Bacon, p.141
      and L. Binder (1964), *Iran: Political Development in a Changing Society*,
      Berkeley and Los Angeles: University of California Press, pp.74–6 and
      passim.
19   E.A. Bayne (1968), *Persian Kingship in Transition*, American Universities
      Field Staff, p.75.
20   A.L. al-Sayyid-Marsot (1977), *Egypt's Liberal Experiment 1922–1936*,
      Berkeley, Los Angeles and London: University of California Press,
      p.190.
21   Smith, op. cit., pp.86–7.
22   B.M. Borthwick (1979), 'Religion and politics in Israel and Egypt',
      Middle East Journal, vol. 33, no. 2, p.154. Also see M. Berger (1970),
      Islam in Egypt Today: Social and Political Aspects of Popular Religion,
      Cambridge: Cambridge University Press, p.128 and D. Crecelius
      (1974), 'The course of secularism in modern Egypt' in D.E. Smith
      (ed.), *Religion and Political Modernization*, New Haven and London: Yale
      University Press, p.91.
23   S.E. Ibrahim (1988), 'Egypt's Islamic activism in the 1980s', *Third
      World Quarterly*, vol. 10, no. 2, p.637.
24   H.A.R. Gibb (1962), *Studies on the Civilization of Islam*, ed. by S.J. Shaw
      and W.R. Polk, Boston: Beacon Press, p.143.

25 H.A.R. Gibb, 'Constitutional organization in Khadduri and Liebesny', op. cit., p.19.
26 Sivan, op. cit., p.91.
27 ibid., p.96.
28 ibid., p.98–9.
29 A. Bligh (1985), 'The Saudi religious elite (ulama) as participant in the political system of the kingdom', *International Journal of Middle East Studies*, vol. 17, no. 1, pp.47–8.
30 H.J. Liebesny (1983), 'Judicial systems in the Near and Middle East: Evolutionary development and Islamic revival', *Middle East Journal*, vol. 37, no. 2, p.205.
31 P.D. Gaffney (1987), 'Authority and the mosque in Upper Egypt: The Islamic preacher as image and actor' in W.R. Roff (ed.), *Islam and the Political Economy of Meaning: Comparative Studies of Muslim Discourse*, Berkeley and Los Angeles: University of California Press, pp.200, 205.
32 ibid., p.219.
33 A.L. al-Sayyid Marsot (1972), 'The ulama of Cairo in the eighteenth and nineteenth centuries' in N.R. Keddie (ed.), *Scholars, Saints, and Sufis: Muslim Religious Institutions in the Middle East since 1500*, Berkeley, Los Angeles and London: University of California Press, pp.158–9 and *passim*.
34 D. Crecelius, 'Nonideological responses of the Egyptian ulama to modernization' in Keddie, op. cit., pp.180ff.
35 D. Crecelius (1966), 'Al-Azhar and the revolution', *Middle East Journal*, vol. 20, no. 1, p.34.
36 B. Borthwick (1967), 'The Islamic sermon as a channel of political communication', *Middle East Journal*, vol. 21, no. 3, p.305.
37 Sivan, op. cit., p.56.
38 ibid., p.38.
39 Crecelius (1966), op. cit., p.35.
40 ibid., pp.38, 40.
41 Mitchell, op. cit., p.212.
42 Kepel, op. cit., p.216.
43 ibid., p.230.
44 ibid., pp.189–90.
45 See Mitchell, op. cit., p.211 and Crecelius (1966), op. cit., p.34.
46 H.N. Ansari (1984), 'The Islamic militants in Egyptian Politics', *International Journal of Middle East Studies*, vol. 16, no. 1, p.124.
47 Ibrahim (1980), op. cit., p.434.
48 S. Akhavi (1980), *Religion and Politics in Contemporary Iran: Clergy–State Relations in the Pahlavi Period*, Albany: State University of New York Press, p.14.
49 N.R. Keddie (1980), 'Iran: Change in Islam; Islam and change', *International Journal of Middle East Studies*, vol. 11, no. 4, p.533.
50 N.R. Keddie (1972), 'The roots of the ulama's power in modern Iran' in N.R. Keddie (ed.), *Scholars, Saint and Sufis: Muslim Religious Institutions in the Middle East since 1500*, Berkeley, Los Angeles and London: University of California Press, p.226.

51   J.A. Bill (1982), 'Power and religion in revolutionary Iran', *Middle East Journal*, vol. 36, no. 1, p.24.

52   H. Algar (1969), *Religion and State in Iran 1785–1906: The Role of the Ulama in the Qajar Period*, Berkeley and Los Angeles: University of California Press, p.18.

53   H. Algar, 'The oppositional role of the ulama in twentieth-century Iran' in Keddie (1972), op. cit., p.245.

54   M. Milani, op. cit., p.139.

55   See H. Algar (1969), *Religion and State, in Iran 1785–1906: The Role of the Ulama in the Qajar Period*, Berkeley and Los Angeles: University of California Press, pp.11ff.

56   Bill, op. cit., p.24.

57   See Akhavi, op. cit., pp.117ff.

58   Y. Richard (1980), 'Ayatollah Kashani: Precursor of the Islamic Republic?', translated by N.R. Keddie in N.R. Keddie (ed.), *Religion and Politics in Iran: Shiʿism from Quietism to Revolution*, New Haven and London: Yale University Press, p.106.

59   *New York Times*, 2 February 1988.

60   N.R. Keddie (1972), 'The roots of the ulama's power', *Scholars, Saints, and Sufis: Muslim Religious Institutions in the Middle East since 1500*, Berkeley, Los Angeles and London: University of California Press, p.211.

61   Akhavi, op. cit., p.171.

62   W.M. Floor (1980), 'The revolutionary character of the Iranian ulama: Wishful thinking or reality', *International Journal of Middle East Studies*, vol. 12, no. 4, pp.501ff.

63   Akhavi, op. cit., pp.63–4.

64   ibid., pp.xvii, 69, 73.

65   ibid., p.66.

66   Richard, op. cit., p.122.

67   A.H. Ferdows (1983), 'Khomaini's and Fedayan's society and politics', *International Journal of Middle East Studies*, vol. 15., no. 2, p.244.

68   Milani, op. cit., p.89.

69   R. Mottahadeh (1985), *The Mantle of the Prophet: Religion and Politics in Iran*, New York: Pantheon Books, p.207.

70   See Algar (1969), op. cit., p.4.

71   H. Enayat (1982), *Modern Islamic Political Thought*, Modern Middle East Series, Austin: University of Texas Press, pp.182–3.

72   Akhavi, op. cit., p.166.

73   Enayat, op. cit., p.194.

74   M. Hegland (1980), 'Two images of Husain: Accomodation and revolution in an Iranian village' in N.R. Keddie (ed.), *Religion and Politics in Iran: Shiʿism from Quietism to Revolution*, New Haven and London: Yale University Press, p.235. Also see M. Fischer (1980), *Iran: From Religious Dispute to Revolution*, Cambridge, MA and London: Harvard University Press, pp.183ff. On the similar transformation of the 'Karbala paradigm' in Lebanon, see F. Ajami (1986), *The Vanished Imam: Musa al-Sadr and the Shia of Lebanon*, Ithaca, NY and London: Cornell University Press, especially pp.123ff.

75   Imam Khomeini (1981), *Islam and Revolution: Writings and Declarations of Imam Khomeini*, translated and annotated by H. Algar, Contemporary Islamic Thought, Persian Series, Berkeley, CA: Mizan Press, p.144.

76   M. Bayat (1983), 'The Iranian Revolution of 1978–79: Fundamentalist or modern?', *Middle East Journal*, vol. 37, no. 1, p.44.

77   Enayat, op. cit., p.25.

78   A. Kelidar (1981), 'Ayatollah Khomeini's concept of Islamic government' in A.S. Cudsi and A.E. Hillal Dessouki (eds), *Islam and Power*, Baltimore and London: Johns Hopkins University Press, p.84.

79   W.M. Watt, 'The significance of the early stages of Imami Shi'ism' in Keddie, *Religion and politics*, pp.27, 31; Algar (1969), op. cit., p.2.

80   Algar, 'The oppositional role', in Keddie (1972), op. cit., p.23.

81   Akhavi, op. cit., p.93.

82   Floor, op. cit., p.520.

83   See Akhavi, op. cit., p.91. There is recent evidence that land reform was not the issue that concerned any of the ulama. See A. Najmabadi (1987), *Land Reform and Social Change in Iran*, Salt Lake City: University of Utah Press, pp.205–9.

84   See Akhavi, op. cit., p.97 for a list of ulama landlords in one province.

85   See Milani, op. cit., pp.90ff.

86   For the text of Khomeini's speech of 27 October 1964, see the Appendix to Floor, op. cit., pp.521–4.

87   Akhavi, op. cit., p.101.

88   Floor, op. cit., p.515.

89   Akhavi, op. cit., p.132.

90   Bill, op. cit., pp.24–5.

91   Akhavi, op. cit., pp.135–6.

92   ibid., p.163.

93   ibid., pp.137ff.

94   Milani, op. cit., p.117.

95   See Bill, op. cit., p.25.

96   Akhavi, op. cit., p.168.

97   Bill, op. cit., p.26.

98   Akhavi, op. cit., pp.168–9.

99   Although Khomeini's official position is that of 'jurist', his official title is 'imam'. This does not mean that he is considered one of the imams in the line that ended with the Absent Imam.

100   Keddie, 'The roots of the ulama's power', in N.R. Keddie (ed.) (1972), *Scholars, Saints, and Sufis: Muslim Religious Institutions in the Middle East since 1500*, Berkeley, Los Angeles and London: University of California Press, p.221.

101   Mottahadeh, op. cit., p.244. Also see G. Rose, '*Velayat-e Faqih* and the recovery of Islamic identity in the thought of Ayatollah Khomeini' in N.R. Keddie (ed.) (1980), *Religion and Politics in Iran: Shi'ism from Quietism to Revolution*, New Haven and London: Yale University Press, pp.166–8.

102   Ferdows, op. cit., p.244.

103   Akhavi, op. cit., p.167.

104   See Khomeini, op. cit., pp.59–60, 79–80 and 137.

105 Akhavi, op. cit., p.174.
106 For the views of a leading medieval theorist, al-Baghdadi, see Gibb, 'Constitutional organization' in Khadduri and Leibesny, op. cit., p.9. For other writers, see E.I.J. Rosenthal (1962), *Political Thought in Medieval Islam: An Introductory Outline*, Cambridge: Cambridge University Press, pp.29, 40 and *passim*.
107 Kelidar, op. cit., p.79.
108 See S.A. Arjomand, 'Revolution in Shi'ism,' in Roff, op. cit., p.119.
109 See Bill, op. cit., p.33.
110 See K. Foroohar (July 1988), 'Leftward lurch at home', *The Middle East*, no. 165, pp.20–1.
111 Milani, op. cit., p.294.
112 See 'Finding places around the table', *The Middle East*, August 1989, no. 178, pp.14–15.

Chapter 5

Politics and religion in contemporary India

Ian A. Talbot

INTRODUCTION

Religion has played an important role in the political evolution of modern India. Hindu reform movements, while regionally based and disruptive of Muslim–Hindu harmony, nevertheless prepared the way for national self-consciousness. Such important nationalist leaders as Tilak and later Gandhi drew their inspiration from religious faith. Religious appeals and symbolism popularized the Congress's message. Eventually it was on the basis of religion that the Subcontinent was divided when the British departed in 1947.

At the outset of Jawaharlal Nehru's premiership of independent India, however, religion appeared a spent political force. Nehru stressed the themes of economic modernization and secularism which he had already espoused during the nationalist struggle. There were enshrined in the legislative provisions of the 1950 constitution which, with its provision for direct elections to a National Assembly and the ending of separate electorates, sought to encourage the existence of an inclusive political community within which groups were differentiated by economic and social interests rather than by ties based on religion, language, ethnicity and locality.

By the late 1950s it had become clear that Indian politics was not operating in the manner predicted by Nehru. Parties gained their support in the villages not on the basis of their policies and programmes, but through the manipulation of powerful ascriptive structures. While the State Congresses had effectively become coalitions of caste and communal groupings, they were led by party bosses who were more concerned with patronage and brokerage than the lofty idealism of the old style Congress elite.

Mrs Gandhi's period of power was marked by her wrestling control of the Congress from the powerful party managers. At the same time, however, caste and religious affiliations far from disappearing from the political arena, assumed new and dynamic forms. Indeed, during the last ten years or so, religion has played a central role in Indian politics. This has been dramatized by the Sikh demand for a separate Khalistan state. It has also been seen in mounting Muslim–Hindu tension and in the resurgence of Hindu communal organizations as religious issues have increased in political importance.

The contemporary significance of religion in Indian politics has received extensive scholarly attention. This chapter will assess some of the major theories. It is first necessary, however, to provide a brief historical background to both the role of religion in Indian politics and the theories concerning this. It will be followed by an overview of the contemporary Indian political scene and a definition of religion and politics in the Indian context.

THE HISTORICAL BACKGROUND

The situation in which religious community rather than caste or class becomes the major determinant of political loyalties has traditionally been known in the Indian context as communalism. Within thirty-five years of the Indian National Congress's formation in 1885, each of the main religious communities had developed communal political organizations in the form of the Hindu Mahasabha, the Muslim League and the Akali Dal.[1]

Despite Congress's secular stance and adherence to a composite national identity, members of communal organizations held dual membership within it during the 1920s. Indeed, such prominent members of the Hindu Mahasabha as Pandit Malaviya and Lala Lajpat Rai exerted considerable influence in its decision-making. They countered concessions to the Muslims sponsored by the Nehrus and their supporters. Gandhi also stood against the Mahasabhites' efforts to Hinduize Indian politics. Early in the 1920s he was able to achieve considerable Muslim–Hindu co-operation over the Khilafat issue.[2] Ultimately, however, Gandhi's own blending of religion and politics alienated the Muslims. Those living in the Hindu-dominated areas gravitated towards the Muslim League. The League raised the demand for Pakistan in 1940, following a period of Congress Provincial Government which had further fuelled Muslim fears about a future Hindu Raj. Wartime social, economic and constitutional developments enabled the Muslim League to swing support behind it in the centres of Muslim population. It faced a particularly fierce struggle, however, to wrest political control from its Unionist party rival in the key region of the Punjab. This paved the way for the creation of Pakistan.

The turmoil which accompanied Partition followed shortly by Gandhi's assassination by a Hindu fanatic, Naturam V. Godse, strengthened Nehru's efforts to suppress political conflicts based on religious differences. The secularism of the Nehruvian Congress did not mean, however, a separation of religion and politics in the western sense, but a giving of equal status to all religions and even a willingness of the state to intervene in, for example, the reform of Hindu personal law and the management of Hindu temples in such states as Tamil Nadu.

The new climate was reflected in the decline of the Hindu Mahasabha and Union Muslim League and the Akali Dal's tactical adoption of secular goals.[3] The dramatic decline in communal riots was another indicator of the changed atmosphere. Communalism appeared defeated. Most observers of Indian politics in the early 1950s responded to this situation by regarding communal and caste loyalties as factors of little importance in the emerging political system, or as problems which could be solved by purely administrative means.[4]

Mounting communal violence and the prevalence of 'casteism' in politics called into question such early assessments of Indian politics. Selig Harrison typified a growing pessimism in his observations of the late 1950s.[5] He foresaw the possibility of the existing political system breaking down under the strain of sectional forces and conflicting group demands which the government would be unable to satisfy in an environment of scarcity.

Harrison's view was quickly challenged, however, by the works of the Rudolphs.[6] They maintained that given the right conditions and incentives, 'natural associations' could foster rather than impede the development of democracy, by integrating their members into the political system. It is of course true that the Rudolphs concentrated on caste associations rather than communal groupings. They also made the important caveat that religious communities posed a greater threat to national integrity than caste associations. Nevertheless, their integration theory concerning 'natural associations' has only recently been questioned. The developments of the last ten years have caused observers to doubt whether groups pressing particularistic demands, can at the same time be socialized into the values of the wider political community. The end of Rajiv Gandhi's honeymoon period in office led to renewed pessimism. By the beginning of 1987, Indian commentators were gloomily declaring that secularism was now no more than a 'myth' and that the Indian state beset by communal violence had never looked so 'fragile', 'decrepit' and 'unreliable'.[7]

RELIGION AND POLITICS IN INDIA

Communalism is based on two main premises, first that because a group of people follow a particular religion they automatically possess common social, economic and political interests, second that religious identity is the sole determinant of political loyalty. These beliefs have undoubtedly exerted a profound impact on modern India's development, but in order to set the interaction between religion and politics in its widest context, it is important to understand that none of the religious communities are monolithic in character and that religion has to constantly compete with other political loyalties.

While Hinduism provides the 'enfolding framework' of over 80 per cent of India's population, caste and economic divisions have prevented the development of a national Hindu identity.[8] In the economically and socially depressed regions of eastern Uttar Pradesh and Bihar, caste conflict is in fact endemic. The rising 'backward castes' of small peasants are locked in competition with the upper caste non-cultivating landowners, at the same time as uniting with the latter against the demands from below of the landless Harijans and the tribals.

The wide range of religious belief and practice also impairs unity. Hindu thought is made up of a variety of philosophical views and traditions and there is no orthodoxy obligatory for the Hindu. Village studies have shown how animist beliefs and the honouring of local goddesses co-exist with the great Hindu pantheon of deities. There are distinctive regional cults and local traditions of spirituality. The worship of Kali, the black earth-mother is, for example, particularly popular in Bengal. The fish-eyed goddess, Meenakshi, is honoured throughout Tamil Nadu. The massive Meenakshi Temple in Madurai, is in fact just one of over 32,000 public temples in Tamil Nadu and bears witness to the temple orientation of south-Indian Hinduism. The western states of Maharashtra and Gujarat have a heritage of saintly figures which Gandhi in the modern period came to fulfil. The looseness of religious ideology has meant that Hinduism has been held together by the social structure of the caste system and the individual's performance of *dharma* or religious duty within this context.

Muslims have historically experienced a greater sense of solidarity than Hindus, because they possess a central revelation to which each must respond and as a natural result, a sharp institutional focus to maintain orthodoxy. Even so, the Indian Muslim community is not monolithic. Muslims are divided by language, region and occupational status. Sectarian conflict continues to disrupt community life in such cities as Lucknow. Sufi practice can stand at variance to the legalism of scriptural orthodoxy. A gulf still remains, although it is narrowing, between the folk beliefs and observances of rural Muslims of often low-caste Hindu origins, and the orthodox beliefs and right practice of the urban population.

The Sikh community similarly contains internal divisions. Despite the Sikh faith's egalitarianism, caste differences continue to exist, both between rural Sikh Jats and Scheduled Caste Mazhabis and Ramdasias, and between Jats and the commercial Khatri and Arora Castes, known in the Punjab as *Bhapas*. Within the countryside, economic divisions (farmer–landless labourer) coincide with the Jat–Mazhabi social division. Sectarian differences are also important, indeed, a key initiating factor in the Punjab crisis was the bloody clash in Amritsar on 13 April 1978 between Akali fundamentalists and the heterodox Nirankari sect.[9]

It is not surprising given the complex character of India's main communities that religious identity has not always been the most important factor in the competition for power and the channelling of group interests during the last hundred years. The Muslim League, for example, struggled until the eve of Independence to win influence in the future heartland of Pakistan, because politics in such regions as the Punjab, Sind and the Frontier had been channelled along ethnic and economic rather than religious lines. The Akali Dal similarly could never automatically count on Sikh support, but had to compete for this with the Congress and Communist parties. In independent India, politics have revolved around caste, linguistic and regional loyalties, as well as communal solidarity.[10]

India's political system is scarcely less complex than its social formations. Each state has its own distinct politics arising from its cultural traditions and social structures. Even within a state there are complex interconnections between the village structure of politics and the wider arena of party politics, as F.G. Bailey revealed in his classic study of Orissa.[11] Two further complicating factors are the different emphases and interests of national and state politics and the linkages between these different levels of political activity.

The complexity of Indian religious groupings and political life makes generalization difficult. It is nevertheless important to identify a number of core assumptions concerning the traditional Hindu, Muslim and Sikh views of politics. Four key elements of Hindu thought can be discovered from the *Vedas*, the *Mahabharata* and the famous *Arthashastra* (Science of Material Gain) text.[12] First, there was a clear separation of religious and secular authority in traditional Hindu thought. The King was never expected to perform priestly functions, his Brahmin adviser, *purohit*, held sole authority in that sphere. Second, politics was autonomous from the non-political sectors of society. What mattered was that society should operate so that each individual could discharge his obligations according to the *dharma* of his caste, not that political power should intervene to transform society. Third, it was accepted as a necessity that the King should use coercion (*danda*) in order to preserve and protect *dharma*. Fourth, it was permissible for the King to act amorally in order to perform his role as protector of the state.

India's participant democracy initially encourages the view that ancient Hindu political theory is irrelevant in understanding contemporary Indian politics. Such writers as Ashis Nandy, however, have demonstrated a connection between them. Nandy sees the institution of the Emergency by Mrs Gandhi in 1975 and the increasing authoritarianism of the post-Emergency decade in terms of the survival of the amoral statecraft found in the *Arthashastra*.[13] Nandy dismisses the high ethical content of Indian politics of the 1940s and 1950s as an aberration brought about by Gandhi's reversal of traditional values with his vision of a 'moral politics'.[14] Nandy controversially maintains that this new approach which W.H. Morris-Jones has dubbed the 'saintly idiom' of politics did not survive Gandhi's death.[15] Moreover, he views with some misgivings the Gandhian emphasis on politics as an instrument for social change and the subsequent ending of the compartmentalization between politics and the *dharmic* order.

A separation between politics and the religious ordering of society has never existed in Islam. From the time of Muhammad onwards, there was a fusion of religious and political authority in the office of the Caliph. His task was to lead the community in submission to God and to safeguard through the exercise of power, the structure for community life which supports the individual Muslim in his obedience. This meant enabling the Muslim teachers (*ulama*) to guard and interpret the Law (*shari'ah*)[16] in which God's will is manifested. Whenever the *shari'ah* has appeared in danger, orthodox Muslims have mobilized themselves in its defence.[17] The celebrated Shah Bano case of February 1986 is the most recent evidence of this historical tradition.

The Sikh community shares with the Muslims, 'an acute sensitivity to the exercise of political power', in maintaining self-identity.[18] This is a legacy of the Sikhs' struggle against medieval Mughal persecution. Also dating from this period are the Sikh traditions of bravery and martyrdom, the concepts of Holy War and the Dal Khalsa (army of the pure) which exert so profound an influence on contemporary Sikh politics.[19] The traditional commitment of Sikhism to the creation of an egalitarian social order is another powerful source of inspiration. The late fundamentalist leader, Sant Jarnail Singh Bhindranwale[20] summed up this theme in the words, 'everyone lives like brothers and each wishes well of the other'.[21] While Bhindranwale's actions belied such honeyed words, his charismatic presence and the traditional respect afforded to a *Sant*[22] in rural Sikh society ensured him a large following during his brief, but momentous career.

COMMUNALISM IN CONTEMPORARY INDIA

Broadly, it is possible to identify five types of communal resurgence during the last ten years. First, there has been a marked increase in the frequency and intensity of communal rioting. Second, there has been the mushrooming of communal organizations and the spread of older ones into new areas. Third, there has been a tendency for local religious conflicts to acquire national political prominence. Fourth, there has been almost continuous political and religious tension and violence in the Punjab. Finally, there has been political encouragement for the spread of militant regional Hindu festivals into new areas.

The curve of communal violence has taken a sharp upward turn during the past decade. Hindu–Muslim riots have occurred in Biharsharif, Pune, Solapur, Ahmedabad, Hyderabad, Meerut, Bombay and Baroda. They have differed from earlier disturbances in their frequency,[23] intensity and duration. The violence in Hyderabad in September 1983 continued unabated for eighteen days. A year later, Bombay witnessed its worst communal riot since Independence: more than 230 people were killed and Army intervention was required to quell the violence.[24] Rioting in Ahmedabad in July 1986 was so intense that some 5,000 people had to shelter in relief camps.[25]

Communal violence has spread to previously untouched towns and communities. The riots of May 1981 in Biharsharif were unprecedented in the town's history.[26] Christians and Hindus came to blows for the first time in the Kanykumari district of Tamil Nadu in 1982. Further evidence of the deterioration in Christian–Hindu relations was seen when a violent altercation occurred at Nilakal in Kerela, over the rights of Christians to build a church on a patch of land where an ancient stone cross had been discovered.[27]

The worst disturbances, however, took place in Delhi in the wake of Mrs Gandhi's assassination on 31 October 1984. Hysterical Hindu mobs, in some instances directed by Congress (I) politicians, raged through Delhi for three days, butchering innocent Sikhs and burning their shops and homes.[28] Over three thousand lives were lost in Delhi's greatest violence since Partition.

Communal conflict has been nurtured and frequently directed by resurgent communal organizations. The last decade has witnessed the revival of the Hindu Mahasabha, the Muslim League and the *Majlis-e-Ittihadul Muslimin*.[29] It has also seen the *Rashtriya Swayamsevak Sangh* (RSS)[30] and Shiv Sena[31] extend their influence. The latter organization had traditionally been centred in Bombay, where it led attacks on Muslims and South Indians who it claimed were enjoying a disparate share of jobs in the state. After winning the 1985 Bombay municipal elections, it began to establish branches throughout the Maharashtran countryside. It raised support in the villages by making use of religious slogans and by taking advantage of the anti-Harijan sentiment amongst the Caste Hindu landowners.

The RSS also increased its strength during the past decade. Since 1977 its membership has more than doubled, without losing the traditional discipline and commitment of the *Shakha* organization.[32] It continues, however, only indirectly to exert political influence, confining itself to 'cultural' and social welfare activities. The old style Jan Sangh was the political mouthpiece of the RSS for many years.[33] At the end of 1980, however, the newly formed Bharatiya Janata Party (BJP) took over this role. Nevertheless, the dramatic events of 1984 led many RSS cadres to join Congress (I) and they continue to exert an important influence in its North Indian organization.

The RSS ideology has changed little since the movement's formation in 1925. The central tenets remain that India belongs to the Hindus, that they should be welded into one ideology and culture and that the RSS itself represents the ideal model of Hindu society. This message is carried into the wider community by the student organization (Akhil Bharatiya Vidyarthi Parishad) which has captured most campuses and was a significant component of the 'JP' movement whose challenge to Mrs Gandhi in 1975 precipitated the imposition of the Emergency.[34] RSS cadres also have influence in the trade union Bharatiya Mazdoor Sangh. The BMS was set up by the Jan Sangh and is today run by the BJP.

Since Independence, the RSS and the Hindu Mahasabha have been joined by a multiplicity of Hindu communal organizations. The Vishwa Hindu Parishad (VHP) and the Virat Hindu Samaj are two of the most important of these and were founded in 1964 and 1981 respectively. They both seek to overcome Hinduism's traditional weakness in terms of central authority and organization by acting as umbrella bodies for Hindu religious groups. In 1982, the VHP launched a series of *Ekatmata Yagya Yatras* (Soul Union Pilgrimages) across the length and breadth of India which transformed its position, at the same time as making a significant impact on Hindu–Muslim relations. Within a year, the VHP could boast 1,000 full-time workers and a network of local branches throughout India's 435 districts.[35] The darker side of this development, however, was mounting Hindu–Muslim tension and violence.

The VHP processions exerted such an enormous impact because they dramatically symbolized Hindu unity and strength at a time when the Hindu population was feeling increasingly insecure as a result of mass Harijan conversions to Islam. Trucks carried in procession huge bronze pots containing water drawn from the Ganges, India's most sacred river. This water was distributed at villages along the route, while the pots were refilled from local temple tanks or sacred rivers. The mixing of sacred water from all parts of India was an emotive symbol of Hindu oneness. From the Muslim point of view, however, the processions were provocative, for they frequently raised anti-Islamic and anti-Pakistan slogans when passing through their quarters. Rioting was the end result.[36]

Further antagonism was caused by the VHP's drawing up a list of Hindu sacred sites which it intended to liberate from their present Muslim occupation. One such site was the Rama Janma Bhumi at Ayodhya in Uttar Pradesh. Hindus believe that it marks the birthplace of Lord Rama, but the Mughal Emperor Babur built a mosque on the spot in 1528. Serious rioting had broken out in December 1949 when Hindus placed an idol of Rama in the mosque. Thereafter it had been placed under lock and key. The VHP reactivated Hindu efforts to secure entrance in October 1984. Mrs Gandhi's death diverted attention from the issue, but early in February 1986, the District Judge allowed the locks to be removed. The highly publicized celebrations which accompanied the site's 'liberation' enraged Muslim opinion. A hastily formed Babri Masjid Action Committee organized strikes and demonstrations in Lucknow and other urban centres. Within a week these were under curfew and a number of leading Muslims were jailed.[37]

The liberation movement was designed to strengthen the VHP's primary aim of Hindu political and social consolidation. 'Outmoded feudal values still prevail in our villages which have kept the caste pollution intact and thus resulted in friction within the Hindu fold', *Vishwa Hindu Samachar*, the VHP's mouthpiece declared in July 1986, '*Savarna* Hindus should now become alert and not widen the gap between the castes and (should) compromise with the *Dalits*'.[38] Such concern arose from Harijan conversions to Islam.

This anxiety had been aroused first in February 1981, when more than a thousand Untouchables had converted to Islam in the small village of Meenakshipuram in the Tirunelveli district of Tamil Nadu. The RSS claimed that a foreign hand was behind the conversions and that such Muslim organizations as the *Jamaat-e-Islami*, *Tabligh Jamaat* and *Ishatual Islam Sabha* were being financed from the Middle East in their proselytizing activities. The RSS joint General Secretary, indeed, maintained that each Harijan was paid Rs 500 to embrace Islam.[39] From June until October 1981, Meenakshipuram was the centre of national press attention. The Lok Sabha, the Lower House, in New Delhi as well as the state legislative assembly (Vidhan Sabha) debated the issues raised by the conversions. The RSS unsuccessfully attempted to secure a ban on all conversions and missionary activity, although 're-conversions' to Hinduism would be excluded from this. The widespread publicity given to the fear of Hinduism in danger, created a favourable climate for the VHP and RSS efforts to create a national Hindu identity which submerged caste divisions, even before events in the Punjab led to a Hindu backlash in North India.

The Meenakshipuram conversions are one of a number of local disputes which have acquired national significance. Other examples are the Ayodhya affair and the Shah Bano case. Tensions arising from the Rama Janma Bhumi dispute at Ayodhya contributed to serious Muslim–Hindu rioting in distant Kashmir. While the dispute over the position of Muslim personal law following on from the Supreme Court judgement in the Shah Bano case[40] undermined the position of secularly minded Muslim supporters of Congress (I).

The Supreme Court ruled that under the constitution a divorced Muslim woman did have the right of maintenance from her husband. This decision was immediately condemned by *Jamiat-e-Ulama*, *Majlis Mushawart*, *Jamaat-e-Islami* and the Working Committee on Muslim Personal Law as it contravened and interfered with *shari'ah* law. Rajiv Gandhi's government brought forward legislation to clarify the position. The Muslim Womens' Bill controversially passed the Lok Sabha on 6 May 1986. It leaned heavily in favour of the fundamentalists' objections and in effect reversed the Supreme Court judgement.[41] A number of leading Muslim Congressmen walked out in disgust, because the measure denied Muslim women the rights to equality, justice and fraternity enshrined in the Indian constitution.

Despite the national attention generated by the Rama Janma Bhumi dispute and the Shah Bano case, all communal issues have tended to be overshadowed by the crisis within the Punjab. The issue of Khalistan stretches back a number of years.[42] It was not until 1981, however, that the Khalistan demand was espoused by a section of the Akali Dal and became associated with the politics of violence. In March 1981, the World Sikh Convention sponsored by a splinter group of the Akali Dal backed a Khalistan resolution. In May, the All-India Sikh Student Association demanded that on religious grounds all cigarette shops should be closed within the walled city of Amritsar. Shortly after, the first prominent Hindu was assassinated in what was to become an increasingly vicious terrorist campaign. The victim was Lala Jagat Narain, a leading newspaper proprietor and outspoken critic of Khalistan and Jarnail Singh Bhindranwale.[43]

Sant Bhindranwale was charged with the crime. His charismatic reputation was enhanced following his dramatic arrest in front of 50,000 followers at his Chowk Mehta Gurdwara (temple) and his release almost immediately afterwards.[44] Bhindranwale's prestige put pressure on Sikh moderates who already faced fierce opposition from those within the Akali Dal such as Jagdev Singh Talwandi and Gurbachan Singh Tohra who were willing to ally themselves with extremists. The moderates' new defensiveness was seen in their addition of religious demands[45] to the forty-five Point

Memorandum which they had initially placed before Mrs Gandhi in 1980, following their fall from power.[46]

Police harassment of Sikhs entering Delhi at the time of the November 1982 Asian Games, undermined the Akali Dal's negotiations with Mrs Gandhi. It therefore turned to civil disobedience to press its demands.[47] The Akali Dal's protests became merged with Bhindranwale's independent agitation over the arrest of his right-hand man, Amrik Singh the President of the All-India Sikh Student Federation.[48] Fearing re-arrest, Bhindranwale moved from Chowk Mehts to the sanctuary of the Golden Temple in Amritsar. He initially stayed in the Guru Nanak Rest House. Eventually, Gurcharan Singh Tohra, the President of the Temple Management Committee allowed him to move to the Akal Takht (the shrine representing the temporal power of God), despite the opposition of the Shrine High Priest. Tohra's decision followed a fight between Bhindranwale's henchmen and those of the Akali Dal President, Sant Harchand Singh Longowal, within the hostel complex.

Bhindranwale rapidly converted the Akal Takht into an armoury. A former Indian Army Major-General, Shahbeg Singh, fortified the temple complex and trained terrorists within it. By the outset of 1984, Bhindranwale was providing an alternative source of authority to the government in central Punjab. At his daily congregations, he dispensed justice, issued statements on religious and political issues and granted interviews to foreign journalists. His supporters in the local police and civil administration ensured that arms went unchecked into the temple. Sympathizers in the local telephone exchange gave his calls priority.[49] Taped sermons calling on young Sikhs to buy arms and motor cycles and attack the enemies of the *Khalsa* (the pure Sikh brotherhood) were openly distributed from the Temple.

In May 1984, Mrs Gandhi entered into a final round of negotiations with the Sikh leaders. By this stage, Bhindranwale held the key to any settlement. Tohra tried unsuccessfully to get him to compromise. Bhindranwale's hold was so great that no Akali leader, including Longowal, would publicly break with him, although his opposition stood in the way of an agreement. The impasse set the stage for military action.

The Army operation against the Golden Temple began on 4 June 1984 and lasted for three days. Longowal and Tohra were 'rescued' from the outer buildings after a Commando-style raid. Tanks had to be used finally to blast their way into Bhindranwale's fortress. Sikh

opinion was subsequently enraged by the damage to the Akal Takht
and the high casualties which arose from this operation. Mrs Gandhi
paid the ultimate penalty for this on 31 October 1984.

Bhindranwale's death did not end Sikh extremism. Indeed,
Talwandi installed the Sant's father, Baba Joginder Singh, as
President of the Akali Dal. Terrorist activity continued unabated.
Rajiv Gandhi, nevertheless, made a determined effort to secure a
political solution. In July 1985, he signed an important Peace Accord
with Longowal.[50] This was followed in September by the election
of a moderate Akali Dal government under the leadership of Surjit
Singh Barnala. Neither the Accord, nor the Barnala government were
destined to survive.

Sikh terrorists murdered Longowal almost before the ink had
dried on the agreement. It is doubtful, however, whether it would
have survived, even without this tragic setback. The Punjab Accord
foundered on the issue of the territorial adjustments between Punjab
and Haryana associated with the transfer of the shared capital
Chandigarh to the Punjab. The Mathew Commission could not
find a solution acceptable to both Barnala and Bhanjan Lal, the
Chief Minister of Haryana, on the transfer of eighty-three Hindi-
speaking villages and two Hindi-speaking towns in the Abohar
and Fazilka tracts of the Punjab to Haryana as they were not
contiguous to Haryana's border.[51] While Barnala faced increasing
Akali Dal criticism of the Accord, Rajiv Gandhi had to contend with
mounting Hindu opposition from within Haryana. The situation had
become communally polarized, as Hindu refugees streamed across
the Punjab border carrying stories of Sikh atrocities. In a vain effort
to woo voters in the June 1987 state elections in Haryana, Rajiv
Gandhi began to trim his attitude to the Punjab Accord. The Eradi
Commission, for example, recommended a river waters deal which
was favourable to Haryana. Presidential Rule was declared in the
Punjab on 11 May on the grounds that the faction ridden Barnala
Government was unable to halt the deterioration in law and order.[52]
These steps, however, failed to impress the Hindu voters in Haryana.
Devi Lal's Lok Dal party in alliance with the BJP dealt Congress
(I) a humiliating defeat which came on top of its earlier setbacks
in Kerela and West Bengal. The Punjab Accord was reduced to
tatters.

The spread of militant Hindu festivals from their original centres
has been another important factor in the communalization of Indian
society. The introduction of new festivals has received considerable

political patronage. It is linked, as were the VHP processions, to the fear that Gulf money is being used by Muslim proselytizing organizations in an endeavour to secure Muslim domination over India. The Ganesh festival, for example, was unknown in Hyderabad until a decade ago, when the Congress (I) Chief Minister, Chenna Reddy brought it to the city.[53] Muslim resentment grew steadily as the idols increased in size and number to such an extent that their immersion threatened to silt up the Hussian Talib Lake in the city.[54] In September 1983, the VHP President, the Maharana of Udaipur travelled all the way from Rajasthan to attend the festival. Hindu houses throughout the city flew orange flags and a huge banner hung on the official platform which read, 'Declare India a Hindu Republic'. The Chief Minister, N.T. Rao, himself wore a saffron cap while listening to the speeches. Communal rioting not surprisingly broke out in this supercharged atmosphere, when Hindu trucks returning after the immersion left the prescribed route and passed through Muslim areas. The riots continued throughout September, claiming over 300 casualties.

There has been a similar pattern of events elsewhere in India. Riots broke out in Tanda in eastern Uttar Pradesh, for example, in November 1983, following the introduction into the region of the Durga puja on a massive scale. The Durga puja with its militant message of *Shakti* (female power force) was originally a festival favoured by the Bengali *bhadralok* (intellectual elite) and was alien to the Rama and Krishna-Bhakti traditions of Uttar Pradesh. Significantly, its introduction was actively sponsored by local RSS leaders because of its association with Hindu militancy. A similar process can be seen at work in the VHP's establishment of *Bajrang* (Hunuman) and *Mahavir* (Shiva) Dals among urban and peasant youth following its pilgrimage through Uttar Pradesh. Both cults were minor strains in the region's popular Hinduism, but were seen as useful symbols of Hindu militancy.[55] Muslims in such centres as Hyderabad have responded to the Hindu challenge, by taking out fresh processions of their own.

EXPLANATIONS OF INDIA'S COMMUNAL RESURGENCE

Writers have attempted, with varying degrees of sophistication, to explain the contemporary communalization of Indian politics and society. The dramatic nature of the Punjab crisis has resulted in its attracting the most attention, but considerable work has also been produced on communal riots. The material can be broadly divided into four approaches: political theories, psychological theories, socio-economic theories and historical analyses. Each will be examined in turn.

Political theories have ranged from broad analyses which set communalism within the context of the de-institutionalization and breakdown of norms which resulted from Mrs Gandhi's political style, to micro-level studies of political involvement in communal riots. Rajni Bakshi, Mathew Kalathil and Asghar Ali Engineer have all produced important findings in the latter area. Bakshi's study of riots in Hyderabad in 1981, clearly reveals that they were instigated by the Chief Minister of Andhra Pradesh in order to provide an excuse for postponing the city's municipal elections.[56] Mathew Kalathil has similarly shown that political motives often lie behind communal riots. His study of the disturbances which broke out in Ahmedabad in July 1986 uncovers the fact that Ministers threatened with dismissal, employed thugs to cause trouble and thereby discredit the Chief Minister.[57] Paul Brass's extensive work on politics in Uttar Pradesh corroborates such findings. Brass has shown that state politicians increasingly require the knowledge of how to use and control violence in order to advance their careers.[58] It is unquestionable that some politicians in Bihar and Uttar Pradesh have links with criminal gangs, although it is perhaps premature to speak, as the Indian political scientist Rajni Kothari has done, of a general 'criminalization of politics'.

Asghar Ali Engineer has examined exhaustively politicians' unscrupulous encouragement of violence in order to consolidate their position. He reveals, for example, that the RSS's efforts to wean Harijans from their traditional support for Congress contributed to the outbreak of Hindu–Muslim rioting in Meerut in September 1982.[59] Engineer views the background to the 1981 Biharsharif riots in a similar light. He points out the detrimental effects of the RSS's efforts to combat the Communist party of India's influence among low-caste Hindus.[60] The riots which resulted from the increased communal tension had the unintended effect as far as the RSS was concerned, of driving Muslim supporters of the CPI into the hands of the fundamentalist *Anjuman-e-Mufidul Islam*. Communal riots in fact frequently consolidate opinion behind fundamentalist groups, as Muslims become more aware of their minority status and seek protection in communal consolidation.

W.H. Morris-Jones, James Manor and Murray Leaf all set communal violence in a wider political context. Morris-Jones partly attributes the crisis in Punjab to Mrs Gandhi's lack of judgement. More important, however, were the institutional changes which accompanied her rule, for the 'dismantling' of the Congress and 'demoralizing' of the administration encouraged 'older more ascriptive loyalties (to) enjoy a revival'.[61] James Manor similarly sees Congress's 'de-institutionalization' since the late 1960s as a mounting factor in both caste and communal violence, as the new style centralized Congress of Mrs Gandhi could not emulate its Nehruvian successor in being the major instrument for conflict management in India.[62] The Congress's failure to fulfil its traditional role of accommodating the demands of newly participant groups coincided with the slowly increasing assertiveness of the 'weaker sections'. The absence of local institutions peacefully to channel this, has resulted in head-on clashes between local Hindu elites and either depressed Untouchable, or Muslim communities.[63]

Another consequence of Indira Gandhi's political style is taken up by Murray Leaf in his analysis of the Punjab crisis. He sees this as primarily not a religious struggle at all, but rather as part of a general crisis in centre–state relations precipitated by Mrs Gandhi's personalization and centralization of politics.[64] Undoubtedly a large part of the Akali Dal's demands was concerned with greater state autonomy. The Akali Dal's 1973 Anandpur Sahib Resolution which formed the basis for all future negotiations, included a demand for a reversal of the Indian constitutional assignment of reserved powers between the centre and the states;[65] a further provision called for the Indian constitution to become 'federal in a real sense'. Moreover, the Punjab was not the only state which found itself in conflict with the centre during the period 1980–84. The question still remains, however, why did the breakdown in centre–state relations in the Punjab have far more explosive consequences than elsewhere in India; Andhra Pradesh, West Bengal and Jammu and Kashmir were all experiencing similar constitutional conflict during this period.

Psychological explanations of communal resurgence centre around the insecurities of majority communities. Undoubtedly by the early 1980s, many Hindus felt themselves members of a beleaguered community, threatened by conversions, minority demands and privileges in terms of job reservations and that behind all this was an 'external hand' which sought Indian destabilization. Hindu neuroses are laid bare in a VHP booklet entitled *Change of Religion. A*

New National Crisis which was distributed in Pune and Solapur shortly before their 1982 riots. Its major theme was the danger of conversion to Islam. This threat was understood in terms of a conspiracy thesis which saw Islamic fundamentalists in Pakistan, Saudi Arabia and Iran orchestrating a campaign to Islamicize India.[66] The VHP and RSS response to such imagined fears sparked off real conflict with the local Muslim population.

Paul Wallace has shown how similar insecurities among the Sikh majority community in Punjab increased support for fundamentalism, if not the Khalistan demand itself. He pinpoints three main factors at work which led orthodox Sikhs to fear that they were about to lose their hard won majority in their Punjab homeland.[67] First, was the emigration of educated Sikh youths to find urban sources of employment. Second, was the immigration of Hindu labourers at harvest time from Uttar Pradesh and Bihar and the fear that they might settle. Third, was the decline in religious identity with the trimming of beards and the 'wheat-whisky' culture brought by the prosperity of the Green Revolution. Wallace concludes that as a result Sikhs manifested 'minority behavioural characteristics in the resurgence of what became known as the Punjab problem'. Sant Jarnail Singh Bhindranwale 'skillfully and demagogically played upon these apprehensions and fears in his efforts to take over or replace the Akali Dal as the major authority for Sikhs'.[68] Such psychological explanations carry considerable power. They fail, however, to explain why the Sikhs attached so much importance to the maintenance of majority status for community survival, or why Hindus felt so insecure in their majority position in India. Such questions can only be adequately answered within a historical context.

Socio-economic theories of communal resurgence fall into three main categories. First, those that concentrate on the threat posed to the Hindu majority by Muslim economic advancement. Second, those that see communalism as an antidote to emerging class conflict within a community. Finally, those that link communalism with a sharpened self-awareness brought about by increased literacy, urbanization and improved communications.

A number of writers have seen communal conflict in terms of economic competition between established Hindu traders and a newly emerging Muslim entrepreneurial class. Asghar Ali Engineer maintains, for example, that the 1980 Moradabad riots were partly occasioned by the antagonism arising from the emergence of Muslim businessmen in the brassware trade as a result of their obtaining lucrative Middle-Eastern contracts. The 1982 Meerut riots displayed a similar background of antagonism between Hindu traders and an 'albeit small, but prosperous Muslim middle class'.[69] Rajni Bakshi has also pointed out that the new wealth and self-confidence brought by Gulf money to a sizeable section of Hyderabad's Muslim population lay behind the 'changing dimensions of communalism' in the city in the early 1980s.[70]

Imtiaz Ahmed has made the most sophisticated attempt to link increased Muslim prosperity with communal resurgence.[71] He traces the emergence of a Muslim entrepreneurial class from small craftsmen and artisans. He identifies its ability to tap Middle-Eastern markets and money and easily to secure a low-wage labour force as posing a threat to Hindu competitors. He then continues to isolate three further factors. These are, the greater cultural and social visibility of Muslims as the newly rich move out of their old localities, the increased political assertiveness of the new entrepreneurial class, and finally the impact on land values as enterprising Muslims invest in real estate. This has not only increased economic competition with Hindu property speculators, but has increased communalism in a direct way, as public lands set aside for religious purposes in city centres have attracted developers' interest. 'Efforts are then likely to be made by vested interests to have these lands vacated for commercial purposes'.[72]

Imtiaz Ahmed's analysis is lucidly presented. It fails to take into account, however, the fact that communal tension is not just confined to localities where Muslims are increasing in prosperity. Religious or educational centres such as Aligarh can also be hotbeds of violence, as can areas of Muslim economic decline. Ahmedabad, for example, has been the scene of Muslim–Hindu riots in recent years, but 75 per cent of its Muslim population is classed as 'destitute'.[73]

A number of Marxist writers have maintained that elites have used communalism to stifle class consciousness and prevent cross-community political co-operation on a class basis. Gopal Singh, for example, has claimed that the leader of the rich landlord Malwa Lobby in the Akali Dal, Prakash Singh Badal, 'couches the demands of his class – the capitalist farmers who have hegemony over the whole of the peasantry – in religious terms whenever it suits him'. The writer has also maintained that the 'increasing politicisation of the landless . . . most of [whom] are hostile to the Jat landlords who are with the Akali Dal' played an important part in impelling the

Akalis to launch their Holy War in 1982.[74]

Marxists have also linked communalism with the colonial legacy of uneven capitalist development. Aspirations aroused by development are achieved by some communities. Others in more 'backward areas' are thwarted. They, so the theory goes, begin to see their deprivation as a result of their religious identity, thus providing politicians with a 'dangerous handle' for the exploitation of communal feelings.[75]

However, such instrumentalist explanations of religion's role in politics all share the important weakness of underestimating the emotive power of religious ideas and symbols. Why should Sikh Mazhabis or backward Muslims respond to them so readily, rather than class appeals? Moreover, are elites sufficiently free from religious influence to make a calculated decision to manipulate communally divisive symbols in order to further their own interests?

Robin Jeffery clearly links increased Sikh communalism with the Punjab's high literacy rates and the explosion of 'print capitalism' during the past decade.[76] He draws attention to the rivalry between the Gurmukhi and Hindi press which contributed as well as reflected the polarizing situation by exchanging 'half-truths and blatant lies' and by reopening 'old scars and wounds'.[77] Similarly he highlights the fact that educational expansion meant that 'more people were capable of being angered by reports of events far away'.[78] This has undoubtedly played an important part in the daily round of retaliatory killings. One of Jeffrey's most interesting findings is the publication programme of illustrated children's history books by the Gurdwara Management Committee. These concentrated on tales of Sikh heroism and martyrdom during the Mughal persecution and were first published in April 1977. Their intention was made plain by the President of the Temple Management Committee, Gurcharan Singh Tohra, when he wrote in the preface of one, 'I am confident that on reading such heart-sending [sic] episodes of Sikh history, a real spirit of a just and righteous struggle for justice will be infused in the community'.[79]

Most studies of contemporary communalism pay some lip service to its historical background. Bipin Chandra, however, goes much further than this in his work. He sees communalism as a modern ideology which did not exist in medieval India. It was a creation of the British divide and rule policies of the colonial era. Nevertheless, he acknowledges that a 'Hindu tinge' was present in the nationalist movement. 'The Congress', he writes, 'although basically secular was prepared to make compromises with communalist ideologies'.[80]

Chandra attributes communalism's continuing influence to two factors; first, its appeal to the trading and other lower-middle-class groups, second, the nationalist elite's failure seriously to challenge it.

Chandra's work draws attention to the continuities which exist between the colonial and contemporary periods of Indian history. When these are acknowledged, new insights can be brought to bear on recent political developments. Earlier Congress compromise with communalist ideologies, sheds light on Mrs Gandhi's dabbling with communal appeals in the early 1980s. Her attempt to head off the BJP's challenge by courting Hindu communal support, does not have to be seen as a complete aberration and betrayal of her father's beliefs.

CONCLUSION

There is no monocausal explanation for the re-emergence of religion as a significant force in Indian politics. The communalism of the 1980s does, however, possess a number of features which were less pronounced in earlier periods. It is important to note, for example, the influence upon communal attitudes of events outside India. Islamic fundamentalism in Pakistan and the Middle East greatly increased Caste Hindu's fears of Untouchables converting to Islam. Without such anxieties, the RSS and VHP would have encountered far more difficulties in expanding their power in the early 1980s. Even Hindu attitudes to the Sikhs were influenced by fears of Islamic fundamentalism. Significantly, journalists likened Jarnail Singh Bhindranwale to 'a religious fundamentalist in the mould of Ayatollah Ruhollah Khomeini', rather than to earlier Sikh *Sants*.[81]

Second, a pronounced feature has been the extent to which Congress (I) politicians have used communalism. This has been noticeable at both the state and national levels of politics. Mrs Gandhi's own dabbling in communal appeals can be traced to the early 1980s. At this time she became aware that many Hindus were antagonized by what they saw as government pampering of the minorities. In the June 1983 elections in Jammu and Kashmir, Mrs Gandhi responded to this by making direct communal appeals to Hindu voters. Ironically she had earlier that year gone out of her way to court the Sikhs in the Delhi municipal elections. Among other things she had promised to nominate a Sikh as mayor. Rajiv Gandhi had in fact made a highly publicized visit to a Gurdwara shortly before polling and had been pictured 'praying' for his party's success.[82] The new strategy paid off in both the state and local elections where fifteen years of BJP rule in Delhi were brought to an end.

The Delhi elections were not the first time, however, that Mrs Gandhi had dabbled in Sikh politics. While in opposition in 1978, she had approached Sant Bhindranwale, through her younger son Sanjay Gandhi, in the hope of using him to break up the Akali Dal–Janata coalition government in the Punjab.[83] It was here that the path began which led to both Bhindranwale's and Mrs Gandhi's death.

Third, communal organizations have achieved greater success than earlier in forging a Hindu political identity which transcends caste divisions. The concept of a Hindu *rashtra* (nation) first voiced by the RSS in the 1930s has gained increasing currency. The RSS itself has grown in respectability and has been joined by a plethora of militant Hindu organizations such as the Vishwa Hindu Parishad, the Virat Hindu Sammelan, and the All India Nationalist Forum. Several new Hindu *senas* (armies) such as the Bajrang Dal have emerged, while Shiv Sena has expanded its base of support. The rise in Hindu self-consciousness has also been expressed in the growth of processions and organized pilgrimages to places of worship and in the movement to 'liberate' Hindu temples with the flash-point in the communally and politically destabilizing dispute at Ayodhya.

This new mood has been politically manifested in a dramatic surge of support for the BJP. Although the Hindu backlash initially swept the Congress (I) to power in the 1984 general elections. Throughout the campaign, the Congress had capitalized on the sense of national insecurity arising from Mrs Gandhi's assassination. A vote for Congress was portrayed both as a vote for national unity and for granting Indira's final wish – 'save the country with every drop of blood'.[84] In many parts of North India, a notion of Hindu unity swept aside Caste divisions. Rajiv Gandhi rode this 'Hindu wave' to victory, securing the greatest majority in post-independence history. By November 1989, however, Rajiv was no longer 'Mr Clean' and the BJP was garnering votes in the communally disturbed Hindi heartland. The eighty odd seats it captured in the Lok Sabha (Lower House) made it along with the Left Front a key supporter of V.P. Singh's National Front government.

V.P. Singh's government staggered through factional crises brought on by the rivalry between the Premier and his deputy,

Devi Lal. On a number of occasions V.P. Singh histrionically threatened to step down. The *coup de grace*, however, was administered by the BJP's withdrawal of support. Its chief, Lal Krishan Advani had in late September begun a highly publicized pilgrimage (*rath yatra*) from Somnath temple in Gujarat to Ayodhya where on 30 October Hindu communal organizations planned to commence the construction of a temple on the Babri Mosque site. When both a Presidential intervention and the convening of a conference of State Chief Ministers failed to head off the looming confrontation, Advani was arrested at Samastipur on 23 October 1990. The BJP immediately withdrew its support from the government and ordered a general strike which sparked off street violence and police action which left at least forty people dead. On 7 November after further violence at Ayodhya, the National Front government was defeated on a no-confidence motion. The BJP eager for fresh elections in which it could further strengthen its position, refused the call of President Ramaswamy Venkataraman to form a government, as also did the Congress. Chandra Shekar, a dissident member of the Janata Dal party of the outgoing Premier, was installed in office, dependent upon the support of the Congress.

Notwithstanding the crisis at Ayodhya, it is important to remind ourselves that every day, the overwhelming majority of India's 750 million people live peacefully together, despite their different religious beliefs. Moreover, the communities are still not monolithic in their feelings, beliefs and values or in political response. This point is clearly illustrated by a study of the earlier stage of the dispute at Ayodhya.[85] This reveals that there was no 'simple expression of Hindu feelings' during the liberation movement at Ram's 'birth-site'. Political and economic considerations led Ramanandis sadhus in Ayodhya 'who believe, of course in Ram's liberating power . . . not [to] desire to liberate the god himself'.[86]

Nevertheless, it is easy to paint a gloomy picture of India's prospects for communal harmony in the 1990s. Nehru's concept of national identity based on the synthetic nature of Indian culture has been largely abandoned. The increase in communal tensions has been palpably revealed in the rash of riots which have spread across India's Hindi heartland. The 1980s began with serious clashes between Hindus and Muslims in Moradabad, and ended with the death of hundreds of Muslims in the Bhagalpur district of Bihar. In 1990 communal tension reached a peak not seen since Independence because of the events at Ayodhya and the repression of unrest in the Muslim majority area of Kashmir. Indeed, it is particularly disturbing for the future to discern growing evidence of the use of state terror to cow the Muslim and Sikh populations of Kashmir and of the Punjab.

The mounting communal crisis in India has been described as a general crisis of 'political alienation' in which the Hindu majority regards the state as endlessly favouring the minorities' interests at the expense of its own, while the latter see the state as failing to afford them protection. At a still deeper level, the crisis has its roots in the twin processes of rapid socio-economic change and the increasing politicization and mobilization of new sets of voters. They both raise the fear of a loss of status and cultural identity for the lower middle-class groups of the Hindu majority community. Such groups have responded by supporting militant Hindu organizations and by voting for the BJP. Hindu militancy is likely increasingly to put India's secular democracy at risk as the country continues to move through a transitional period of rapid socio-economic and political change.

NOTES

1 The Hindu Mahasabha was founded in 1915 as an All-India body to consolidate the Hindu *rashtra* or nation by Hinduizing politics and protecting and promoting Hindu interests. The Muslim League was founded at Dacca in 1906 to protect Muslim interests. Politically this meant securing separate electorates for Muslims so that they were not swamped by the Hindu majority.

   The Akali Dal was formed in 1920 to spearhead the struggle to bring temples and shrines under Orthodox Sikh control. In 1925 the aim was achieved. The Akali Dal's control of the newly formed Temple Management Committee gave it vast patronage.

2 For details see, G. Minault (1982), *The Khilafat Movement*, New York: Columbia University Press.

3 A. Major (1985), 'Sikh ethno-centrism, 1967–1984: Implications for the Congress', *South Asia*, vol. VIII, no.2, p.172.

4 The ideas for this and the following paragraph were drawn from, R.I. Duncan (1979), 'Levels, the communication of programmes, and sectional strategies in Indian politics', unpublished, Sussex D.Phil.

5 S.S. Harrison (1960), *India: The Most Dangerous Decades*, Princeton: Princeton University Press.

6 L.I. Rudolph and S.H. Rudolph (1967), *The Modernity of Tradition: Political Development in India*, Chicago: The University of Chicago Press.

7 *Tribune*, 1 January 1987.

8 Although in North India, since the early 1980s, a sense of a monolithic Hindu community has begun to emerge.

9   Dyal Das established the Nirankari sect in the middle of the nineteenth century. By the 1980s it had moved towards a Hindu 'god man cult' under the leadership of Gurbachan Singh. Despite its unorthodoxy, it drew support from Mazhabia and Ramdasias.

10   Harrison, op.cit.

11   F.G. Bailey (1963), *Politics and Social Change: Orissa in 1959*, Berkeley: University of California Press.

12   This work has been attributed to Kautilya, the Brahman Prime Minister of India's first Imperial unifier Chandragupta's (reign, 324–301 BC). As a textbook in *realpolitik* it has been likened to Machiavelli's *Prince*.

13   F.A. Presler (1984), 'Studying India's political culture', *Journal of Commonwealth & Comparative Politics*, vol. XXII, no. 3, p.231.

14   ibid., p.226.

15   W.H. Morris-Jones (1963) 'India's political idioms', in C.H. Phillips (ed.) *Politics and Society in India*, London, pp.135–54.

16   The *shari'ah* was developed on the bases of the Qur'an, *hadiths* (traditions of the sayings of the Prophet Muhammad) analogy and consensus.

17   See, for example, the activities of Shah Waliullah, or a century later of Hajji Shariat Ali. The twentieth century equivalents are the Khilafat and Pakistan movements, although not all orthodox ulama supported the latter, as they were opposed to secular Muslim nationalism.

18   J.M. Brown (1985), *Modern India*, Oxford: Oxford University Press, p.30.

19   In 1978, for example, a Dal Khalsa was founded to fight for a Sikh State.

20   Jarnail Singh took the name Bhindranwale after the village of Bhindran, where the Damdami Taksal missionary movement he headed from 1977 onwards, had been founded.

21   Major, op.cit., p.173.

22   *Sants* were a central part of the rural Sikhs' religious experience. They travelled the countryside, as Bhindranwale did, giving readings of the sacred Sikh texts.

23   Baroda, for example, witnessed eighteen riots between September 1981–May 1982.

24   R.L. Hardgrave (Feb 1985), 'India in 1984: Confrontation, assassination and succession', *Asian Survey*, vol. XXV, no.2, p.134.

25   I. Narain and N. Dutta (1987), 'India in 1986', *Asian Survey* vol. XXVII, no. 2, p.186; M. Kalathil (1986), 'Riots with a political motive', *Economic and Political Weekly*, vol. XXI, no. 30, p.1300.

26   A.A. Engineer (ed.) (1985), *Communal Riots in Post-Independence India*, Hyderabad: Sangham, p.239.

27   J.R. Siwach (1985), *Dynamics of Indian Government and Politics*, New Delhi: Sterling, p.427.

28   Hardgrave, op.cit., p.140.

29   G.R. Reddy (1979), 'Language, religion and political identity. Majiis-e-Ittihadul Muslimin', in D. Taylor and M. Yapp (eds) *Political Identity in South Asia*, London: Curzon, pp.113–37.

30   The RSS was founded in 1925 by Dr Keshev Hedgewar. Its aim was Hindu cultural and spiritual regeneration.

31 Shiv Sena was founded in Bombay in 1966. For details of its aims see, N.F. Katzenstein (1979), *Ethnicity and Equality: The Shiv Sena Party and Preferential Politics in Bombay*, Ithaca, NY: Cornell University Press; R. Joshi (1970), 'The Shiv Sena: A movement in search of legitimacy', *Asian Survey*, vol. X, no. 11, pp.967–78.

32 The *Shakha* was the basic unit of RSS organization. Its members known as *Swayamsevaks* were divided into four sections according to age. The *Shakha* included in its day-to-day activities training in the use of swords and javelins.

33 Jan Sangh was founded in 1951 by a former President of the Hindu Mahasabha, Dr S.O. Mookerjee. Although it claimed to be a non-sectarian party, it sought to promote national unity by Hinduizing the minorities. Significantly, it refused to recognize the Partition of India.

34 R.L. Hardgrave (1980), *India. Government and Politics in a Developing Nation*, 3rd edn, New York: Harcourt Brace Jovanovich, p.139.

35 *Link*, 9 January 1983.

36 Engineer, op.cit., p.268.

37 *Link*, 2 March 1986.

38 A.A. Engineer (1985), 'Gujrat burns again', *Economic and Political Weekly*, vol. XXI, no. 31, p.1343.

39 G. Mathew (1982), 'Politicization of religion. Conversions to Islam in Tamil Nadu', *Economic and Political Weekly*, vol. XVII, no. 25, p.1070.

40 For details see *Link*, 15 September 1985.

41 For details see *Asian Recorder* 11–17 June 1986.

42 The demand for a Sikh State had been brushed aside by the British in 1946. In 1971 Dr Jagjit Singh Chauhan took out an advertisement in the *New York Times* in favour of Khalistan. In July 1977 he returned to India and helped form the Dal Khalsa. In March 1980 he hoisted a Khalistan flag at a Gurdwara at Anandpur and formed a twelve-man Khalistan Council. This issued Khalistan stamps and passports. But it was seen at this time as little more than an eccentric gesture.

43 Bhindranwale was already being sought at this time for the murder of the Nirankari leader, Gurbachan Singh on 24 April 1980.

44 Bhindranwale himself said, 'The Government has done more for me in one week, than I could have achieved in years.'

45 These included that Amritsar should be declared a Holy City and that the constitution should be amended to guarantee the Sikhs a separate religious identity.

46 They were replaced by the Congress (I) government of Darbara Singh which in 1983 was superseded by President's Rule.

47 Such action included blocking the Punjab's roads and railways and an attempt to prevent the digging of a new Sutlej-Jamuna Canal which Sikh farmers regarded as 'stealing' the Punjab's water.

48 Amrik Singh was the son of Bhindranwale's guru, Kartar Singh.

49 M. Tully and S. Jacob (1985), *Amritsar. Mrs. Gandhi's Last Battle*, London: Jonathan Cape, p.130.

50 For details see P. Wallace (March 1986), 'The Sikhs as a "minority" in a Sikh Majority State in India', *Asian Survey*, vol. XXVI, no. 3, pp.363–77.

51   Narain and Dutta, op.cit., p.182.
52   Barnala had been excommunicated by the High Priests of the Golden
     Temple on 11 February 1987 for defying their order to resign and merge
     his party into a new militant Akali Dal which would bring together all
     the rival Sikh factions.
53   The Ganesh festival had previously been associated with Maharashtra.
54   T. Singh (1985), 'The secular myth', *Seminar* March.
55   *Link*, 2 March 1986.
56   R. Bakshi (1984), 'Changing dimensions of communalism', *Economic and
     Political Weekly*, vol. XIX, nos 51 & 52, p.2152.
57   Kalathil, op.cit., p.1300.
58   P. Brass (1984), 'National power and local politics in India: A twenty-
     year perspective', *Modern Asian Studies*, vol. XVIII, no. 1, pp.89–118.
59   Engineer, op.cit., pp.273 ff.
60   ibid., p.241.
61   W.B. Morris-Jones (1984), 'India – more questions than answers', *Asian
     Survey*, vol XXIV, no. 8, p.814.
62   'De-institutionalization' refers to the reduction of political participation
     in this case through the ending of elections to local Congress organi-
     zations. The Congress structure as a result became increasingly
     centralized.
63   J. Manor (1983), 'Anomie in Indian politics', *Economic and Political
     Weekly*, vol. XVIII, no. 19, pp.725–34.
64   M. Leaf (1985), 'The Punjab crisis', *Asian Survey*, vol. XXV, no.5,
     pp.475–98.
65   The division of powers laid down in the Union List, State List and
     Concurrent List, gives the centre a paramount position. Residual power
     also lies with the union and union law prevails over state law in any
     conflict.
66   A.A. Engineer (1982), 'Behind the communist fury', *Economic and
     Political Weekly*, vol. XVII, no. 10, p.356.
67   The campaign for Punjabi Subha had been launched by the Akali Dal
     in 1960. Akali volunteers filled the jails, while Master Tara Singh and
     Sant Fateh Singh engaged in abortive fasts. In 1966, Punjabi Subha
     was conceded by the centre as a reward for the Sikhs' role in the 1965
     war with Pakistan.
68   Wallace, op.cit., p.377.
69   A.A. Engineer (ed.) (1985), *Communal Riots in Post-Independence India*,
     Hyderabad: Sangham, p.272.
70   Bakshi, op.cit., p.2152.
71   I. Ahmed (1984), 'Political economy of communalism in contemporary
     India', *Economic and Political Weekly*, vol. XIX, no. 23, pp.903–6.
72   ibid., p.905.
73   This figure was arrived at following a survey undertaken by Gujarat
     University in 1982–83.
74   G. Singh (1984), 'Socio-economic bases of the Punjab crisis', *Economic
     and Political Weekly*, vol. XIX, no. 1, p.43.
75   *Link*, 5 August 1984.
76   R. Jeffrey (1986), *What's Happening to India?*, London: Macmillan,

pp.83–5.
77   ibid., p.85.
78   ibid., p.86.
79   ibid., p.90.
80   A.A. Engineer (1984), 'Understanding communalism. Report on a seminar', *Economic and Political Weekly*, vol. XIX, no. 18, pp.754–5.
81   Jeffrey, op.cit., p.88.
82   A. Rao (1983), 'Delhi civic elections and after', *Economic and Political Weekly*, vol. XVIII, no. 18, p.682.
83   Jeffrey, op.cit., pp.135–6; Tully and Jacob, op.cit., pp.57–62.
84   Jeffrey, op.cit. p.15.
85   PVD Veer (1987), '"God must be liberated!" A Hindu liberation movement in Ayodhya', *Modern Asian Studies* vol. XXI, no. 2, pp.283–301.
86   ibid., p.294.

Chapter 6

Politics and religion in Southern Africa[1]

Adrian Hastings

INTRODUCTION

Southern Africa is characterized, in religious terms, by the dominance of Christianity among its black population as much as among its white. In no area of the world has the missionary movement of the nineteenth century, and its aftermath, proved more effective. The presence of Islam is quite limited until one reaches the northern parts of Mozambique and nowhere in the region is it politically significant. While the spirit mediums of traditional religion remain influential in Zimbabwe and some use was made of them by both sides during the war of the 1970s, there is even here no really coherent or systemic interaction of religion and politics requiring analysis in an assessment of this length. The relationship of Church and state in southern Africa has been a fascinating one, an almost classical case of both mutual support and conflict, but it is the Christian Church (or rather the Christian Churches) which is in question. This indeed has been the case ever since the beginning of the modern period in southern Africa. If the support which the Churches have provided colonial states in the region has been very considerable, there has also been a long tradition – ever since Vanderkemp and John Philip in the early nineteenth century – of Church–state tension.[2]

Fundamental to the situation has been on the one hand a considerable degree of unity provided by some sort of Church–state alliance, even of state Church, and on the other hand the diversity provided by a multiplicity of Churches, often out of sympathy with one another. In South Africa the Dutch Reformed Church (DRC) has always had a special official character, ever since the days when South Africa was a Dutch colony; at the British takeover in Napoleonic times, its position was guaranteed, though by the late nineteeth century the Anglican Church had assumed the central establishment position. Since the Second World War, the original 'state Church', the Dutch Reformed, has been effectively restored to power. In May 1948, the Nationalist party led by Dr Malan won a general election and has been in office ever since. Almost all its members belong to the Dutch Reformed Church and the inter-locking of leadership has been and remains exceptionally close. The University of Stellenbosch provided the training ground for both. Nevertheless, if it is a majority Church among whites, it has few members in the English-speaking white community and constitutes a relatively small proportion of the black majority. The long period of British rule over South Africa and the continued highly British character of Cape Town, Natal and even Johannesburg has made for an alternative Anglican Church establishment. Ever since Bishop Gray in the mid-nineteenth century, the Archbishops of Cape Town have to some extent behaved as heads of a quasi-established Church. A not unimportant dimension of the Church–state relationship of the twentieth century has been the way in which this quasi-establishment has, as a result of the long monopoly of power of the Nationalist party, been converted into a status of established opposition.

In Mozambique and Angola the 1940 Concordat between Portugal and the Vatican established a highly privileged position for the Roman Catholic Church, but there are also Protestant Churches of importance. In Namibia, linked with its pre-First World War German colonial status, the majority Church among blacks and whites is the Lutheran, but Anglican and Catholic Churches are also strong. In Zimbabwe (Rhodesia until 1980), there was at least a 'state Church'. Nevertheless it was British enough for there to be here too something of an Anglican quasi-establishment, visibly obtrusive in the cathedral and its cloisters in Harare (formerly Salisbury) which were decorated with the names of the Pioneer Column and regimental banners. The very strong Roman Catholic presence, however, reinforced by the fact that the first Prime Minister (Sir Charles Coughlan) was a Catholic and that the premier white school, St George's, was run by the Jesuits, provide again a sort of secondary establishment, this time Catholic, made easier by the fact that here (as in few other parts of Africa) the major body of Catholic missionary priests, the Jesuits, consisted of Englishmen, and often rather upper-class Englishmen at that.

The complexity of the Church–state relationship throughout the region derives in no small measure from the initial closeness in relationship between state and chosen quasi-established Church, and the sense of conservative political and social responsibility and support of the state to be found in the latter, but also in the increasing reluctance of the state Church to be controlled and the emergence of highly vocal minority groups within it. At the same time that was never the whole story. The multiplicity of Churches in each country ensured that there were always some which felt far from privileged and – despite attempts to establish a single ecclesiastical line – there was always in fact a multiplicity of viewpoints.

Before 1950, however, that multiplicity had generally not been excessively obvious in political terms. The principal Churches all had both white and black members; their white members provided most of their financial support and they included, in one or another Church, the principal political leaders of the white community. Effectively, no large Church either wanted or could afford to alienate this powerful minority of its membership by taking up a position opposed to that of government. Furthermore, most Churches received considerable financial support from the state for their educational and medical work among black people. On the one hand, missionary work had developed immensely through state subsidies, on the other hand, financial dependence required a high degree of public conformity with state policy. There was in practice a large measure of colonial consensus. The Roman Catholic Church was least obviously dependent upon the white community in that most of its priests came from overseas and its bishops were appointed directly by Rome. By 1950 it had just begun to appoint some white South Africans (e.g. Bishop Hurley of Durban) to the episcopate. The Anglican Church had a larger number of local clergy and its episcopal elections were local but by tradition its bishops, especially its senior bishops, were selected from abroad. In the case of the Dutch Reformed Church control by the local white community was absolute. In the Catholic Church in Mozambique all bishops had to be of Portuguese nationality, were appointed by Rome after consultation with the government of Portugal, and were paid a salary by the state equal to that of a provincial governor. The clergy were also paid their travelling expenses and priests and nuns were entitled to travel first class.

Behind the various relationships between governments and Churches – tightest between state and Catholic Church in Mozambique, loosest between any state and, say, Methodists or Lutherans – there was a large measure of common mind: what we may call a theology of Romans 13 ('he who resists civil authority resists what God has appointed'). This was generally held without qualm or question to apply to the colonial state. The colonial takeover of Africa was not a problem. It was held to be manifestly advantageous for black people. It had brought them peace and progress. It had also made the advance of Christianity far easier. It was something providential. The harsher sides of the early conquest were now well in the past and were largely forgotten by whites. Any hard criticism of colonial rule was likely to be seen as evidence of 'communism'.

On the other hand, the churches had a strong sense that they were trustees for the black community whom they had, in many cases, come explicitly to convert, and they were able to recognize that, at least on occasion, the latter had been treated with less than fairness.[3] They were prepared in principle to speak out against injustice and a few leading Churchmen had done so emphatically – the Congregationalist John Philip and the Anglican John Colenso in South Africa, more recently the Methodist John White and the Anglican Arthur Shearly Cripps in Rhodesia (Zimbabwe), the Catholic Dom Sebastian Soares de Resende, Bishop of Beira, in Mozambique. In South Africa, English language Church leaders had frequently opposed the introduction of new measures of racial discrimination. In general they held, more or less correctly, that the best way to strengthen the position of blacks was to educate them in European ways so that they could show themselves the equals of white people on white terms, and enter into the political, journalistic and economic areas effectively.

By no means all missionary education had such goals clearly in mind. For many missionaries the point was to provide just sufficient education to be a basis for catechetics and inferior paid work; to do more would be dangerous. For others – notably the American Board at Adams College or Scottish Presbyterians at Lovedale – the intention was to provide much more. African political leaders like Albert Luthuli and Z.K. Matthews had come out of such schools and remained staunch Churchmen. There was then a significant, if small, missionary minority which long before 1950 had seriously, if generally cautiously, challenged the direction of white political power. Church leadership more widely, however, while not entirely rejecting the idea that the Church had such responsibilities, held to the view that authority as exercised was essentially beneficent and the black majority manifestly unfitted to exercise power. To rock the boat, fortified by so many subsidies, on account of some injustice here or there, would be unwise. All in all, Church–state relations in the late colonial period in southern Africa were very harmonious.

SOUTH AFRICA UNTIL THE 1960s

By the later 1950s this harmony was fast disappearing. The reasons were various. The international understanding of colonialism had altered profoundly. In the age of the United Nations Organization and the ending of the British Empire in Asia, it was impossible to continue with the ostensibly unquestioning acceptance of white rule over black majorities which had characterized the previous period. In 1957 Ghana became independent and black nationalism was organizing all across the continent. At the same time, in South Africa, under the formula of apartheid, racial discrimination was being massively strengthened and black rights (so far as they had ever existed) eroded. The 1950 Suppression of Communism Act both provided machinery for the crushing of opposition and defined communism exceedingly widely. The English-speaking Churches were almost bound to take up a position opposed to what was now the deliberate policy of government and they did so, fairly emphatically in word, though doubtless many of their white members more or less agreed with government policy. The clergy of these Churches and particularly the senior clergy were influenced far more than their laity by the outlook of the world outside South Africa. In the era of Archbishop Temple and then of the postwar Labour government in Britain, there was to be found a significantly different outlook towards social and political issues from that of an earlier clerical generation. It was to be found in particular among Anglican priests like Trevor Huddleston, Michael Scott, Joost de Blank and Ambrose Reeves. Cripps or White were indeed of a comparable outlook a generation earlier, but they had been clerically in a far smaller minority. All six were Englishmen.

It was the Bantu Education Act of 1953 which more than anything else permanently undermined the traditional Church–state relationship by largely withdrawing black education from Church to state control: government could not trust the kind of more or less liberal education the church provided, but the termination of the educational alliance between the two effectively terminated too the principal reason for Church compliance in state policy – fear of the loss of subsidies. Then in 1956 Albert Luthuli, Z.K. Matthews, Oliver Tambo and 153 other people of all races were arrested one

December morning and the great Treason Trial was set to begin. Five years later the last of the accused were acquitted but by then the Sharpeville massacre had taken place (21 March 1960) and the African National Congress had been banned: these events were crucial for Church–state relations. It was impossible for a general condition of largely unanalysed harmony to continue further. Trevor Huddleston's fierce *Naught for your Comfort* was also published in 1956.[4] For him apartheid and the whole gamut of government policy was 'fundamentally evil and basically un-Christian'. Most of his fellow clergy at first regarded him as a dangerous radical, but in the light of the Treason Trial, Sharpeville and much else, it would be increasingly difficult for the Church not to agree with him. The state of public politics – the politics of Verwoerd (now Prime Minister) on the one hand, the independence of most states in black Africa after 1960 on the other – forced a polarization upon the Churches and upon Church–state relations which most Church people were all the same extremely reluctant to face up to.

In December 1960 an important consultation between all the Churches in South Africa (other than RC) took place at Cottesloe, a Johannesburg suburb, presided over by Dr Franklin Fry, chairman of the Central Committee of the World Council of Churches. Its General Secretary, Dr Visser 't Hooft was also present. The Dutch Reformed Church was fully represented and its delegates a little surprisingly accepted the moderately anti-racialist note of the concluding statements. The aim of the exercise, to bring together the DRC and the main English-speaking Churches in response to the current polarization which was threatening to tear them apart (de Blank, the Archbishop of Cape Town, had even called for the expulsion of the DRC from the WCC) seemed to have been successful. At once, however, Dr Verwoerd declared his great displeasure with the position of the DRC delegation and in due course the Synods of the Church repudiated the actions of their representatives and even went further by withdrawing from the WCC altogether.

At this point the characteristic Church–state position of South Africa for at least the next twenty-five years was established. It consisted of the following: the emphatic alliance between the Dutch Reformed Church and state policies; more or less open hostility between the leadership of most other Churches and the state in which the former could count on the full support of the WCC and most Churches overseas. Hostility inevitably flares up from time to time largely in response to wider political tension, but it is dampened by the reluctance of most Church leaders to go much further than verbal condemnation of government policies and by the fact that a majority of the white members of every Church largely back government policy. Furthermore, many of the more radical clergy remain foreigners subject to deportation or simply the non-renewal of their residence permits (a particularly large number of such cases, no fewer than fifty, took place in 1971). This greatly weakens the Church's ability to protest.

A small minority of DRC Christians were equally determined to speak out against apartheid policies. Most notable was Beyers Naudé, at that time vice-chairman of the Transvaal Synod of the DRC and one of its representatives at Cottesloe. He refused to repudiate the Cottesloe resolutions and in his own words 'put it clearly to the Synod that with all respect which I have for the highest assembly of my Church, in obedience to God and my conscience I could not see my way clear to giving way on a single one of the resolutions, because I was convinced that those resolutions were in accordance with the truth of the Gospel'. Two years later, in August 1963, the Christian Institute was founded in Johannesburg as an ecumenical body intended to struggle for justice and reconciliation.[5] Naudé became its director and was at the same time deprived of his status as a minister of the DRC. His final sermon to his congregation at Aasvoelkop was upon the text of Acts 5:29, 'We must obey God rather than men'.

Up to 1960 clerical opposition to government policy in South Africa was most obviously the opposition of foreigners. It was indeed a point that government made much of. With the deportation of Bishop Reeves of Johannesburg in 1960, the resignation of Archbishop de Blank in 1963 and the founding of the Christian Institute, this changed. The expulsions around 1971 further diminished foreign involvement. From now on the leadership of the Church in the anti-apartheid struggle would be taken predominantly by South Africans such as Naudé and Denis Hurley, the Catholic Archbishop of Durban, South African but white. At this date the main Churches still had next to no senior black leadership while the independent black Churches, particularly the more numerous ones of so-called Zionist character, tended to be cautiously apolitical or even apparently pro-government. In being 'black only' Churches they were, after all, in their way practising apartheid spiritually. Their very growth – especially among the poorest and least educated – and the consequent movement of Africans away from mixed Churches was bound to please government and, in regard to a few of the largest, such as the Zion Christian Church of Lekganyane in the Transvaal, this was particularly clear. Black initiative of this sort was not politically sensitive.

Clearly the opposition of Naudé and other Afrikaner critics like Professor Geyser was felt far more acutely by government than that of English-speakers, Roman Catholic English-speakers above all. Naudé was a graduate of Stellenbosch and a former member of the inner Afrikaner secret society, the *Broederbond*. Effective opposition from this angle was bound to be threatening, because the whole strength of the Nationalist position lay in the effective unity of Afrikaner *volk*, DRC and Nationalist party.[6] English-speakers were seldom members of the party any more than they were of the DRC. Clerical criticism from their ranks could be expected. Revolt from an inner member of the Afrikaner power circle in the name of the gospel was quite a different thing.

MOZAMBIQUE

The position in Mozambique was in almost every way different, yet here too in the course of the 1960s a Church–state conflict developed, in due course almost more acute, as a response to the mounting conflict between black nationalism and white government. The Concordat, the historical tradition of Portuguese colonialism (including the *Padroado* (patronage) of the state over the missionary church granted by the papacy in the fifteenth century), and the current policy of Salazar (continued after 1968 by Marcello Caetano) all tied the Catholic Church to the Portuguese state in a way which might have seemed commonplace in the seventeenth or eighteenth century but was extraordinarily anachronistic by the 1960s.[7] Its official and explicit task was to engage not only in evangelization but in something described as 'Portugalization'. However, the number of Portuguese missionaries available for work in Africa was very limited and the one creative effect of the Concordat had been that it allowed a large increase in the number of non-Portuguese priests and nuns to work in Mozambique. There were very few black priests and next to no local white ones. The local Church itself was exceptionally passive. The conflict as it developed, though in Africa, was entirely one between white people born in Europe: Portuguese colonial authorities and some Portuguese clergy upon the one side, Portuguese and non-Portuguese clergy upon the other.

Dom Sebastian Soares de Resende was Bishop of Beira from 1940 to 1967. He was a strong and courageous man who frequently criticized government injustices, published a newspaper, the *Diario de Mozambique*, which was the only paper moderately free from government censorship in the country, and gathered round him a group of priests – both Portuguese and non-Portuguese – who were increasingly critical of the government's refusal to admit that Mozambique could have a future other than as a 'province of Portugal'. Among them was a very international group of White Fathers as well as several quite radical Portuguese secular priests.

In 1964 Frelimo, the Mozambique nationalist movement, began a war of liberation from bases in Tanzania in the north of the country. The war spread south and engendered an increasing ruthlessness on the part of the Portuguese authorities. In January 1967, Bishop de Resende died and was in due course replaced by Dom Manuel Fereira Cabral, someone of entirely opposed outlook. He soon sold the *Diario de Mozambique* to its greatest enemies and forced many of the priests who had worked with his predecessor to return to Portugal. In 1971 the group of forty White Fathers decided they could cope with the situation no longer and their Superior General in Rome publicly declared that they were leaving the country, and why:

> The confusion between Church and state, which is sustained by the constant practice of both civic and religious authorities, does a great disservice to the presentation of the gospel message and of the real face of the church. . . . We wanted, we asked for and for a long time we waited for the hierarchy to take a definite stand to dispel these ambiguities in face of injustice and police brutality. Faced with a silence which we do not understand, we feel in conscience that we have not the right to be accounted the accomplices of an official support which the bishops in this way seem to give to a regime which shrewdly uses the church to consolidate and perpetuate in Africa an anachronistic situation.[8]

When this decision was made public the Fathers were expelled from Mozambique by the DGS (secret police) at forty-eight hours notice. With them was expelled the most senior Portuguese priest left in the diocese, the former editor of the *Diario*, Mgr Duarte de Almeida. There can be no doubt that the withdrawal of the White Fathers, something unheard of in Catholic missionary history, was a major shock alike for Portugal and for the Vatican. Portugal prided itself on the highly Catholic character of its African policy. Yet here was the largest and most respected missionary society in Africa declaring in the most public manner that the two were now simply incompatible.

Later in 1971 Spanish priests of the missionary society of Burgos working in the diocese of Tete protested about even larger scale atrocities taking place around them, especially at Mucumbura.[9] Two of them were arrested and confined for nearly two years in Machava prison in Lourenço Marques. On 1 January 1972, World Peace Day, a Portuguese diocesan priest in Beira named Fr Joaquim Sampaio, in charge of Macuti parish, moved by the protests of the Burgos Fathers, preached a sermon on the theme 'If you desire peace, work for justice' and spoke of the recent massacres at Mucumbura. He and his curate were arrested a few days later and brought to trial in Beira in January 1973 accused of attempting to separate Portuguese territory from the mainland.[10] After a remarkably fair trial in which several bishops appeared for the defence, the two men were found guilty of rather minor offences, given suspended sentences and returned to Portugal, where the trial was never reported in the newspapers. In Mozambique, as in South Africa, the judiciary was never wholly co-opted by the regime.

In June 1972 a rather different event took place: a considerable number of black Protestant leaders, particularly those of the Presbyterian Church, were arrested and placed in Machava. Six months later, in December, Zedequias Manganhela, the sixty-year-old President of the synodal council, was found hanged in his prison cell. The Protestant Churches were relatively small and politically insignificant, except that they were suspected of sympathizing with Frelimo. Their only protection was international sympathy (in this case especially that of Switzerland whose missionaries had been at work in Mozambique). The contrast between the treatment of Sampaio, the white Catholic from Portugal, and Manganhela, the black Protestant native, was striking. Nevertheless the fact that the Churches were actually being brought together for the first time in opposition to the state and the consequent increasing width of opposition were equally significant.

Five days after the death of Manganhela, on 16 December, a particularly large and horrible massacre took place in and around Wiriyamu, a village near Tete.[11] With the help of survivors and a Portuguese chaplain at the army base, a group of Spanish Burgos Fathers and an African priest at the nearby mission of San Pedro compiled a detailed report including a list of 180 victims which they sent to the bishops. The publication of this report in London through the Catholic Institute of International Relations the following July caused an international storm. The protests of priests and nuns multiplied, culminating in the deportation of the Portuguese Bishop of Nampula, Mgr Manuel Pinto, together with eleven Italian Verona Fathers in April 1974. They had signed a statement recognizing the justice of the aims of the liberation movement and calling for an end to the Concordat. Just a fortnight later the Armed Forces Movement overthrew Caetano's government in Lisbon and effectively brought Portuguese rule in Africa to an end. It seems likely that the publication of the Wiriyamu report, together with the continued Church struggle, played a considerable part in stimulating the Portuguese revolution.[12]

The evidence would suggest that the Vatican was far from happy with the position taken up by an increasing minority of missionaries in Mozambique. It had not only challenged the Concordat with the state, it had also produced a complete division in the Mozambican Church because the large majority of bishops, headed by the Archbishop of Lourenço Marques, Mgr Custodio Pereira, rejected any public criticism of the government. Nevertheless, with the coming to power only a few months later of Frelimo led by Samora Machel, with its strongly Marxist and anti-religious orientation, Rome may have been grateful that at least some priests had shown themselves prior to the April 1974 Portuguese revolution to be in sympathy with African aspirations. In no other part of Africa did political independence immediately involve such a total alteration in the status of the Church and the shape of Church–state relations. Over the next two years most of the Portuguese bishops and many of the clergy left the country. Only the Bishop of Nampula, returned from exile, retained any authority. An African Archbishop of Maputo was appointed with several other Mozambican bishops. Much Church property was taken over by the state (including all minor seminaries) and a considerable anti-Church propaganda, based on Chinese or earlier East European models, was carried on by the government: the Catholic Church was a reactionary organization, hitherto cocooned in Fascist privilege. Everything good in Mozambique came from Frelimo: 'If we want to proceed on the road of socialism and communism, it is necessary to stop once and for all the influence and activities of the church'.

In the pre-Independence situation the strength of the Church on the conservative side lay wholly in its support by the government and the government's need for the Church in terms of the national mystique as developed by Salazar. On the radical side what strength there was lay in, first, the personal courage and determination of a relatively small number of mostly foreign clergy; second, in international support. The protesting missionaries in Mozambique included Italian, Spanish and Dutch priests as well as Portuguese and increasingly they were backed by a world lobby, both Catholic and liberal. The appeal of Spanish priests to British newspapers in the 1970s angered the Portuguese government, just as the appeal of Trevor Huddleston or Michael Scott to British newspapers in the 1950s angered the South African government, but the moral credibility of priest protesters in international terms was in both cases an important element in such strength as the Church possessed *vis à vis* the state. But it was not simply a matter of protest. It was a matter of providing trustworthy evidence of crimes suspected but otherwise unproven. The international strength of the Church lay especially in the reliability of its witness.

In the post-Independence situation the immediate strength of the Mozambican Church was minimal. It depended upon the basic support – disorganized, unprepared, but not non-existent – of a good many ordinary black people. Faced with a highly critical government, the Church could do little but survive in a somewhat confused condition, led as best he could by the Bishop of Nampula, now chairman of the episcopal conference. Nevertheless after some years the position slowly improved. The somewhat doctrinaire Marxist anti-Church attitudes of Frelimo declined as Frelimo's own troubles multiplied and it was able to recognize that the Church could be a moderately useful ally in the struggle for development, food and international co-operation. It became clear that the sort of systematic attack on the Church which had happened in the early period of some Marxist governments in other continents would not be repeated here. Perhaps the harmony between Church and state in Mozambique's closest backers, Tanzania and Zambia, helped to ensure that too sharp a confrontation would not develop here and that the reaction to the ending of the 'padroado' was less ecclesiastically disastrous than might have been anticipated.[13]

ZIMBABWE

The history of Church–state relations in Zimbabwe (Rhodesia) is different again. Here too, however, the story is one of the progressive breakdown of the long-established working agreement between Church and state under the mounting pressure of the nationalist movement. The high point of the working agreement was the prime ministership of Garfield Todd from 1953 to 1958. Todd had been a New Zealand missionary of the Church of Christ. While by no means a radical (at least at that period) he was sufficiently favourable to African advancement and racial partnership to lose white confidence. The subsequent premiership of Edgar Whitehead, however, still witnessed a battered survival of the old relationship. It was the coming to power of Ian Smith and the Rhodesia Front which provided the irrevocable moment of change. Three months later Ralph Dodge, the American Bishop of the United Methodist Church and first President of the new Christian Council of Rhodesia (CCR), was deported. He had been the most outspoken of Church leaders in opposition to the increasing racialism of government policy, while the CCR was seen (not unfairly) as a tool to unite the Churches in resistance to that policy. The next year, in November 1965, Smith made his Unilateral Declaration of Independence, 'a blow', as he said 'for the preservation of justice, civilization and Christianity'. The CCR declared it 'an unlawful act'. Kenneth Skelton, the Anglican Bishop of Matabeleland and Dodge's successor as President of the Christian Council, became the most outspoken Church critic of government over the next few years.[14] In general, Church leaders insisted upon the illegality of what had been done and this point had theoretical importance in that it threw doubt upon whether the subsequent government could be covered by the guidance of Romans 13. Nevertheless, in practice, the degree of conflict was not great and Bishop Alderson, the Bishop of Mashonaland, was soon objecting to any preacher in church referring to 'the illegal regime' as a contradiction of charity. It would upset too many white Anglicans. In 1970 Bishop Skelton resigned and left the country, while Paul Burrough, the new Bishop of Mashonaland, proved considerably more sympathetic to the government position.

It was, all the same, only at this rather late date that a crisis could be said to have arisen in Church–state relations. It was as a result of the new, more explicitly racialist, constitution of 1969 and a new Land Tenure Act which the Churches (and especially the Roman

Catholic Church) believed could grievously affect their day-to-day working. The Christian Council emphatically rejected both. Bishop Skelton's personal role as leader of the ecclesiastical opposition was at this point taken over by the Catholic Bishop Donal Lamont of Umtali (Mutare), a man much influenced both by participating in the Second Vatican Council and by the example of Bishop de Resende of Beira (little more than a hundred miles from Mutare). Shortly before leaving Skelton had declared in a sermon: 'Justice is more important than law and order – and can sometimes be incompatible with it . . . the church is being challenged today'. With his departure such statements would hardly be heard any more from Anglican pulpits. They would, however, be increasingly heard from two other types of pulpit – Catholic and Methodist. In this, the Catholics had the advantage of numbers and effective institutions (the Catholic Church being by far the largest single religious body in the country), the Methodists of being black.

The majority of Catholic bishops and clergy were anything but radical, and that is especially true of the English Jesuits in Salisbury with their very strong connections with the white population, many of them Catholics, and overwhelmingly supporters of Smith – just as the white Anglicans were. Outside Salisbury, however, Swiss missionaries in Gweru and Spanish Burgos missionaries in the north-west of the country had far less contact and sympathy with the white community. Their work lay overwhelmingly with blacks. The teaching of the Second Vatican Council and the emergence of liberation theology in Latin America were affecting a political radicalization of at least some sections of the Catholic clergy comparable to what was going on next door in Mozambique. Nevertheless the Church and the bishops as a whole did their best to avoid confrontation with government after the land and schools crisis of 1970–71.[15]

If confrontation did, all the same, escalate throughout the 1970s, it was the doing of a tiny but powerful Catholic minority: the Justice and Peace Commission, the vernacular *Moto* newspaper and Bishop Lamont. The Justice and Peace Commission, consisting of a group of white priests, sisters and laity, all radically minded, was set up in November 1971. For the first time the Catholic Church had an instrument specifically concerned with social justice. Though *Moto* (edited by the Swiss Fr Traber) was definitively banned in November 1974, the Justice and Peace Commission was able to publish a number of precise and highly damaging accounts of the civil war and the treatment of civilians by the armed forces through the assistance of the Catholic Institute of International Relations (CIIR) in London. Most effective were *The Man in the Middle* (1975) and *Civil War in Rhodesia* (1976).[16]

The power of the Church lobby, as in Mozambique, lay in its intrinsic credibility, in its possession of damaging evidence and its ability to publish that evidence internationally. But this depended not upon the Church in general so much as upon a rather small group of highly dedicated and efficient people (by no means all of them in point of fact Catholics) in touch again not with the international Church in general, but with a network of small but effective organizations within it. If the Catholic Church in Rhodesia came out from the civil war with a rather high standing, this had relatively little to do with the hierarchy as a whole within the country and nothing at all to do with the hierarchy abroad.[17] It was the work of the Justice and Peace Commission, the CIIR and related individuals who had received from the hierarchy little more than a general blessing on their work and an absence of formal repudiation. Nevertheless, the role of Bishop Lamont as President of the Justice and Peace Commission was exceedingly important. Ecclesiastically it validated the whole operation. His personal statements (for instance his Open Letter to the Rhodesian Government of 11 August 1976) were also extremely outspoken. It is hardly surprising that he was put on trial, charged with not reporting the presence of 'terrorists' at missions in his diocese, and in due course (March 1977) was deported from the country.[18]

In 1971 when the British Conservative government had just negotiated a possible settlement with the Smith regime, but insisted upon sending a commission (the Pearce commission) to the country to test its acceptability to Africans, the African National Congress was established with Bishop Abel Muzorewa as President and the Rev. Canaan Banana as Vice-President with the purpose of demonstrating that it was not acceptable. At the time all the principal black political leaders (Nkomo, Sithole, Mugabe) were in detention. For a while the ANC represented practically the whole black community. The commission came to recognize that the settlement was not acceptable and the British government did not pursue it. This brought Bishop Muzorewa to the centre of the political scene where he remained, more or less, for nearly ten years to become in due course the country's first black prime minister. He was Bishop Dodge's successor as head of the small (American formed) United Methodist Church and henceforth combined the headship of the Church with that of the ANC. A fiery preacher and highly determined personality, he was in the early 1970s undoubtedly performing a national role, 'a bishop-in-politics' standing in for the imprisoned politicians. He was at the time almost the only black with a senior ecclesiastical position in any Church. The position changed after three years when the politicians were released and, after a while, he found himself unable to work with them so the ANC developed into a nationalist but less radical party competing with ZANU and ZAPU, particularly for the Christian and middle-class constituency. By the late 1970s he was inside the country pursuing a peaceful solution and Nkomo and Mugabe were abroad organizing the liberation war. With the advance of the guerrilla forces and as a last desperate ploy Smith arranged for him to take office in April 1979 as black Prime Minister of Zimbabwe–Rhodesia (as it was then briefly named) in a government still very effectively controlled by the white Rhodesia Front. Muzorewa himself now became 'the man in the middle', only too quickly reduced in his black support while receiving – as apparently the only alternative to the victory of the liberation armies – a good deal of international white backing. He had become, ostensibly, the black Christian alternative to communism.

When at length in 1980 after the Lancaster House Conference Britain resumed formal control of the country, a free election was held and overwhelmingly won by Mugabe's ZANU, Muzorewa retained only three seats in Parliament. The Rev. Canaan Banana, a former minister of the British Methodist Church and originally Muzorewa's Vice-President in the ANC, but now a leading member of ZANU, became Zimbabwe's first president. Despite attempts to regard Muzorewa as the Christian politician still struggling within a 'Marxist' Zimbabwe (and Mugabe and ZANU were theoretically indeed committed to Marxism) and despite his continued control for some years of the United Methodist Church and even more briefly of the Christian Council, there was very little hostility between the Churches and the new state – certainly nothing comparable to what had happened initially in Mozambique. On the contrary, Mugabe stressed his gratitude to organizations like the Justice and Peace Commission and CIIR for their support during the war and ministers frequently attended religious services. The great difference with Mozambique was the far wider penetration of Christianity in Zimbabwe in the lives of ordinary people. Nearly all the leaders of ZANU had close Church family connections, Mugabe's sister was a full-time Catholic Church worker, his wife and mother were to be seen as active participants at services Sunday by Sunday.

The advance of explicit nationalist sentiment in rural Zimbabwe had coincided with, rather than conflicted with, the advance of Christianity. Undoubtedly there were tensions in the war. Quite a number of missionaries and Church workers were killed (whether by covert government forces or revolutionary groups of one sort or another, it was often almost impossible to know), church attendance temporarily went down in many places and there was a revival in the influence of spirit mediums.[19] Locally and within the immediate context of the war, these things were of undoubted importance. Nevertheless in the longer term (judged at least from the standpoint of five years or so after the war's termination) they proved to be of secondary and rather temporary significance – just as did the more stridently 'Marxist' note in ZANU rhetoric. At one time it might have seemed credible that Bishop Muzorewa would fill the role of carrying black Christians across to the Smith camp and thus accentuate the anti-Christian character of the liberation forces. Effectively he quite failed in this. While some middle-class black Christians undoubtedly sympathized with such an approach and feared a ZANU victory, as a whole the black Christian community (including some of its white leadership) had grown far too opposed to Smith over the years to be reconciled in this way.

There was some Church–state tension after 1980 in the post-Independence era, particularly in regard to the unrest in Matabeleland and the behaviour of the security forces there, producing at times quite fierce attacks by individual ministers on white Church leaders, but such tension was neither generalized nor prolonged. The Catholic Church, which had through the Justice and Peace Commission contributed so much in the earlier period, was all the same now in a seriously leaderless state, unable to adapt appropriately to the new dispensation. Most of its priests and several of its bishops remained white and its charges of brutality against the security forces in Matabeleland were weakened by precisely this: the accusers were white clergy, some of them people who had been known prior to 1980 for their Rhodesian sympathies (the Marianhill priests of the Bulawayo diocese had not been noted for any liberationist stance). The efficiency of the Justice and Peace Commission and the link overseas with CIIR were largely lost. While the membership of the Church was overwhelmingly black, its effective leadership remained too predominantly white and expatriate to be well adapted to relate to the new state. However, as the state was clearly most anxious not to precipitate any Church–state conflict, the effect was to engender not disharmony but ineffectiveness.[20]

SOUTH AFRICA FROM THE 1960s

The 1960s were on the whole a quiet time for South Africa: the repression following Sharpeville left little room open for opposition. The Anglican ecclesiastical opposition had almost faded away with the resignation of Joost de Blank and for the time being there was no comparably loudspoken alternative, but the Christian Institute under Naudé began quietly to develop a far more systematic approach, both theological and sociological, to the task of being a Christian within apartheid society. This was again made possible both by its autonomous character and in part by financial support from abroad, but it made relatively little public impact for some years. In 1968 the South African Christian Council (SACC), hitherto a rather ineffectual body, began to take the lead, co-operating with the Christian Institute and supported by the small minority of, mostly white, radical Christians to be found in all Churches. Both had the official backing of the main English-language Churches but in practice this might still have meant little, though it was, again, important for its ecclesiastical validation that Archbishop Selby-Taylor of Cape Town was the SACC's president. *Message to the People of South Africa*, published by the South African Council of Churches in 1968, represents the beginning of a new phase in Church–state conflict: 'A thorough policy of racial separation must ultimately require that the Church should cease to be the Church'. Six hundred ministers signed the message which, for days, was vigorously supported or attacked in different branches of the national press. John Vorster, the Prime Minister, whose brother was moderator of the Cape Synod of the DRC, personally replied, warning those 'who wish to disrupt the order in South Africa under the cloak of religion. . . . Cut it out, cut it out immediately for the cloak you carry will not protect you if you try to do this in South Africa'.

At this point the internal confrontation in South Africa was greatly affected by the World Council's Programme to Combat Racism and its 1970 decision to make grants for humanitarian purposes to liberation movements,[21] among them the South African ANC banned within the country since Sharpeville and now committed to violent revolution. Anti-apartheid Christians in South Africa were deeply divided about the propriety of making the grants. Most whites condemned the grants, but most Churches were unwilling all the same to be pushed by the government into withdrawing as a result from the World Council. The few people, on the contrary, who supported the WCC position were now open to full government attack and the large number of deportations and refusals of employment permits in the following years was an immediate consequence. One leading liberal cleric, the Anglican Dean of Johannesburg, Gonville ffrench-Beytagh, was first put on trial and then deported.[22] In 1972 a special 'Commission of inquiry into certain organizations' (the Schlebusch Commission) was set up and focused particularly upon the Christian Institute. When Naudé refused to testify before it on account of its secretness and non-judicial character, he too was brought to trial and convicted.[23] The Christian Institute was subsequently banned. In 1974 the further issue of conscientious objection arose after the National Conference of the SACC meeting at Hammanskraal passed a resolution, proposed by the Presbyterian Douglas Bax and seconded by Beyers Naudé, asking the Churches to consider whether in the current situation in South Africa Christian discipleship should not be expressed in the form of conscientious objection to military service. The wrath of the government in response was expressed in its turn by the passing through parliament of a draconian bill for the punishment of those inciting persons to refuse military service.

In March 1978, Bishop Desmond Tutu was appointed General Secretary of the SACC. Up until the later 1970s the Church–state struggle in South Africa, in so far as it existed, was predominantly a relationship between whites. It has been possible to chronicle it with little or no reference to individual black people. But in South Africa, as in Zimbabwe, the 1970s brought the beginning of a complete change in this regard. With the passing of the Hammanskraal resolution and the banning of the Christian Institute the long history of white minority Christian protest against racialism came effectively to a close. It did, of course, continue, but it had gone as far as it could go. It never had the support of the majority of white Christians and its role of defending the rights of black people or speaking in the name of black Christians could hardly go on when black people and black Christians were now so clearly able to speak up for themselves. Desmond Tutu as General Secretary of the Council of Churches and, later, as Archbishop of Cape Town, represents a new generation, as do black theologians like Manas Buthelezi, Alan Boesak and Joe Chikane. Quietly the centre of gravity of the main Churches has moved across to the black majority. Tutu is undoubtedly the heir of Trevor Huddleston, Joost de Blank and Beyers Naudé: the voice of Christian prophecy has remained remarkably constant across the years. The difference is that none of his predecessors had any large constituency to which he could turn for support. The new black Church leaders have. If Tutu confronts the state today, he is conscious of having the support of at least four times as many people as the State President. Even now, with Mandela out of prison and Tambo no longer in exile, the Church leaders can still exercise to some extent the provisional role of 'bishop-in-politics' held by Muzorewa in the early 1970s, though of course the far more complex character of the South African situation limits its exercise in comparison with what was possible in Rhodesia. They are, however, likely to have learnt the lesson from Muzorewa of the danger of over-stepping their legitimate function or even of being drawn at length into some sort of latter-day 'Christian' white–black alliance in defence against the 'communist' African National Congress. Such a scenario in South Africa is implausible.

Behind the relatively moderate and diplomatic leadership of Tutu, a new Christian radicalism has been developing far more in the spirit of South American liberation theology than almost anything which has existed hitherto. The work of Alan Boesak is especially important in this regard because Boesak is himself Moderator of the coloured branch of the DRC.[24] The much discussed Kairos document published by the Institute of Contextual Theology in Johannesburg in 1985 is perhaps the most notable expression of this new radicalism.[25] Signed by 152 ministers and lay people of all Churches but mostly drawn up by Joe Chikane, Director of the Institute of Contextual Theology, and the Dominican, Albert Nolan, the Kairos document could in a way be said to stand in a line with the Cottesloe Declaration of 1960 and the *Message to the People of South Africa* of 1968. It is much more forthright than either, however, (even, one might suggest, simplistic) in its condemnation both of the basic principles evoked by government and – still more devastatingly – the half-truths previously appealed to by the Churches. Again and again it could be claimed that in the past the undermining weakness of the position of the Churches was the failure adequately to challenge their own complicity with the practice of apartheid.[26] Perhaps surprisingly there was little government response to the Kairos document. Maybe this was due to a recognition that, for the present, its proponents remain relatively impotent.

GENERAL CONSIDERATIONS

In the last forty years the Churches in southern Africa have increasingly demonstrated that they are by no means just white domination and racialism at prayer. Even the Dutch Reformed Church which was starting to pull away from such a role in the 1950s, but appeared to fall back into it after Cottesloe, has been attempting of late to recover a greater theological and spiritual independence from the state.[27] To a large extent they have all been prisoners of their history and primary status as colonial Churches, developed to provide moral support for white Christians in the southern hemisphere. What is significant first, is the degree to which, they managed to get beyond that; second, the way in the last ten years they have begun to shift their leadership, voice and public persona to express the fact that today they are all, 80 per cent or more, black churches.[28]

In their rather different ways, Malan, Verwoerd, Vorster and Botha, Ian Smith and the Portuguese government of Salazar and Marcello Caetano, all endeavoured to use Christianity as a pillar of the state and of white domination. They have had the backing of many local white Christians, some of them undoubtedly devout. They have, after all, not done anything particularly new, for the traditions they have represented stretch far back into the past. Despite the rather different histories of the three countries considered, this position broke down in all three. That breakdown was most noticeable at the end of the 1960s and the beginning of the 1970s. Prior to those years it might have seemed that opposition could be contained. After those years a confident, if inexperienced, black Church was rather evidently taking over as the principal local incarnation of the central Christian tradition. What were the factors which brought about this sea change?

There are at least five factors of which we should take note. The first was the effect of the inevitable ruthlessness of minority governments faced with a challenge to their power by a progressively more disaffected majority. It may well be said that a great ruthlessness already preceded that challenge. The Churches were in fact always more or less bound to protest about manifest tyranny and cruelty. They had done so at times in the early years of the western conquest of Africa; they did so in the face of the incoming tide of nationalist apartheid in the 1950s. By the late 1960s, however, liberation wars were multiplying and the violence of the reaction of the state in each country ensured a rising level of ecclesiastical protest which, while at first related only to individual incidents, almost inevitably developed into a more wholesale questioning of the state by elements in the Church.

The second factor was simply that of powerful charismatic personalities. It would be impossible to write the history of Church–state relations in southern Africa perceptively without stressing the immense role that a very few people performed in raising issues, challenging preconceived notions, and providing a new symbolic vision of the nature of the Church exceedingly different from that which had previously been held. Michael Scott, Trevor Huddleston, Ambrose Reeves, Joost de Blank, Colin Winter, Cosmos Desmond, Beyers Naudé, Donal Lamont, Desmond Tutu – these and a number of other people achieved a spiritual transformation of the image of Christianity in regard to the political world which both infuriated the white state and largely prevented African alienation. From the viewpoint of an analysis of the structural functioning of charisma it is useful to distinguish between the impact of personalities who also have institutional authority and those who do not: Reeves, de Blank and Lamont on one side: Scott, Huddleston and Desmond on the other. Public trials of ecclesiastics like those of ffrench-Beytagh, Naudé and Lamont were an immense bonus offered by the state for the strengthening and purification of a still timid and ambiguous Church.

The third factor was the efficiency of small, largely autonomous, Christian organizations in replacing a largely passive Church leadership at moments of crisis: Defence and Aid, established in the early 1960s by Canon Collins, was the first. The Christian Institute was a second. The Justice and Peace Commission in Rhodesia and the CIIR in London were others. The Christian Council in Rhodesia and then in South Africa fulfilled at times a similar function. Somewhat comparable were religious orders like the Burgos Fathers and the Maryknoll Sisters, though their larger numbers and greater susceptibility to hierarchical control, meant that their role from this point of view might be less continuous or secure. Such mobilization as the Church achieved in terms of ability to challenge the state at the level of prolonged debate, international propaganda or the provision of help for the victims of oppression, has come almost wholly through groups of this sort consisting not so much of charismatic figures but of a small handful of almost nameless individuals committed to long hours of hard work for justice.

The fourth factor was a significant change in world theology which came about in the course of the 1960s, as a result of a more radical approach to secular realities, the influence of the Second Vatican Council, the World Council of Churches Conference at Uppsala in 1968, the life and death of Martin Luther King, and the emergence of liberation theology in Latin America. As a result of all this, attitudes among the younger clergy towards the state and the pursuit of justice were markedly different in 1970 from those of 1960. The shift from the predominance of a theology centred upon Romans 13 to one centred upon Exodus and the Magnificat (simplistic as the interpretation of all these texts might be) was not universal but it was considerable enough to alter fairly decisively the image of the church militant in the eyes of white and black alike. This shift was particularly marked among Roman Catholics: they were the least likely to get away from a 'Romans 13' style theology in the early part of the postwar period; by the 1970s, however, they were among the most likely to respond wholeheartedly to a 'Magnificat' style theology.

The fifth and final factor was simply the steady advance, numerically and in group consciousness, of the black Christian community.[29] By the 1970s a sense of Christianity being native to this or that rural area had a naturalness and a depth to it which – in many cases – was certainly not there in the 1940s (though there were, especially in South Africa, areas where it had arrived long before, while in most of Mozambique it was not so obvious even at the end of the period). There were far more Christians of second and third generation standing. There were far, far more black clergy. The impression of a white Church speaking to and for blacks rather suddenly fades as a much larger black Church emerges from its swaddling clothes, stronger and more confident in its convictions than its mentors had dared to anticipate.

What was achieved in the Church–state relationship in this period? We may summarize an answer under five headings. First, undoubtedly the Churches initially provided the colonial and settler states with a considerable sense of validation and even purpose. 'Christianity' was part of the high function of their existence. It could be seen as justifying the establishment of white rule over black 'heathens' in the first place. Ian Smith's description of UDI as 'a blow' for 'Christianity' might appear in 1965 rather laughably anachronistic, but it would not have seemed so twenty or more years earlier. Above all, in South Africa among Afrikaners the role of the DRC in providing a high sense of unity and providential purpose was of immense importance. When on 16 December 1958 Verwoerd, the newly appointed Prime Minister, declared 'We are standing like a Luther at the time of the Reformation, back against the wall', battling for the survival of 'everything which has been built up since the days of Christ' he was appealing to a religious mystique at least as strong as that of his black nationalist opponents. Many Christians of other traditions such as Arthur Lewis, Anglican priest and senator of Ian Smith, who regularly denounced the way his brethren were replacing the gospel 'according to Mark' with that 'according to Marx', felt a profound sense of betrayal that the old alliance of Church and state which had achieved so much in earlier colonial history was being abandoned by the 1970s.

Second, the relationship had included (long before the 1940s) the possibility of Churchmen doing a good deal to defend African rights. Doubtless the opportunity had been exercised by some more than others. Nevertheless it was a significant part of the old relationship, at least in English-speaking Africa, and it is probable that if there had been little missionary presence, the abuse of African rights would have been a great deal worse than it was in fact. The sheer presence of missionaries, as well as their occasional interventions, was protective, just as their opening of schools provided the basis for any long-term African counter-attack. This leads us to a third point. The Churches, at least in South Africa and Rhodesia, educated the black nationalist leadership from Luthuli to Mugabe. However critical the latter later became of the Churches, a considerable personal gratitude remained; gratitude not only for secondary schooling but also, in a number of cases, for subsequent friendship and assistance with tertiary education overseas. Individual friendship between liberal white Christians and black nationalists remains a significant element in the overall Church–state picture. Fourth, during the civil wars in Mozambique and Zimbabwe, Church agencies did an influential job in documenting and publishing state-organized atrocities. The effect of documents like the Wiriyamu report and *Man in the Middle* in affecting international public opinion was very considerable. It was obvious how grateful ZANU, for instance, was to the CIIR. Finally, and more generally, in many different situations the Churches have acted as a sort of temporary opposition party when none other was possible. The position of Muzorewa and Banana in Rhodesia in the early 1970s or Tutu, Boesak and Chikane in South Africa in the 1980s has been of such a kind.

With the coming of black rule almost everything changes. It is too early to define the new lines of tension and accord with confidence. The Church's old white leadership, except for its most liberal wing (and even there Bishop Lamont, for instance, found himself quite at sea in post-Independence Zimbabwe) lacks both the standing and the sense of direction to be influential in the new order, but black Church leadership remains mostly very limited in experience and education to cope with the new government (in South Africa that may well not be the case). Apart from general appeals to seek the common good, but not in too Marxist a way, the Churches may seem to have little to say to the new states. The black state on the other hand is almost everywhere almost as impatient of Church interference in politics as was its white predecessor. However, it again (except in Mozambique and this, too, may be changing) sees the church, despite some irritating qualities, as a natural ally and it soon recognizes that it needs whatever allies it can get. The Churches with some moral credit, the loyalty of many ordinary people, international links and considerable overseas funds remain useful friends and awkward enemies. Moreover the new political order is full of Christians or people from a Christian background and it has little alternative to offer to the continuing spread of a multitude of churches in country and town alike. For the most part, Church–state relations are defused by the coming of independence and for the foreseeable future they are likely to remain that way.

NOTES

1   It should be noted that recent events in South Africa are not included in this chapter. These events approximately begin with the resignation of President Botha and the release by his successor, President de Klerk, of Nelson Mandela in February 1990.

2   For a review of the historical background to Church–state relationships in the area see, *inter alia*, W.A. De Klerk (1975), *The Puritans in Africa*, London: R. Collings, J.W. De Gruchy (1979), *The Church Struggle in South Africa*, Cape Town: David Philip, esp. Ch. 1; F. Wilson and D. Perrot (eds) (1973), *Outlook on a Century: South Africa 1870–1970*, Lovedale: Lovedale Press.

3   For a recent account see A. Hastings (1985), 'Mission, church and state in southern Africa' in *Christian Mission and Human Transformation*, Report

of Sixth International Association for Mission Studies Conference, Harare, Leiden: IAMS, pp.22–32.

4 T. Huddleston (1956), *Naught for your Comfort*, London: Collins.

5 See P. Walshe (1977), 'Church versus State in South Africa: The Christian Institute and the resurgence of African nationalism', *Journal of Church and State*, vol. 19, no. 3, pp.457–79.

6 See T.D. Moodie (1975), *The Rise of Afrikanerdom: Power, Apartheid and the Afrikaner Civil Religion*, Berkeley: University of California Press.

7 See C. Bertulli (1974), *Croce e spada in Mozambico*, Rome: Coines.

8 White Fathers (1973), *Mozambique, une église, signe de salut . . . pour qui?* Rome: White Fathers Generalate, 400pp. mimeograph collection of documents.

9 See *Terror in Tete* (1973), London: International Defence and Aid Fund.

10 See *O Julgamento dos Padres do Macúti* (1973), Porto: Afrontamento.

11 See A. Hastings (1974), *Wiriyamu: My Lai in Mozambique*, London: Search Press.

12 For further discussion see A. Hastings (1974), 'Some reflections upon the war in Mozambique', *African Affairs*, vol. 73, no. 292, pp.263–76, and, by the same author, 'Portugal's other rebellion', *The Observer*, London, 21 April 1974 and 'Christianity and revolution', *African Affairs*, vol. 74, no. 296 1975, pp.347–61.

13 See also Dutch Missionary Council (1977), *A New people, A New Church? Mozambique*, 's-Hertogenbosch; Dutch Missionary Council.

14 See M. Lapsley (1986), *Neutrality or Co-option? Anglican Church and State from 1964 until the Independence of Zimbabwe*, Gweru Zimbabwe: Mambo Press.

15 See R.H. Randolph (1971), *Church and State in Rhodesia 1969–1971*, Gweru Zimbabwe: Mambo Press.

16 The two reports, by the Catholic Commission for Justice and Peace in Rhodesia, are *The Man in the Middle* (1975), London: Catholic Institute of International Relations and *Civil War in Rhodesia: Abduction, Torture and Death in the Counter-Insurgency Campaign* (1976), London: Catholic Institute of International Relations.

17 See also I. Linden (1980), *The Catholic Church and the Struggle for Zimbabwe*, London: Longman.

18 See D. Lamont (1977), *Speech from the Dock*, London: Catholic Institute of International Relations.

19 See D. Lan (1985), *Guns and Rain: Guerrillas and Spirit Mediums in Zimbabwe*, London: James Currey. For a case study see T. Ranger (1984), 'Religions and rural protests in Makoni district, Zimbabwe, 1900–80', in J.M. Bak and G. Benecke (eds), *Religion and Rural Revolt*, Manchester: Manchester University Press, pp.315–35.

20 See also N.E. Thomas (1985), 'Church and state in Zimbabwe', *Journal of Church and State*, vol. 27, no. 1, pp.113–33.

21 See E. Adler (1974), *A Small Beginning: An Assessment of the First Five Years of the Programme to Combat Racism*, Geneva: World Council of Churches. See also, more generally, D. Hudson (1977), *The World Council of Churches in International Affairs*, Leighton Buzzard: Faith Press.

22 See his *Encountering Darkness* (1973), London: Collins.
23 See International Commission of Jurists, Geneva (1975), *The Trial of Beyers Naudé*, London: Search Press.
24 See his *Black Theology, Black Power* (1978), London: Mowbray.
25 See Kairos Theologians (1985), *Challenge to the Church: A Theological Comment on the Political Crisis in South Africa*, London: Catholic Institute of International Relations.
26 For a discussion of the Churches and the issues of apartheid and racism from different viewpoints see Z. Mbali (1987), *The Churches and Racism: A Black South African Perspective*, London: SCM Press; A. Paton (1973), *Apartheid and the Archbishop: The Life and Times of Geoffrey Clayton, Archbishop of Cape Town*, London: Jonathan Cape; D.M. Paton (ed.) (1958) *Church and Race in South Africa*, London: SCM Press; A. Prior (1982), *Catholics in Apartheid Society*, Cape Town: David Philip; and L. Cawood (1964), *The Churches and Race Relations in South Africa*, Johannesburg: South African Institute of Race Relations.
27 See General Synod, Dutch Reformed Church (1976), *Human Relations and the South African Scene in the Light of Scripture*, Cape Town: Dutch Reformed Church Publishers.
28 See A. Hastings (1981), 'The Christian churches and liberation movements in southern Africa', *African Affairs*, vol. 80, no. 320, pp.345–54 and, for a more general review by the same author, *A History of African Christianity 1950–1975* (1979), Cambridge: Cambridge University Press.
29 See, for example, T. Sundermeier (ed.) (1975), *Church and Nationalism in South Africa*, Johannesburg: Raven Press.

Chapter 7

Politics and religion in Latin America

Kenneth Medhurst

INTRODUCTION

Latin America looms large in contemporary discussions of the relationship between politics and religion. Changes within the Church of that region have provoked or contributed to debates that have had a significant impact on the global Christian community. Shifts in the perceptions and alliances of many Latin American Churchmen have opened up political and theological controversies whose effects have been experienced in many other parts of the world. A Church once relatively united in defence of conservative doctrinal and social positions has become an important centre and source of international ecclesiastical division. Equally, a Church inclined to follow in the wake of European ecclesiological or theological trends has become one of the universal Church's pace-setters in such matters.

In thus speaking of the Church, reference, of course, is principally being made to the Roman Catholic Communion. Much of the significance of Latin America's religious situation stems from the fact that the region supplies the world's largest single grouping of those officially designated as Roman Catholic. For the Vatican, therefore, local ecclesiastical developments have a special strategic significance. Not least there is an awareness that the region is the only part of the Third World with a preponderantly Christian inheritance. Particularly for Roman Catholics the future global prospects of Christianity could therefore be seen as being especially dependent upon developments within this strategically significant area.

Nevertheless, attention cannot be exclusively focused on the Roman Catholic Communion. One of the latter's dilemmas is that it now faces unprecedented pressure, not only from the proponents of secular ideologies but also from representatives of alternative religious traditions. This is partly a matter of syncretic or non-Christian religions especially associated with the descendents of imported African slaves; it is still more a matter of Protestant and, especially, Pentecostal groups. The inroads these groups have made constitute an important part of the background against which Catholic debates are being conducted. Equally, non-Catholic bodies contribute, in their own right, to unfolding discussions about the nature of relationships between the religious and political domains.

THE ROOTS OF THE PROBLEM – THE CHURCH AND COLONIAL SOCIETY

Christianity was implanted in Latin America by the Roman Catholic Church as an integral feature of the Spanish and (in Brazil's case) the Portuguese colonial enterprise.[1] Churchmen were to be found working alongside the original conquistadores and, subsequently, in conjunction with official imperial representatives. In each case the priorities of those concerned may have varied. Thus the friars, who were among the first Churchmen to arrive in the area, were primarily concerned with offering salvation to the indigenous population and this sometimes brought them into conflict with laymen interested particularly in military conquest or economic exploitation. Nevertheless, the relationship between Church and colonists was an essentially collaborative one. Churchmen saw their missionary task in terms of incorporating Indians into an extension of 'Christendom'. They contemplated the creation of an empire constituted on Christian foundations and within which Church and society could be viewed as co-terminous. Equally, they looked to the secular arm for the creation of a stable political framework within which their evangelistic work could proceed. They also looked to the secular authorities to uphold their doctrinal monopoly. The latter, for their part, were moulded by Castile's anti-Moorish crusading traditions and by a Counter-Reformation Catholicism that equated the task of military conquest with the pushing back of Christendom's frontiers.

Just as the initial period of conquest gave way to the more orderly rhythms of a centrally administered empire, so the era of mass evangelization yielded to more routine patterns of ecclesiastical life. Significant missionary work was sustained, by friars, on the empire's expanding frontier. Also, Jesuits established their own independent, paternalistically run, Indian communities. But the initiative increasingly tended to pass to more obviously bureaucratized clergy operating within conventional diocesan and parochial structures. Equally, Church and state co-operated closely in the task of imperial administration.

Thanks to special papal concessions imperial authorities enjoyed an unprecedented degree of control over their ecclesiastical partners. Senior clerical appointments were in the hands of the Spanish or Portuguese Crowns and the publication of even official papal communications required royal approval. Senior Churchmen also assumed official governmental responsibilities. In return the Church was guaranteed a privileged social position. Imperial authorities and private individuals showered the institution with land and other forms of wealth. Its control over education also ensured it an important role in the formation of the region's limited upper strata groups. The net result was closely to identify ecclesiastical institutions with the hierarchically ordained structures of post-conquest society. From the local level upwards the Church's official clerical spokesmen tended to be closely allied with landed or bureaucratic elites of European extraction, rather than the majority indigenous or *mestizo* populations. An orthodox Thomist theology which perceived established hierarchies as an expression of the divine will offered no basis for a radical critique of this social order. It also underpinned a clerically dominated vision of the Church itself.

THE POST-INDEPENDENCE PERIOD

This situation helps to explain why the Church, especially at its senior levels, did not throw its weight behind the early nineteenth century pro-independence cause. A handful of junior clergy, notably in Mexico, were actively engaged on the anti-Spanish side in the wars of independence, but they were the exception. Most Churchmen were, at best, ambivalent in their attitudes toward the region's emergent republics. Moreover, they became caught up in struggles between freshly established governments, anxious to assume those controls over the Church that had formally been exercised by imperial authorities, and the papacy which saw in the new situation an opportunity to retrieve lost authority. They also became the subject of divisive struggles within the new states' governing elites. Some less traditional and commercially orientated groups linked to liberal parties and subject to contemporary rationalist or positivist influences, sought to limit the Church's social and political significance. They were not necessarily anti-Catholic but they did see the curtailing of clerical power as a pre-condition of national development. Others, associated with traditional upper-class controlled and largely rural-based conservative parties, mobilized in defence of established clerical interests. Neither liberals nor conservatives had incentives to disturb existing social hierarchies. But in a number of countries differences over the Church's economic status, its educational influence and its impact on law-making processes, constituted an especially significant source of intra-elite ideological conflict.

Such conflicts had varying outcomes. At one end of the scale was Colombia where a still extant Concordat, initially signed in 1887, guaranteed the Church a privileged and legally established position.[2] At the other extreme was post-revolutionary Mexico which briefly experienced militantly anti-clerical attempts definitively to eradicate ecclesiastical influence. These gave way to a largely peaceful *modus vivendi* but one which left the Church in a politically marginalized position.[3] Between these two points there fell, for example, Chile where, in 1925, the Church was officially disestablished yet retained considerable *de facto* political and social influence.[4] The end result was an institution which, for the most part, still felt itself relatively secure and lacking in incentives radically to question inherited alliances, assumptions, structures and practices.

This sense of security tended to distract attention from underlying long-term challenges. At the institutional level the Church emerged from nineteenth-century struggles stripped of a good deal of its once great wealth and frequently short of adequately trained clergy. In the medium term, at least, this entailed intellectual dependence on European mentors and some reliance upon clergy introduced from abroad. At the cultural level there was a tendency to overlook the limited extent of the organization's hold upon lower strata social groups and the restricted nature of Orthodox Catholicism's impact upon popular religious practice. The early mass conversions of indigenous peoples often produced no more than superficial results which subsequent pastoral practice frequently did little to amend. Many continued to espouse a syncretic religion that combined Catholic practices or values with beliefs and rites of pre-colonial origins. In societies like Brazil and Cuba that had experienced the importation of slaves, African cults also attracted large followings.[5] Those concerned had, at best, tenuous links with official ecclesiastical structures. Other more apparently orthodox believers embraced Catholic symbols or rituals associated with the prevailing popular culture, but without doctrinal understanding or strong institutional ties. Such ties tended, most frequently, to characterize middle or upper-class groups – groups whose Catholicism remained essentially individualistic and pietistic in nature. Their largely unquestioning acceptance of the status quo paralleled the fatalistic passivity generally nurtured among practitioners of the more popular forms of religiosity.[6]

THE EROSION OF THE TRADITIONAL ORDER IN THE FIRST FOUR DECADES OF THE TWENTIETH CENTURY

Socio-economic and political changes, ultimately threatening to the status quo, exposed by degrees the underlying weakness of the Church's position. They also prompted some re-evaluation of the institution's relationship with the surrounding society. The form taken by this re-evaluation was significantly affected by the then influential currents of European Catholic thought, but the process was, in the first instance, a response to changes in the Latin American Church's immediate environment. In particular urbanization and a measure of industrialization ate away at the base of the relatively stable rural and agrarian society within which the Church had long been embedded. In transformed urban settings new middle and lower strata groups emerged who were relatively free from traditional forms of clerically inspired social control. Especially in such countries as Argentina, Brazil, Chile and Uruguay, which received many late nineteenth- and early twentieth-century European immigrants, such groups were particularly open to the influence of new secular or even Protestant movements of opinion. In the political domain the net results were novel challenges to the hegemony of those upper-class groups upon whom the Church's leaders had particularly relied for the underwriting of institutional privileges. In the ecclesiastical domain the result was an unprecedented level of competition from non-Catholic sources.

Initial Catholic responses to the transformed situation were of an essentially defensive kind. Catholic laity were mobilized under clerical auspices, within the framework of Catholic Action, with a view to consolidating an effective Church inspired 'counter-culture'. Similarly, such trade union bodies as the Colombian UTC were established at the behest of clergy in order to offset the influence of secular unions.[7] In other instances, especially during the 1930s and 1940s, clerical reactions to novel challenges took the form of support for populist movements of a sometimes authoritarian, nationalist or even quasi-fascist variety. The movements associated with Getulio Vargas in Brazil and Juan Peron in Argentina, initially seemed to offer viable ways of safely incorporating newly politicized groups into their respective polities. Church leaders were consequently to be found as one element within the broadly-based coalitions that such leaders assembled.[8]

Underlying all these responses was a desire to resist or pre-empt challenges to traditional forms of clerical authority and to the inherited hierarchically structured pattern of social organization which had come to be associated with the Church's own institutional interests. There was a desire to hang on to the essence of the Christendom model of Latin American society. There was also a presumption in favour of that traditional Catholic triumphalism which denied any significant degree of autonomy to secular society and which instead sought the perpetuation of a social order ultimately subject to clerical tutelage. It expressed itself in support for a 'fortress Church' able to ward off threats from the surrounding society, pending its re-conquest. The necessary defences, within this frame of reference, were to be supplied by lay organizations, tied closely to ecclesiastical hierarchies, and/or by institutional alliances with political leaders in search of the legitimacy which Churchmen could confer.

The fate of the Argentinian hierarchy's alliance with Peron (1946–55) points to the possible dangers of such strategies. Initially Church leaders saw association with the latter's broadly-based populist regime as an appropriate way of conserving their influence. In the longer term, however, this largely opportunistic alliance left the Church vulnerable to threatening shifts in the balance of forces represented within the populist coalition. Thus Peron, constrained by economic difficulties and confronted by the ultimately irreconcilable demands of competing groups of supporters, was increasingly driven to embrace demagogic responses. Not least there was an effort to rally disenchanted urban labour support which involved 'the playing of the anti-clerical card'. Such a move highlighted the extent to which urban labour had become alienated from the Church. It also suggested that tactical alliances with political power holders could not be a lasting substitute for the development of the Church's own institutional resources or popular base.[9]

REFORMIST STRATEGIES – THE 1950s AND EARLY 1960s

During the 1950s support grew for initiatives which recognized some of the limitations of earlier and largely defensive responses to change. As before they were partly inspired by influences of European provenance. Theologians like Jacques Maritain, associated with the postwar development of Christian Democracy, encouraged a more positive evaluation of secular society and of calls for the extension of popular political participation. They also propounded a Christian humanism which saw secular demands for greater economic and social equality as being consistent with reformulated Catholic understandings of man's nature and destiny. It remains significant, however, that such changes of perspective were first and most clearly evident in the Latin American society which seemed to present the Church with particularly direct challenges. Thus the initial pace-setter in the matter of spelling out new possibilities was the Chilean hierarchy which confronted especially strong competition from Marxist-inspired parties and from unusually dynamic Protestant groups, of a generally Pentecostal variety. The appeal of such bodies to lower strata urban dwellers indicated the extent to which the Catholic Church had lost contact with such groups and provided the institution's more adventurous leaders with unusually strong incentives to re-assess their positions. The Chilean situation left less room for the complacency or rigidity that had perhaps been evident, for example, in the case of Argentina. It certainly seems significant that Chilean Churchmen were among the first in Latin America seriously to advocate the cause of land reform. They were in the vanguard when it came to recognizing that, in the interests of justice, a measure of generally agreed but serious structural change might be required.[10]

Of particular interest, in the Chilean context, was the emergence of a strong Christian Democratic party.[11] Similar parties emerged elsewhere in the region and continue to play some part in national politics. El Salvador presents one example. It was in Chile, however, that Christian Democracy made its most obvious impact. The party in question was not directly linked with the hierarchy and was not confessional in character. Indeed, it deliberately sought to extend its electoral appeal beyond the frontiers of the Catholic community and, to that extent, manifested a relatively new acceptance of the now ideologically pluralistic nature of Chilean society. On the other hand, it owed its creation to socially progressive Catholics who, having become impatient with Chile's traditional Conservative party, had sought a more appropriate vehicle for creating a society constituted in accordance with their reformulated understandings of Catholic social doctrine. Their objective was to build a cross-class electoral coalition that would take account of Chile's new political realities. It was not only designed to embrace reform-minded middle-class or professional groups but also to incorporate hitherto largely unmobilized groups to be found among the peasantry, the working class and urban shanty town dwellers. Their support was to be secured through a reform programme designed to foster industrial growth, agrarian reform, and increased public welfare expenditure. Equally, they were to be won over by novel opportunities for participation in economic and political decision-making. Not least, new forms of economic management were supposed to offer the possibility of an alternative to unbridled pro-capitalist authoritarianism, on the one hand, and Marxist-inspired revolution, on the other.

The advent of Cuba's revolutionary regime (1959) appeared to many to give a new urgency to such a reformist strategy. Certainly, developments in Cuba formed an important part of the background to subsequent debates within the Latin American Catholic community. In Chile they were amongst the factors underlying the emergence (in 1964) of Eduardo Frei's Christian Democratic administration. He was the beneficiary of both national and international support attracted by the possibility of an apparently credible and progressive alternative to revolutionary change.

Despite a promising start the expectations initially attached to Frei's experiment went largely unfulfilled. Great difficulty was experienced in bridging the gap between short-term political necessity and the realization of Christian Democracy's long-term goals. The daily demands of managing an economically vulnerable and politically divided society impeded the pursuit of the original strategy. In particular, it ultimately proved impossible to preserve an alliance between radical Catholics, moderate reformists and the many conservatives who had seen Christian Democracy as no more than the best available defence against a growth of the secular left. Finally (in 1970), the Christian Democrats fell victim to a process of political polarization which first resulted in the election of President Allende's Marxist-inspired coalition and which ultimately (in 1973) led to the Chilean military's total destruction of democratic government.[12]

THE EMERGENCE OF RADICAL CATHOLICISM

Well before that denouement the general terms of Latin American ecclesiastical debate had begun to shift in the direction of more obviously radical understandings of Catholicism. Chilean developments were, in some measure, associated with broader Latin American trends that entailed important challenges to earlier reformist approaches. Such challenges arose out of a mounting sense of crisis in the region's economic, social and political life that Chile's experience of Christian Democracy helped to exacerbate. In this instance the initial pace-setters were particularly to be found within the Brazilian Church. A vocal and well-organized minority within this latter institution became caught up in a more general process of popular political mobilization and radicalization that, in the late 1950s and early 1960s, significantly affected their national polity.

In part this was a matter of Churchmen responding, along with other groups, to difficulties associated with maintaining the populist mode of governance bequeathed by Getulio Vargas. Intensifying competition between the governing coalition's constituent elements helped to propel some Catholic activists, along with their secular counterparts, in unprecedentedly radical directions.[13] Student, working class and even some peasant groups fell into this category. But, in part, it was also a matter of some official Catholic leaders positively re-evaluating traditional doctrinal and political commitments in the light of these shifting realities. In particular a group within the Brazilian episcopate, led by Archbishop Helda Camara, sought to move the Church towards more socially critical and politically radical positions.[14]

Institutions and programmes of action were devised with a view to improving the social conditions and to raising the political consciousness of the lower strata groups whose passive acceptance of traditional social hierarchies had once been taken for granted. A new ethically inspired stress came to be laid upon enabling such groups to press for significant changes in their material and cultural circumstances. A preoccupation with justice began to compete with previously prevalent preoccupations with order or stability. Thus some official Church protection was given to the radical Catholic 'Movement for Basic Education' which sought to equip peasant groups with the cultural tools needed to prosecute their own political cause.[15] Equally, the famous educational specialist, Paulo Freir, developed the influential concept of *'conscientizaçao'*

– namely the attempt to raise the individual and corporate self-awareness of lower strata groups in order that they might assume greater responsibility for their own political destinies, free from the manipulation of traditional patrons.[16]

The Brazilian military coup of 1963 put an end to all such activities. The Church, in common with all other institutions, experienced the new military regime's attempts to de-politicize Brazilian society.[17] Equally, much of the national hierarchy to some degree shared in a reaction against previous radical trends and so closed ranks in at least provisional support of military rule. Nevertheless, their more radicalized colleagues had established significant precedents and they were subsequently to bear a special responsibility for fostering radical currents of opinion within the wider Latin American church.

Their activities have, in part, to be seen against the background of the Second Vatican Council.[18] This gathering, convened by Pope John XXIII in order better to equip the Church for witness in the modern world, helped both to legitimize and to give added impetus to those more radical currents of opinion that had already begun to surface among the region's Catholics. During the Council's own meetings the still generally conservative bishops of the area made few positive contributions. They generally tended to respond to initiatives emanating, in particular, from more reform-minded European and North American colleagues. But, thereafter, significant numbers within their ranks, as a consequence of their new experiences, became more open to novel possibilities.

In terms of the Church's own internal life this meant some acceptance of more decentralized decision-making and a more widely shared responsibility, on the part of bishops, clergy and laity, for the institution's worship and welfare. In the matter of Church relationships with the wider world it meant support for ecumenism. It also meant some recognition of the pluralistic nature of modern society and of the legitimacy of secular or left-wing ideologies. If only at the level of theory there was some at least initial willingness to contemplate 'Christian–Marxist' dialogue. It further meant a willingness to abandon reliance upon traditional forms of state protection in favour of greater dependence upon the Church's own mass membership. In principle there was some move away from the notion of a 'fortress Church', largely at odds with the surrounding society, and toward the concept of 'a Pilgrim People' open to some of the fresh challenges or possibilities presented by historical change.[19] Within this framework, unfolding historical dramas are perceived as a locus of divine activity. Part of the Church's task is correctly to read 'the signs of the times' in order that it may proclaim the underlying meaning of events and the moral imperatives to which they point. A somewhat static understanding of faith, particularly grounded in tradition, to some extent yields to a more obviously dynamic and biblically-based approach.

Within Latin America such new possibilities came to be especially associated with the second meeting of the regional bishops' conference (CELAM) held in Medellín, Colombia, in 1968.[20] This assembly, and the prior creation of the permanent secretariat which prepared its agenda, testified to growing awareness of a shared Latin American identity. More concretely it provided a framework within which to work out Vatican II's implications for Latin America and to address the region's perennial problems in the light of revised theological understandings. It was in preparing bishops for this reconsideration of corporate priorities and policies that radical Brazilian advisers, aided by some episcopal allies, were able significantly to influence the terms of subsequent Latin American ecclesiastical debates. By thus seizing the initiative they helped to push the area's Church leaders towards radical positions that went somewhat further than simply applying Vatican II's findings within a specific regional context. The Medellín Conference, in reality, helped to catalyse processes whereby the Latin American Church became something of a trendsetter in the matter of relating the Christian faith to contemporary social and political realities. It also marked the beginning of a new era in Latin American ecclesiastical history which, for the first time, saw the local Church establishing its own regional priorities on the basis of its own distinctive analysis of the area's development.

This analysis, following upon Vatican II's challenge to enter into dialogue with secular currents of thought, presented Latin America's problems in terms of imperialism, economic dependency and class conflict. Equally, fresh consideration was given to inherited theological categories. Once prevalent Thomist approaches gave way to that biblically-based understanding of faith which believes God is revealing His purposes within the context of mundane conflicts and which challenges Christians, in alliance with others of 'goodwill', to co-operate consciously in the realization of such purposes. The Church's task, in this setting, is not so much to preserve a sacrilized social order as to sustain a prophetic ministry based on a biblically-inspired reading of the contemporary 'signs of the times'. Among such signs, identified in the conclusions reached at Medellín, are spreading demands for greater equality between and within nations. Calls for Third World citizens to share in the shaping of their own destinies are similarly regarded.

The quest for justice implied in these calls was clearly viewed by the drafters of the Medellín documents as wholly consistent with biblical ethics. Moreover, the quest is no longer seen in purely individualistic terms. Whereas traditional Catholic piety in Latin America had tended to see salvation as an essentially private and other-worldly matter, it was now emphasized that the process had a corporate and historical dimension. In particular, room was found for the notion of sin as something which is not merely personal but also 'structural'. Impersonal economic, social and political structures are now seen as being under judgement because of their exploitative or dehumanizing properties. From now on, therefore, participation in the task of challenging, transforming or eradicating such structures is officially seen by Latin American Church leaders as a necessary feature of the institution's witness. By implication, at least, the Christian gospel is seen to point towards a radical political commitment.

LIBERATION THEOLOGY

Much of the Latin American Church's recent life has been taken up with exploring the implications of such revised understandings of Christian commitment. Above all, the impact of the Medellín gathering has been felt in the subsequent emergence of 'liberation theology'.[21] The general and controversial approach to the religious life suggested by this latter term, can, in large measure, be seen as an attempt to spell out the consequences of the Medellín findings in more specific or concrete forms. Indeed, liberation theology's first internationally renowned expositor, the Peruvian priest Gustavo Gutiérrez, was one of the episcopal advisers who helped to shape that conference's original agenda.[22] It may also be viewed as an especially radicalized and politicized version of the new orthodoxies. Thus Gutiérrez, and such other practitioners as José Luis Segundo, Hugo Assman and Leonardo Boff have, in varying ways, emphasized radical, social or political commitment as the appropriate starting point for their theological reflections. In common with Marxists the stress is upon 'praxis' or upon theology considered as a meditation upon pre-existing socially committed activity. Theological truth, it is assumed, emerges from direct involvement in historical dramas rather than from the musings of ostensibly detached academics. It is particularly assumed that deeper Christian understanding will be a fruit of active commitment to the cause of the poor and oppressed. The gospel is now seen as necessarily pointing Christians towards solidarity with the victims of injustice and hence towards participation in the struggle for their 'liberation'. Theological insight, it is suggested, comes in the wake of this prior, overriding and divinely prompted imperative.

In the case of Gutiérrez, for example, such understanding is associated with the biblical theme of the Exodus. The God who led the Israelites out of their bondage in Egypt now comes to be seen as the God who challenges Christians to share in the freeing of those enslaved by unjust structures. Similarly, Jesus is seen as a figure who most closely identifies with the poor and oppressed. He proclaims the reality of a 'Kingdom of God' which challenges or even inverts the assumptions conventionally undergirding temporal institutions. This Kingdom is not equated with the Church. Whereas traditional Catholic theology had spoken of the latter as 'a perfect society' whose hierarchy constituted the unchallengable guardians of definitively revealed truths, ecclesiastical institutions are here seen as having a more provisional or contingent quality. According to this latter vision the Church itself is challenged constantly to renew itself in the light of the values of the Kingdom. That Kingdom's purposes, it is intimated, will be finally realized beyond the historical realm. In the meantime, it is the Church's task actively to witness to their present significance and to assist in the task of bringing them closer to fulfilment within the sphere of mundane secular affairs.

Some opponents of liberation theology insist that its practitioners have indiscriminately absorbed Marxist categories of thought.[23] They suggest, for example, that there is a tendency to equate Christian understanding of 'the Kingdom' with Marx's vision of a classless society and so to introduce an unacceptably utopian element into Catholic social thought. Likewise, they point to the danger of reducing Christianity to the level of a political movement that will almost inevitably lose its distinctive spiritual identity. Not least, they express the fear of indentifying the Church too exclusively with particular partisan political causes and so introducing divisive conflicts into an institution that exists to witness to the values of harmony and reconciliation.

Other commentators concede the existence of some dangers while maintaining a more generally favourable attitude. In common with the theologians of liberation themselves they seek to distinguish between Marxism as a materialistic philosophy, which they reject, and as a tool of social analysis which, in the Latin American context, is deemed to have particular relevance and explanatory power. From this vantage point, coming to terms with Marxism is viewed as yet one more example of a perennial Christian quest for intellectual frameworks through which the faith, within a changing world, may find contemporarily relevant expression. In particular it is maintained that Marxist critiques of the part played by ideology in perpetuating exploitative economic relationships can serve a useful, socially critical, function. They may, not least, unmask the extent to which the Church itself could have been co-opted into the service of privileged elites.

To the charge that liberation theology signifies an undue politicization of faith there comes the reply that adherence to consensual models of society has tended, in practice, to legitimize the interests of the dominant minorities who benefit from the status quo. Previous Church postures, it is argued, have either entailed overt politicization of a conservative kind or an ostensibly apolitical viewpoint which, in reality, implies tacit support for the established order. Proponents of such thinking argue that Latin American society is so divided that political choices become inescapable. For them the Christian task, within this context, is to espouse that 'preferential option for the poor' to which the gospel is deemed to point.[24] This, it is conceded, may mean forming alliances with secularized left-wing forces. But it is also asserted that these alliances have constantly to be kept under critical review in the light of overriding Christian commitments. The concept of 'the Kingdom' is proffered as a relatively autonomous vantage point from which to sustain authentically Christian commentary upon secular events and contingent ideological frameworks.

Such general approaches have gained currency as both effect and cause of a post-Medellín process whereby members of the clergy and of religious orders have increasingly been disposed to identify closely with Latin American society's least privileged elements. The Church's human and material resources remain substantially committed to such traditional activities as the education of established elites but work among urban shanty town dwellers, peasant groups and other socially disadvantaged sectors has acquired an unprecedentedly high priority. Indeed, the movement of ecclesiastical opinion testified to by these developments extends well beyond those obviously committed to elaborating liberation theology. Those clearly associated with the latter 'school' have helped to catalyse currents of opinion which have been widely felt within the Catholic community in, and even beyond, Latin America.[25]

ECCLESIASTICAL BASE COMMUNITIES

Of particular importance within this context has been the spread of 'ecclesiastical base communities'.[26] These novel sub-parochial groups have offered the universal Church an influential new model for the structuring of its relationships with surrounding societies. In Latin America they have been, in part, a fresh and flexible response to the region's chronic shortage of trained clerical leaders. They have enabled small locally-based groups of lay people to come together, often under their own auspices, for the purposes of worship, prayer and Bible study. Equally, they have helped to raise levels of religious awareness and commitment amid lower strata groups who have traditionally been on the Church's margins. Their impact can be exaggerated. Probably more Latin Americans have recently joined Protestant bodies than have become members of base communities. Nevertheless, they have provided unusually large numbers of the region's poor with previously missing opportunities for religious education and self-expression.

Such opportunities are primarily intended to satisfy conventional pastoral needs. However, they have also had significant 'spill over' effects of a more obviously social or political kind. Thus emphasis is frequently placed on relating Bible study to the everyday experience of participants with a view to increasing the latter's awareness of their situation and of their latent power to effect change. The result has sometimes been the enhancement of solidarity among locally disadvantaged groups and an increased willingness or capacity to demand concessions from traditionally unresponsive local elites. Likewise, ecclesiastical base communities have sometimes served as a previously absent 'training school' for genuinely local leaders – leaders able to assume responsibilities within the wider community. Initially such leaders may simply have played a part in the articulating of highly localized grievances. But sometimes they have been drawn into the service of broader based political or labour movements.

The long-term consequences of such developments are hard to gauge but, in the medium term, it seems likely that, in some areas, base communities have facilitated not insignificant changes in the local political culture. An increased sense of political efficacy has sometimes been created which could ultimately place at least a small question mark against those traditional clientilist forms of politics that, in the past, have depended upon the ability of upper strata 'patrons' to manipulate their largely acquiescent lower class 'clients'.

In the shorter run base communities have played a significant part in sustaining opposition to those authoritarian military regimes that have recently characterized much of Latin America. In the face of repression and bans on all conventional political activity they were often the only locally-based institutions capable of nurturing a spirit of resistance to official policies. They were also one of the initial recruiting grounds for more broadly based opposition forces. In Central America (as indicated in Chapter 8 of this volume) they have even played a part in mobilizing support for revolutionary movements.[27]

THE CHURCH AND OPPOSITION TO MILITARY GOVERNMENTS

The role played by base communities in such situations clearly cannot be divorced from more general Catholic reactions to recent authoritarian military governments. Initially there was a relatively widespread tendency for Church leaders to acquiesce in or even welcome takeovers by the armed forces. In Brazil and elsewhere the military was seen to rescue society from the disorder, political instability and economic mismanagement that large segments of middle- and upper-class opinion had come to associate with competitive or populist politics.[28] Particularly (though not only) in Chile, perceived Marxist threats worked to the same end.[29] In the latter case most of the local hierarchy at first maintained an officially correct attitude to their country's legitimately elected left-wing government but, especially as a consequence of developments in the educational sphere, Church–state relationships became progressively more fraught. In the same country the impact of political struggles upon the Church's own internal life was an additional cause of anxiety for the institution's leaders. The fairly substantial 'Christians for Socialism' group not only offered positive support to Salvador Allende's administration but also openly challenged their ecclesiastical superiors.[30] The net result was that even in the case of a relatively progressive episcopate there was little initial opposition to military intervention.

Longer term experience of military rule, however, significantly altered official Church responses. In Argentina most of the traditionally conservative hierarchy kept silent during the years of military dictatorship (1976–84).[31] The difficulties of the Peron era seem, in this instance, to have reinforced traditional conservative dispositions. But in Brazil and Chile (most notably) there were enough socially critical Churchmen to mount protests against violations of human rights and the socially damaging consequences of official economic policies. In Chile the Catholic Church, in co-operation with other religious bodies, took the lead in providing legal or other services for the victims of state oppression and in organizing relief for improverished working-class groups. In Brazil Church leaders went onto the offensive in support of workers, peasants and Indians whose welfare was sacrificed in the interests of rapid capital accumulation and growth. Equally, they offered support to local Church activists engaged in parallel opposition activities.

The process whereby official Church spokesmen moved to such positions was complex. At least four main factors were involved. First, it was partly a matter of responding to pressure from priests, members of religious orders and lay activists caught up, at local level, with the victims of social crises and, in many instances, radicalized by such experiences. Second, it was partly a matter of conservative ecclesiastical leaders at least partially redefining their attitudes in the light of both the Church's recently revised social teaching and unfolding political events. In some instances the priorities and methods of military regimes helped to clarify the underlying options and to give a fresh sense of urgency or relevance to the official Church analyses offered at Medellín. Not least, government-sanctioned attacks upon Church personnel induced some Church leaders to extend their protection to radical causes that might have previously met with some official ecclesiastical disapproval. Third, it was also a matter of new developments giving radical Church leaders, like Helda Camara, a fresh credibility. Governmental provocations helped to create a climate of opinion that enabled such prophetic figures to sieze or regain the initiative within the Church's decision-making bodies. Certainly, in Brazil's case, the local hierarchy, taken as a whole, emerged during the 1970s as one of the most socially and politically radical in the world. Finally, revised attitudes were, in some measure, the product of encouragement or pressure from the international ecclesiastical community. Thus, international Church networks served as a means of communicating fresh ideas and of disemminating re-interpreted values. Equally, the Vatican was generally supportive of hierarchies engaged in conflict with repressive military regimes. Such support gave added encouragement and authority to Churchmen concerned to challenge government policies.

The extent and efficacy of such challenges was always variable. Even in the Brazilian case significant numbers of Church leaders remained cautious or hostile in the face of the new ecclesiastical postures. A small minority associated themselves with those ultra conservative Catholic groups, like 'Tradition, Family and Property', which tended to support authoritarian regimes. Larger numbers remained wedded to apolitical postures and so, at least by implication, dissassociated themselves from more outspoken colleagues. Equally, there were variations in the scope and effectiveness of attempts to mobilize Catholic opinion in support of official positions. In Brazil, for example, there were indications of considerable discrepancies as between regions or dioceses. A significant factor was the capacity or willingness of diocesan bishops to offer sustained support to radical local groups or to assist in the elaboration of well-institutionalized political strategies.[32] Success in mobilizing popular support significantly depended upon the devising and nurturing of coherent programmes of mass pastoral activity. Where lack of resources or will inhibited the development of such official Church commitments, radical political activity tended to remain at the level of symbolic protest or was of a somewhat diffuse and localized kind.

The diocese of São Paulo (the most populous in the Catholic world) indicated what could be achieved when the necessary commitment was present. An outspoken and supportive archbishop, Dom Paulo Evaristo Arns, raised the creation of base communities, the defence of human rights and the cause of the poor to the top of the local Church's list of priorities. The Archbishop himself was responsible for relatively little in the way of pastoral or organizational innovation. Prior to his appointment significant numbers of Catholic activists had become committed to such enterprises and there had already been a substantial number of relevant grass roots initiatives. His contribution was to co-ordinate such activities, to extend their scope and to grant them a new officially recognized status. In the process he not only gave a new dynamism to work of this kind, within the diocese, but he also gave an important lead to the entire Brazilian Church. Because of the size and strategic significance of his diocese, within both Church and society, he was able to play an important

part in tilting the balance of forces within the national hierarchy
in a radical direction. The Archbishop's evident capacity to speak
for significant numbers of activists effectively mobilized in support
of a socially radical understanding of Christianity, helped to place
him in the vanguard of a 'popular Catholicism' whose influence was
widely and deeply felt.[33]

The medium-term effectiveness of this 'popular Catholicism' was
made evident in the course of the political processes which eventually
led to the termination of Brazil's experiment in military rule. The
military's inability to offer durable or widely acceptable solutions
to the country's chronic economic problems made the problem of
establishing its own political legitimacy ever more difficult. The
attempt to create viable new institutions, in place of those destroyed
after 1963, floundered in the face of mounting dissent. The resulting
pressures first induced some liberalization of the military regime
and, ultimately (in 1985) a return to civilian rule.

The Church's contribution to this process was substantial. At the
symbolic level its withholding of legitimacy from a regime ostensibly
dedicated to the defence of western Christendom helped significantly
to undermine the dictatorship's credibility. Ecclesiastical voices
raised in opposition to the social implications of the military's
economic priorities and to its record on human rights did much
to focus the attention of national and even international opinion
upon the dubious nature of many of the institution's claims. At a
more substantive level it played a significant part in the mobilization
and sustaining of mass popular opposition. This was partly a result
of the part played by base communities in promoting solidarity
amongst socially disadvantaged groups and in nurturing new forms
of lower strata leadership. Of perhaps even greater importance,
it was also a matter of placing its unprecedently comprehensive
organization at the disposal of wider opposition groupings and of
extending a protective umbrella to other elements within the society,
seeking to bring military rule to an end. In the face of repression,
and in the absence of alternative channels for the articulation of
dissent, the Church provided opposition groups with otherwise
unavailable opportunities for rallying their forces. Church personnel
and organizations were by no means exempt from official repression
but ecclesiastical structures had a relative autonomy or freedom of
manoeuvre that was denied to all other national institutions. The
result was an ability on the Church's part to provide opposition
forces with valuable organizational infrastructure. Equally, such

forces sought out alliances with Church spokesmen on a scale that was otherwise unlikely to have occurred. Thus, particularly in São Paulo, diocesan structures played an important role in facilitating the formation of unofficial trade unions and in sustaining illegal union activities. Church support was also an important factor in sustaining the *Partido dos Trabalhadores* (PT) which was formed in 1979 under the auspices of labour leaders and in competition with established clientelist parties. The Church was able to offer such groups a measure of 'sanctuary' and to provide them with valuable support from its own intellectual, organizational and pastoral resources.

THE QUESTION OF VIOLENCE

Such developments can be seen as a success for an essentially non-violent approach to politics. It is an approach that became associated in the public mind with figures like Helda Camara and Dom Paulo Evaristo Arns. Despite their radical analyses of Latin America's problems they remained opposed to those Catholic spokesmen who saw the use of force as a sometimes appropriate application of recently re-interpreted Christian commitments. Pope Paul VI, at Medellín, officially precluded violence from otherwise legitimate struggles for justice and this remains clearly the majority view among those anxious to implement the findings of that gathering. But those concerned have had to confront questions posed by that minority of radicalized Catholics who have seen violence, in response to the 'institutionalized violence' of established elites, as a sometimes appropriate option. The latter have drawn some sustenance from traditional Catholic understandings of 'the just war'. They found a pre-Medellín model in the person of Camilo Torres, the Colombian priest who joined a Marxist guerrilla organization and, in 1966, was killed in an encounter with his country's security forces.[34] Above all, they have felt themselves vindicated by recent Central American developments. They particularly point to Nicaragua as an example of a society where violent revolution seemed to be the only way of creating an obviously more just society.[35] On the other hand, most Catholic radicals have doubts about the long-term prospects of a polity created as a consequence of violent struggle. They would also, at a more pragmatic level, point to the proven capacity of armies, in such relatively developed countries as Brazil, to deal with insurrection and to the longer term success of more obviously peaceful strategies. Equally, they would point to the way in which violent challenges have frequently done more to consolidate support for conservative forces than to promote the cause of radical change.

CONSERVATIVE RESPONSES TO THE POST-MEDELLIN SITUATION

Anxieties about the prospect of violence have been not least among the factors underlying conservative reactions within the Catholic community to the more radical post-Medellín developments. Certainly, the most obviously politicized expressions of Catholicism have evoked a response from more cautious elements within the Church – elements who have regrouped with a view to stemming the radical tide.[36] Leadership for this exercise was particularly provided by members of the traditionally conservative Colombian hierarchy and, above all, by the Cardinal Archbishop, Alfonso Lopez Trujillo, of Medellín. He spearheaded a movement which led to the capturing of CELAM's bureaucracy by declared opponents of liberation theology. Advocates of the latter who had been in control of this important agency were nudged aside.

From this vantage point a continent-wide series of publications and seminars was launched in order to counter liberation theology's influence. Equally, Lopez Trujillo, in conjunction with the celebrated Belgian Jesuit, Father Vekermans (previously associated with Chile's Christian Democratic experiment) sought to develop alternative theological models. They highlighted what they saw as liberation theology's undue and potentially dangerous politicization of faith. They particularly perceived a danger of losing sight of the Church's identity and its transcendental claims amid divisive political struggles. They stressed the need of a Church less obviously committed to one particular side of the political argument and more clearly committed to conventionally defined pastoral tasks. They also stressed the danger of Christianity being 'diluted' through the influence of Marxist categories of thought and of being betrayed as a consequence of involvement in revolutionary politics. Their approach to the development of Latin American society continued to be essentially consensual and evolutionary in character. Within this framework the Church was seen as having a responsibility for urging the claims of social justice but more through its conventional preaching ministry than through political activism. Evangelism rather than the direct challenging of existing structures was asserted as the first priority. The latter task was seen to be more a matter for individual politically conscious Christians than for ecclesiastical institutions and their official spokesmen. Not least, they saw the growing strength of Protestant Churches as a particular challenge to evangelistic activity.

During the papacy of John Paul II supporters of such viewpoints have received considerable support from the Vatican. The Pope himself has made clear his opposition to overt clerical involvement in revolutionary or radical politics. He has also made plain his support for traditional understandings of clerical authority rather than the more communally orientated understandings associated with base communities and 'popular Catholicism'. Vatican officials, for their part, have been involved in attacks upon liberation theology and in the silencing of such exponents of the latter as Leonardo Boff.

THE THIRD CONFERENCE OF LATIN AMERICAN BISHOPS – PUEBLA, 1979[37]

Such a background clearly offered much encouragement to more conservative Latin American Churchmen and, as a consequence, they saw the Third Conference of Latin American Bishops, convened in Puebla (Mexico) in 1979, as a special opportunity for putting post-Medellín developments into reverse. By contrast with the earlier gathering, the agenda for Puebla was in the hands of a bureaucratic machine controlled by 'neo-conservatives'. Draft documents put before the conference clearly bear their imprint. Ultimately, however, conclusions were reached that did not so much represent a conservative triumph as a series of compromises between the main contending forces. Renewed stress was placed upon the Church's traditional pastoral responsibilities and upon the importance of evangelism. But adherence to the cause of justice was also strongly proclaimed and there remained a strong official commitment to a 'preferential option for the poor'. The more theologically or politically radical were clearly far too numerous, well-organized and confident to be wholly overriden. Their contribution to the conference's final outcome provided continuing legitimation for the more socially critical or politically radical exponents of Catholicism. They kept open the possibility of continuing debate about appropriate ecclesiastical responses to Latin America's social and political crises.

The course of such debates continues to be conditioned by complex interactions between changes in the Latin American Church's cultural, economic, social or political environment, on the one hand, and dilemmas arising out of the nature of the Roman Catholic Communion itself, on the other. In terms of the Church's environment there have been two things of particular importance. First, the retreat from military dictatorship which has recently characterized the region, necessarily entails some change in the expectations or pressures to which the institution must respond. In Brazil, most notably, the resumption of more obviously competitive politics has diminished the Church's perceived need to operate as a focus or enabler of political activity.[38] Given the opening up of alternative channels for political expression Church leaders have generally become more inclined to put some distance between themselves and the political arena. Equally, political leaders now have less incentive to seek out clerical allies. The net result appears to be some diminution of the relevance attached to that 'popular Catholicism' which, during the years of military rule, acquired a particular salience. Within the changed situation the Church may have rather more incentives or opportunities to focus upon the traditional pastoral activities preferred by conservative Churchmen.

The second important environmental factor points in the same direction – namely a continuing awareness of the inroads being made by non-Catholic religious bodies. Despite the considerable success of base communities it remains evident that, particularly among lower strata groups, the Catholic Church is losing ground to Protestant fundamentalist or Pentecostal groups. Their appeal seems to testify to the frequent inability of the local Roman Catholic community to meet pastoral needs or to convey a sense of community and personal significance to its potential members.

Such long-established Protestant bodies as the Lutheran Church, first established in the region by European immigrants, are no longer widely perceived as significant challenges. Post-Vatican II ecumenical developments have, to some extent, softened old divisions. The most important cleavages frequently cut across such frontiers. Conservative middle-class Protestants share many of the preoccupations of similarly situated Catholics. Equally, more radical Catholics have their Protestant allies. Such Protestant theologians as the Brazilian Ruben Alves and the Argentinian Jorge Bonino are in essentially the same camp as Catholic theologians of liberation. Catholics of all tendencies, however, can, in some measure, unite in opposition to the more recently established and often numerically stronger groups located on the fundamentalist wing of Protestantism. Conservative Catholics have particular cause to resent the frequently strident character of the latter's anti-Catholicism. Radical Catholics have cause to resist the sectarian, otherworldly or individualistic thrust of many of the groups in question. They also have reasons to believe that some Protestant groups are being promoted, for largely political reasons, as a form of 'antidote' to post-Medellín expressions of Catholicism. Especially among some United States-based evangelical groups there is a perception that the Roman Catholic Church in Latin America has been 'subverted' by Marxists and that, as a consequence, special effort has to be put into missionary endeavours within the region. United States foreign policy-makers and even some Latin American governments have encouraged the same groups for still more obviously political reasons. The net result is some willingness on the part of otherwise divided Catholics to unite in support of their own communion's evangelistic endeavours.[39]

Recent ecclesiastical debates have been further conditioned by dilemmas of a more purely internal kind. Thus, at the episcopal level, even the more radical leaders have been somewhat inhibited by their concern for the Church's own unity. As the institution's guardians, charged with the maintenance of inherited structures and orthodoxies, they have been made aware of the potentially divisive effects of some post-Medellín developments. On the one hand there is a concern that active pursuit of the 'preferential option for the poor' could alienate those more traditionally orientated middle- and upper-class groups upon whom the institution has, in the past, particularly depended. On the other hand there is the fear that the new decentralized understandings of ecclesiastical authority could become associated with institutionally damaging centrifugal forces.[40] The nature of such tendencies has been made graphically evident in Nicaragua where the hierarchy, supported by traditional elements, has come into open conflict with a 'People's Church' that has been generally supportive of the Sandinista cause. In less polarized situations within South America there remains the latent threat of Catholic base communities, subject to their own indigenous lay leadership, escaping from the effective control of nominal superiors.

Relations between the Church's leaders and its grass roots constituents have been further complicated by changing attitudes to the matter of unofficial 'folk Catholicism'.[41] The latter, as noted at the beginning of this chapter, might be deeply embedded in local cultures but have little directly to do with Orthodox institutionalized Catholicism. The Church's traditional attitude to such popular devotion tended, at best, to be one of benevolent aloofness. In the immediate aftermath of Vatican II these attitudes were, if anything, strengthened. The stress on '*aggiornamento*' and dialogue with the modern secular world sometimes tended to reinforce official reserve in the face of popular religiosity and its inherited culturally determined accretions. In more recent times, however, some priests, members of religious orders and lay activists, closely involved with poor lower strata communities, have come to perceive folk Catholicism as a potentially positive spiritual resource. They no longer see it solely as an indicator of superstitious fatalism but as a source of communal identity and meaning that can be deployed or built upon in the quest for more socially critical forms of religious consciousness. However, such 'dialogue' between official and popular religion can be seen by some institutional guardians as a further cause for anxiety. It may aggravate the fear of 'popular' locally-based Church communities with a propensity to slip beyond the control of official leaders. Such reservations, on the part of even relatively moderate Church spokesmen, tend further to strengthen the bargaining hand of their more obviously conservative colleagues who are resolved to check overtly radical Catholic impulses.

There are developments, however, which seem to point in a different direction. As the Puebla Conference made plain, some of the changes associated with the Medellín watershed have acquired such widespread currency as to be virtually irreversible. The once dominant conservative consensus has been shattered and, within the foreseeable future, there is no realistic prospect of it being restored. Even such leading theological conservatives as Cardinal Lopez Trujillo, who reject the analyses and methods of their more radical colleagues, share the now widespread view that the Church must manifest special concern for social justice and the needs of the poor. Those ultra conservative Catholic groups who have unapologetically favoured authoritarian solutions to Latin America's developmental and political problems, are not only in a small minority but also find themselves largely discredited as a consequence of their links with recently failed and brutal experiments in military rule.

Moreover, it is plain that the papacy, despite a reassertion of traditional theological and ecclesiological understandings, remains officially wedded to socially critical positions. John Paul II has restated an apparently apolitical definition of the clergy's role while attacking materialism of both the Marxist and capitalist varieties. Equally, as a papal visit to Chile exemplified, he has made plain his opposition to the methods and priorities of oppressive military regimes. Catholic defenders of human rights and ecclesiastical opponents of unbridled free market capitalism can, in large measure, legitimate themselves by reference to the Church's supreme teaching authority. They consequently remain open to the possibility of being drawn into political controversy and of crossing the necessarily uncertain line that separates the enunciation of general theological principles from attempts to influence specific public debates. Thus, even following the demise of military regimes, and despite a certain post-dictatorial process of disengagement from the political arena, Church leaders have continued to exercise a socially critical ministry. Early in 1988, for example, the Brazilian hierarchy denounced the corruption that they saw as a feature of their country's restored democracy and warned against what they perceived as its dangerous long-term social or political consequences.

Such an intervention suggests the impossibility of being simultaneously loyal to an apolitical vision of the clerical function and to the call to witness prophetically in the face of what the Church sees as social and political evils.[42] It also indicates the extent to which Catholic radicals have both reflected and strengthened broader movements of opinion within the Church. By remaining ultimately loyal to the institution, and by deliberately choosing to work within it, they have helped to focus widespread attention upon the causes to which they are committed. This has so modified external perceptions of the Church that, for example, the leadership of Cuba's revolutionary regime can now talk of Christians as potentially important allies in the quest for a radically changed and more just Latin American social order.[43] Equally, it has so modified the Church's own internal life that Latin American Catholics are now internationally regarded as an important source of ecclesiastical innovation. For example, South African Churchmen, locked in conflict with their government, have acknowledged a debt to liberation theology.[44] Likewise, the concept of the base community has become a universally influential model for Christians concerned with liturgical experimentation, pastoral renewal, enhanced lay participation and increased social relevance. Amid the tensions and debates engendered by the collapse of the old conservative

consensus the Latin American Church has made unprecedentedly
significant contributions to perennial debates about the relationships
of religion, society and politics.

CONCLUSION

General reflection upon the background to such developments
points to some tentative concluding observations concerning Latin
America's experience of interactions between the religious and
political domains. Thus it is apparent that from the time of the
conquest onwards the Church has been powerfully constrained or
conditioned by its social and political environment. In the context
of a history characterized by important underlying continuities, the
values, practices and institutions of Latin American Catholicism
even now bear the imprint of formative experiences associated with
colonial or early post-colonial society. Contemporary dilemmas in
the sphere of the Church's relationships with local cultures, societies
and states frequently have their roots in much earlier social and
political realities. In particular, Latin American Catholics continue
to wrestle with problems arising from the existence of a society which,
in principle, was an extension of Christendom but where, in practice,
the religion of the official Church tended to a disproportionate extent
to be an upper strata affair. Equally, twentieth-century changes in
the Church's life have frequently represented defensive responses to
changes, emanating from the surrounding community, that seemed
to imperil the traditional Christendom model of Church–society
relationships.

Institutional developments, from the 1920s onwards
have, in substantial measure, indicated the existence of attempts to
regain ground lost amid challenges to the traditional Christendom
concept and, to conserve as much as possible of those inherited
social frameworks with which the Church came to identify its
interests. It is noteworthy that significant institutional changes
were initially most evident in that society (namely Chile) where
the hegemony of traditional upper-class elites was most strongly
contested by secular left-wing parties and where the Church itself
met a particularly effective challenge from Pentecostal Churches
well-rooted amongst lower strata groups. It is equally significant
that the Catholic hierarchies generally most resistant to change
have either been in a country like Colombia, where traditional
elites have clung onto the political initiative, or in a nation like

Argentina, where the populist alternative to inherited arrangements tended to reinforce the Church's affinities or alliances with society's most conservative if not reactionary groups. In all such cases the initial willingness to contemplate change significantly depended on the existence of external incentives to re-assess traditional strategies. Equally, responses to such incentives have frequently been inspired by particular culturally conditioned understandings of the Church's relationship with society – understandings grounded in specific pre-existing political frameworks.

The traffic in influence between Church and society, however, has not been one way. Even in the context of particularly close co-operation between conservative political elites and senior Churchmen it has often been more a matter of complementary or converging rather than wholly identical interests. In Colombia, for example, the interests of the Church's traditional Conservative party allies were undoubtedly served by the creation of clerically inspired trade unions but, from the hierarchy's point of view, the primary objective was to secure their own influence within an emergent working class that was in the process of being politicized under anti-clerical auspices. Similarly, shifts of ideological or theological perspective in the Church have enabled the institution to act as a relatively autonomous catalyst, facilitator or agent of change within the wider community. While remaining necessarily constrained by the society within which it is embedded the Church has nevertheless sometimes manifested a simultaneous capacity to contribute creatively to the process of social or political change and to parallel public debates. Thus, late twentieth-century challenges to the Latin American Church precipitated re-assessments of Christianity's social and political implications that, in their turn, enabled many Churchmen actively to encourage changes in the political culture or to assist in the promotion of movements pressing for structural change. A new dynamic understanding of faith, and its potentialities within the political realm has been part effect and part cause of wider social transformations. The relationship between social change and changing images or understandings of God is a subject deserving a detailed treatment that lies beyond the scope of this work.[45] Here it suffices to suggest that contemporary Latin America's socio-economic and political crises were at least partly instrumental in directing the attention of some Christians to elements within their own tradition that had become obscured or lost. At the same time the retrieval of such insights enabled significant portions of the local Church to move away from socially conservative and towards socially radical or even prophetic positions. For students of the perennial tension between the socially conserving and the socially questioning dimensions of institutionalized Christianity, Latin America continues to provide a rich field for investigation.

NOTES

1   For a general history of the Church in the region see J.L. Mecham (1966), *Church and State in Latin America*, rev. edn, Chapel Hill: University of North Carolina Press.
2   On the subject of the Colombian Church see D.H. Levine (1981), *Religion and Politics in Latin America: The Catholic Church in Venezuela and Colombia*, Princeton: Princeton University Press. See also K.N. Medhurst (1984), *The Church and Labour in Colombia*, Manchester: Manchester University Press.
3   See R. Quirk (1973), *The Mexican Revolution and the Catholic Church, 1910–1929*, Bloomington: Indiana University Press.
4   See B.H. Smith (1982), *The Church and Politics in Chile: Challenges to modern Catholicism*, Princeton: Princeton University Press.
5   See T. Bruneau, M. Mooney and C. Gabriel (eds) (1984), *The Catholic Church and Religions in Latin America*, Montreal: Centre for Developing Area Studies.
6   See E. Pin (1963), *Elementos para una Sociología del Catolicismo*, Bogotá: Centro de Estudios Sociales.
7   See Medhurst, op. cit.
8   On the Brazilian Church, see S. Mainwaring (1986), *The Catholic Church and Politics in Brazil 1916–1985*, Stanford: Standford University Press. Also of importance is T. Bruneau (1982), *The Church in Brazil: The Politics of Religion*, Austin: University of Texas Press, and T. Bruneau (1974), *The Political Transformation of the Brazilian Catholic Church*, Cambridge: Cambridge University Press. On the Argentinian Church, see J.J. Kennedy (1958), *Catholicism, Nationalism and Democracy in Argentina*, South Bend, IN: University of Notre Dame Press.
9   For general studies of the Church's varying attempts to adjust to processes of social, economic and political change, see I. Vallier (1970), *Catholicism, Social Control and Modernization*, Englewood Cliffs: Prentice-Hall; F.C. Turner (1971), *Catholicism and Political Development in Latin America*, Chapel Hill: University of North Carolina Press; and H.A. Landsberger (ed.) (1970), *The Church and Social Change in Latin America*, South Bend: University of Notre Dame Press.
10   See Smith, op. cit., esp. pp.86–105.
11   On the general subject of Christian democracy in Latin America, see E.J. Williams (1967), *Latin American Christian Democratic Parties*, Knoxville: University of Tennessee Press. Chilean Christian democracy is the subject of a special study in M. Fleet (1985), *The Rise and Fall of Chilean Christian Democracy*, Princeton: Princeton University Press.

12 For the effects of this process on the Chilean Church see Smith, op. cit., pp.165–280.
13 See Mainwaring, op. cit., pp.43–75.
14 For examples of Helda Camara's own writings see H. Camara (1969), *The Church and Colonialism: the Betrayal of the Third World*, Danville: Sheed and Ward, and *The Desert is Fertile* (1974), Maryknoll, Orbis Books.
15 See E. de Kadt (1970), *Catholic Radicals in Brazil*, Oxford: Oxford University Press.
16 See P. Freire (1968), *Pedagogy of the Oppressed*, New York: Seabury Press. Also, P. Freire (1974), *Education for a Critical Consciousness*, New York: Seabury Press.
17 For the effects of military takeover on the Brazilian Church see Mainwaring, op. cit., pp.79–141.
18 The findings of the Council can be found in W.M. Abbott (ed.) (1966), *The Documents of Vatican II*, New York: American Press. For an account of the Council's proceedings, see R. Caporale (1964), *Vatican II: Last of the Councils*, Baltimore, MD: Helicon Press.
19 For an important discussion of different models of the Church see A. Dulles (1976), *Models of the Church*, Dublin: Gill & Macmillan.
20 For the documents published as a consequence of the conference at Medellín see CELAM (1970), *La Iglesia en la actual transformación de América Latina e la luz del Concilio*, 2 vols, Bogotá: CELAM. A commentary on the Council is to be found in H. Parada (1975), *Cronica de Medellín*, Bogotá: Indo American Press Service.
21 Liberation theology is the subject of a large and still growing literature. For some general discussions, together with an ample bibliography, see P. Berryman (1987), *Liberation Theology*, London: I.B. Tauris & Co. Ltd. Also see E.L. Cleary (1985), *Crisis and Change: The Church in Latin America Today*, Maryknoll, NY: Orbis Books, esp. pp.51–103.
22 For Gutiérrez's seminal work see G. Gutiérrez (1988), *A Theology of Liberation*, 15th Anniversary Edn, Maryknoll, NY: Orbis Books.
23 Critiques of liberation theology are contained in *C.E.L.A.M. Liberación: Diálogos en el C.E.L.A.M.* (1974), Bogotá: CELAM. Also, J.V. Schall (ed.) (1982), *Liberation Theology in Latin America*, San Francisco, CA: Ignatius Press. Recent Vatican inspired criticisms have especially come from Cardinal Ratzinger, see *National Catholic Reporter*, USA, 21 September 1984.
24 See J. Pixley and C. Boff (1986), *Opción por los Pobres*, Buenos Aires: Ediciones Paulinas.
25 On liberation theology's impact beyond Latin America see Berryman, op. cit., pp.162–78.
26 On the subject of ecclesiastical base communities see T. Bruneau (1979), 'Basic christian communities in Latin America: Their nature and significance (especially in Brazil)', in D.H. Levine (ed.), *Churches and Politics in Latin America*, Beverley Hills, CA: Sage, pp.111–34. Also Mainwaring, op. cit., Chaps 5–10 and Berryman, op. cit., pp.63–79.
27 On the Central American situation see P. Berryman (1984), *The Religious Roots of Rebellion: Christians in the Central American Revolutions*, London: SCM Press.

28 On the Brazilian military regime and the Church see Mainwaring, op. cit., pp.79–141. For a more general study of clashes between the Church and military regimes, see P. Lernoux (1982), *Cry of the People*, Harmondsworth Penguin Books.

29 On the parallel Chilean situation see Smith, op. cit., pp.283–335.

30 See J. Eagleson (ed.) (1975), *Christians and Socialism*, Maryknoll, NY: Orbis Books.

31 See E.F. Mignone (1988), *Witness to the Truth: The Complicity of Church and Dictatorship in Argentina*, Maryknoll, NY: Orbis Books.

32 See Bruneau, op. cit., esp. Chap. 6.

33 On the subject of Brazil's 'popular Church' see Mainwaring, op. cit., pp.145–253.

34 For Camilo Torre's writing see J. Gerassi (ed.) (1971), *Torres: Revolutionary Priest. The Complete Writings and Messages of Camilo Torres*, London: Jonathan Cape. For a biography see W.J. Broderick (1975), *Camilo Torres*, Garden City, NY: Doubleday.

35 Berryman, op. cit.

36 See Levine, op. cit. Also D.H. Levine (ed.) (1986), *Religion and Political Conflict in Latin America*, Chapel Hill: University of North Carolina Press.

37 The findings of the Puebla Conference were published in *Third General Conference of Latin American Bishops. Puebla* (1980), Middlegreen, Slough: St Paul Publications. For a commentary upon Puebla and its aftermath see P. Berryman (1979), 'What happened at Puebla' in D.H. Levine (ed.), *Churches and politics in Latin America*, Beverley Hills, CA: Sage, pp.55–86.

38 On the changing Brazilian situation see Mainwaring, op. cit., pp. 237–53.

39 For a very critical perspective on some Protestant activities in the region see D. Stoll (1982), *Fishers of Men or Founders of Empires*, London: Zed Press. Also, D. Stoll (1990), *Is Latin America Turning Protestant?*, Los Angeles: University of California Press.

40 An acute analysis of these dilemmas as they particularly affect the Chilean Church is contained in Smith, op. cit., Part I. For a generally more sympathetic view, see D. Martin (1990), *Tongues of Fire*, Oxford: Blackwell.

41 See D.H Levine (ed.) (1986), *Religion and Political Conflict in Latin America*, Chapel Hill: University of North Carolina Press.

42 It should be noted that such interventions have continued despite Vatican pressures to moderate the Brazilian Church's radicalism. Also, in 1988, for example, it was proposed to sub-divide the diocese of São Paulo in a move apparently designed to weaken the position of its head, Dom Paulo Evaristo Arns.

43 On the Church in Cuba see M. Crahan (1979), 'Salvation through Christ or Marx: Religion in revolutionary Cuba', in D.H. Levine (ed.) *Churches and Politics in Latin America*, Beverley Hills, CA: Sage, pp.238–66.

44 For example, see A. Boesak (1987), *Farewell to Innocence: A Socio-ethical Study on Black Theology and Power*, Maryknoll, NY: Orbis Books.

45 See, for example, D. Nicholls (1989), *Deity and Domination: Images of God and the State in the Nineteenth and Twentieth Centiries*, London: Routledge.

Chapter 8

Politics and religion in Central America:
a case study of El Salvador

Jennifer Pearce

CHURCH AND STATE AT THE CROSSROADS

'Religion' and 'politics' have never been entirely separate spheres of social existence in the history of western Christianity. From the days of Constantine, the institution of the Church has been deeply involved in political life. The power of the system of beliefs it represents, has enabled the Church to build a great spiritual system of authority with enormous secular power and influence. Long before 'liberation theology' emerged in Latin America, 'religion', it might be argued, was already the 'pursuit of politics by other means'.

The precise relationship between the two is the subject of intense debate. Marxists have produced elaborate theories on the class basis of the Church and religious ideology[1] and non-Marxists have sought to treat the two spheres of politics and religion somewhat independently but to stress their close relationship. Levine writes, for instance, 'religion and politics necessarily impinge on one another; their goals and structures overlap and run together as a matter of course'.[2] But what has intrigued social scientists of all persuasions in recent years is that, particularly in the Third World, the 'politics' with which the Church has traditionally been associated and which religious values have sought to sustain, has shifted dramatically. Durkheim, Marx, Weber and a host of other political thinkers of the nineteenth and early twentieth century witnessed a deeply conservative Church, engaged in constant battle against liberal, scientific, socialist and other alternative belief systems. They could hardly see the Church as anything but a reactionary force.

Today's Church, however, has divided on the major social questions of our age. More than that, significant sectors of the church have become agents, catalysts and even protagonists in the pursuit of radical social change. Priests, members of religious orders, and, in some countries, bishops, have taken an 'option for the poor', often an overt challenge to those who control the state in particular countries. Marx, who saw religion as an 'opium', a generator of passivity, would not recognize the popular Church of the Philippines or El Salvador, where it has helped mobilize people into political activism in a way many left-wing political parties in industrial societies would dream of.

A Church which is no longer unified and which is unable to fulfil its most valuable function to the state – the transmission of values conducive to order and respect for authority – risks its privileged position in the eyes of the state. When a sector of that Church advocates that the Church should no longer serve the state but the poor, as it has in most countries of Central America, the relationship of Church and state is in deep crisis, with far-reaching implications for the social order. Pope John Paul II recognizes this fact, and is on the offensive to halt the advance of those associated with liberation theology. The political authorities have also recognized the problem. The Central Intelligence Agency under the Reagan administration promoted a right-wing evangelical Protestantism in Central America, which preached non-political responses to hunger and injustice, once so successfully advocated by the Catholic Church in the region. Clearly, the relationship of religion to politics, of the Church to the state in Central America, is at a crossroads; the outcome is not yet clear.

The countries of Central America share many similarities of socio-economic development, but there is considerable variation in the experiences of the Catholic Church in each. This is inevitable if one considers the Church to be an institution in constant interaction with the material reality of which it is part, influenced by it and in turn influencing it. The Churches of Central America are both reflecting and acting upon the deep crisis in the region, which has reached different points in each country.

Throughout the region, capitalism has failed to produce the means of life for the majority of the people. Traditional power structures based on alliances between a small ruling class, the armed forces, the United States and, until the last two decades, the Catholic Church, are now seriously challenged. Guerrilla groups, new social movements, the breakdown of traditional ideologies and emergence of powerful new influences, have offered the excluded majority alternatives to their misery.

The Church in Central America has not just been caught up in the social conflagration which has swept the region, and in particular, Nicaragua and El Salvador over the last decade, it has openly participated in it – on both sides. Although many have questioned the Church's political neutrality in the past, this is the guise under which it has always tried to operate. This has now clearly been abandoned in Central America. Today the Church is a political actor in a direct sense, divided in its allegiances, with each side associating its religious understanding with a set of political beliefs. It is apparent in Central America that religion and politics have taken on quite distinct meanings for different sectors of the Church. Nicaragua and El Salvador illustrate this very clearly.

In Nicaragua, the radical clergy formed part of the Sandinista government, until its electoral defeat in early 1990. During that period these clergy's conservative superiors, often backed by the Vatican, waged a fierce battle from outside the government against the Sandinista social experiment. Indeed, the Archbishop of Managua, Mgr Obando y Bravo was considered the leading figure of the political opposition in that country; he associates his religion with a certain type of anti-communist political praxis. The Jesuits and other religions in the Sandinista government, on the other hand, came to share a system of political values in which Christian humanism, nationalism and Marxism intermingled to provide a unique, often misunderstood, ideology of government. For them, religion relates to politics in a way inconceivable to the Archbishop, challenging the hierarchical and traditional structures of the Church – and society as a whole – in a very political sphere. This challenging, active Christianity, which focuses on 'consciousness raising' (*concientización*) is diametrically opposed to the Christianity which sought to promote passive allegiance to the state.

In El Salvador, it is the radical Church which remains in opposition to the government, engaged in a variety of activities in pursuit of the shared goal of a more just social order. This chapter will focus on the changing role of the Church in El Salvador as one of the most illuminating examples of shifting definitions of the relationship of religion to politics in the late twentieth century. It will be particularly concerned with the way sectors of the Church have transferred allegiance from the state to grass roots Christian communities often in direct opposition to the state as well as the hierarchy of the Church. It offers one of the most interesting experiences available to social scientists of what happens when sectors of the Church shift their allegiance from the rulers to the ruled.

THE CHURCH, THE STATE AND THE PEOPLE IN EL SALVADOR: AN HISTORICAL PERSPECTIVE

Historians of the Latin American Church have tended to concentrate on the Church's relations with the state. But the Church has always had to relate itself to both the state and the people. Many writers have drawn attention to the close relationship it developed with the former, few have highlighted the problematic relationship it has frequently had with the latter. The 'people' only seem to enter Latin American Church history with the twentieth century, when urbanization, industrialization and external and internal migration brought the 'masses' into the political arena and under the influence of ideologies in direct competition with Catholicism.

In El Salvador, where these processes of 'modernization' were delayed somewhat, and were never as far-reaching as the more advanced societies of Latin America, the Church did not have to confront the problems raised by them until the 1960s. Prior to that, the Salvadorean Church was the Church of the ruling elite, its institutional interests closely identified with the status quo. Its relationship with the peasant communities, which were and are its major constituency, remained ambivalent and complex. The reasons for this date from the Conquest itself, the process of conversion in Central America and the subsequent organization of peasant society.

Mass conversion of the indigenous population of Central America by the Spanish was as much a political necessity of the Conquest as a spiritual one. Acceptance of the beliefs and values of the conquerors enormously facilitated control of the vanquished. The background to the Conquest, it should be recalled, was the process known as the *Reconquista* (Reconquest) in the Iberian peninsula. The Iberian Kingdoms had won back former Christian territory from the Islamic invaders. The success of the enterprise strengthened the view that faith could be propagated by military means and that commitment to one religion should be the foundation of the modern state.

Significant also for the future role of the Church in Latin America, was the extent to which the state came to control it. The worldly Popes of the sixteenth century were intensely preoccupied with European politics and their own wealth and power. They could not spread the faith to the New World alone. Spiritual conquest of the Indies would always have to await the establishment of Spanish authority through military and political conquest. After 1517, the rise of Protestantism posed a new threat and gave further impetus to expanding the Catholic empire through conversion of Indian souls. For these and other reasons Popes gave the Crown of Castile unprecedented control over the life of the Church in the new territories.

The Church legitimized the Conquest, while obliging the Catholic monarchs to promote the conversion of the conquered peoples and protect the interests of the Church. The Crown gained the right to present candidates for ecclesiastical appointment (the *Patronato*), paid wages and built churches, monasteries and hospitals and authorized the passage of Church personnel to the Indies. 'The Church in America had a practical mission assigned to it' writes the historian Josep M. Barnadas, 'it was to hasten Indian submission and Europeanization and to preach loyalty to the crown of Castile. Any resistance by the church to the fulfilment of this function was viewed as a political problem and dealt with accordingly'.[3]

As a result, the history of the Church during the colonial period is one of increasing identification with, and subservience to, the state. As the Church became institutionalized, it became richer, initially through the bequests of settlers and the levy of tithes, and more conservative. The Jesuits alone stood out for some independence from the Spanish Crown, but they were expelled in the eighteenth century. Inevitably therefore, when the legitimacy of the colonial state was challenged by the independence movement in the late eighteenth century, the Church's authority was also questioned. But, unlike the former, the Church survived Independence, though considerably weakened and at the centre of bitter political conflicts between anti-clerical liberals and conservative forces.

THE CHURCH AND THE LIBERAL STATE

The confrontation between the Church and the state in the nineteenth century did not in any sense mean the neutralization or annihilation of the one by the other. The Church had sufficient flexibility to replace itself in the new economic, social and political order. In this way, the Church has not only shaped historical Central American reality but the latter has shaped the Church. 'This mutual influence of reality on the Church and the Church on reality, constitutes the basis of the political dimension of the Church'.[4]

The liberals were intent on building a modern secular state in which loyalties were first and foremost to the nation not to any corporate remnants of the colonial era such as the Church. Progress meant liberating the individual from past prejudices and entrenched privilege. The Church was seen to embody both. Its wealth and political power made it, in the minds of many liberal politicians, a rival authority to that of the nation-state they were building and they determined to destroy both. This did not necessarily mean they were anti-religious as such, but they were anti-clerical to the extent that the Church was an obstacle to their modernizing project.

The Church turned to its natural allies, the conservative politicians, in search of a political defence. The conservatives, like the liberals, essentially represented a conflicting economic interest. Unlike the liberals, however, the conservatives believed that the Church held the social fabric together, and its defence was a defence of order over anarchy. But history in El Salvador was on the side of the modernizers; the conservatives proved incapable of resolving the prolonged economic and institutional crisis of the post-Independence period. The liberals, on the other hand, took advantage of the land's suitability for coffee production and growing European demand for the commodity. They expelled the peasant communities who had traditionally farmed the land, and created a powerful – and secular – state, representative of the rising coffee bourgeoisie.

The Church tried in vain to defend its independence and sovereignty, but the liberal state could not tolerate such a challenge to its authority. The rise of the secular state stripped the Church of its monopoly in the fields of education, marriage and burials, reducing its income and political influence. But its presence within civil society, as opposed to the institutions of the state, remained strong. For the peasants, displaced from their land by the rise of coffee, religious faith was as important as ever, if not more so. Ecclesiastical power, not religion as such, had come under attack. The debates and battles on the issue of that power took place mainly within a small elite of wealthy individuals, while the ordinary people carried on their time-honoured practices of worship.

The Church did not give up its hopes of regaining its privileged position in the state, recognized by the constitution. But it considered that its best means of attaining such an end was through accommodation to the liberal state, and the establishment of family and personal connections to strengthen its influence. Thus, although it was the coffee bourgeoisie which had stripped it of its institutional power, the Church soon chose to adapt itself to the new status quo and to give it full support.

The Church was an ideal vehicle for giving the state the legitimacy which the daily hardship suffered by those excluded from the economic benefits of growth under the coffee (and later cotton) boom would surely have denied it. It provided the belief-system, the rituals, the comfort of priests, saints and myths, which made an unjust world less bleak and incomprehensible for a people whose ancestors had explained the vicissitudes of nature in almost the same way. The Church was clearly aware of the social problems in the country, but it called for resignation, humility and suffering.

For the Church, however, its support for the ruling order was 'apolitical'; 'politics' was the act of opposing that order. The clergy were closely watched for any imprudence which might have caused embarrassment to the state, assisted by the fact that canon law forbade them to participate in politics. Similarly the Catholic press was strictly censored to avoid offence to anyone in government.

In 1932, the peasants working on El Salvador's coffee estates rebelled. The rebellion was crushed mercilessly and was followed by the establishment of a rigorous system of social control based on the army and local police forces. This succeeded in restoring order to the countryside and the peasants returned to lives of passivity and hardship. The coffee boom was followed in the 1950s by a cotton boom and in the 1960s by a sugar boom, as landowners tried to diversify and modernize. Cotton took over the lands of the Pacific coast, once again forcing peasant farmers off the land. Landowners throughout the country began to expel peasants from the small plots on their estates which they had been given in exchange for their labour. The pool of landless peasants provided sufficient cheap labour for the little work needed for most of the year. Labour is only in real demand during harvest periods in El Salvador, and there were enough peasants increasingly unable to survive on their subsistence plots to provide the harvest labour as required. The landless population grew from 11 per cent of the active rural population in 1961 to 41 per cent in 1975. A war between Honduras and El Salvador in 1969 had resulted in the expulsion of those Salvadoreans who had gone there in search of the means of life, and their return increased the pressure on the land. Manufacturing industry developed in El Salvador in the 1960s, but failed to produce sufficient jobs for those forced off the land. People flooded to the cities, but most ended up in the impoverished informal sector, living in shacks in sprawling shanty towns.

The most disadvantaged sector of the population was the landless and land poor (those with less than one hectare of land), who by 1975 comprised an estimated 75 per cent of the rural population (60 per cent of the population of El Salvador can be called rural). They saw their incomes decline between 1961 and 1975 to below the minimum level of subsistence.

Indices of poverty, however, do not necessarily have a political impact. What is of interest is how rural discontent in El Salvador translated into a peasant movement, which by the late 1970s was the embryo of arguably the most effective guerrilla movement Latin America has seen, and which has only been prevented from taking power by vast injections of US military aid and expertise. More pertinent to the discussion of this chapter, is the role the Church has played in this process. In particular how, within the heart of the conservative Church described hitherto, a radical and politically challenging wing emerged which has contributed to the growth of an extraordinary popular movement.

THE NEW PASTORALISM

In December 1968 I was asked to take Suchitoto parish for a while. The message of Medellín was very familiar to me. I immediately started to try and inform my people about the message from Medellín, and to think about the possibilities of organizing Christian 'base communities'. . . . In 1970 we looked at baptism, the role of prophets and priests, and applied our study to the socio-economic realities of El Salvador. The peasants discovered they were not kings, they were slaves. So we discussed how to have domain of the land in order to be lords not slaves, and we discovered that the way was through land reform.

Jose Alas, Salvadorean priest[5]

The shift in the Salvadorean Church has been highly dependent on the attitudes of individuals within the hierarchy, in particular the Archbishop of San Salvador. The Archdiocese has been at the forefront in promoting the Church's social role. Archbishop Luis Chavez y Gonzalez, who occupied the Archbishopric from 1939 to 1977, was a humane man with a sense of social justice which he displayed even before the Vatican began to re-evaluate the social role of the Church in the 1960s. He had taken a keen interest in Catholic Action, but he went further, promoting co-operatives in the 1950s in an effort to find ways of improving the lives of the peasants, founding parish schools and supporting social communication media in the Archdiocese. He also encouraged his most able priests to go abroad to study, and with the help of the Jesuits established an important seminary where many priests from Central America came for training. The Second Vatican Council, and subsequently the meeting of Latin American bishops at the Medellín Conference, were to help him considerably to strengthen and develop this early work. His concern with social issues and his openness to change were crucial to the early development and success of the movement for pastoral renewal within the Salvadorean Church. It was considerably reinforced by his successor, Archbishop Romero. Underlying the efforts of both Archbishops to re-examine the Church's role has been the unfolding social crisis in the country: the 'mutual influence of reality on the Church and the Church on reality'.

The 1960s was a decade of ferment everywhere. In Latin America, the decade opened with the success of the Cuban Revolution, launching intense debates on issues of justice, oppression and dependency throughout the continent. The Church was inevitably caught up in the process. The new sense of social concern emerging in the Church was immensely strengthened when the Second Vatican Council (Vatican II), inaugurated by Pope John XXIII in 1962, began a far-reaching re-evaluation of the role of the Church in the modern world. The Church abandoned its claim to be the exclusive means of salvation and with it the belief that bringing people to salvation or a 'state of grace' was its only role. The Church's purpose was to offer the means of a more meaningful and dignified human life. The idea that the Church should identify itself unquestioningly with western capitalism was also abandoned, and in the 1963 encyclical, *Pacem in terris*, the possible existence of 'good and commendable elements' in Communism was recognized.

This had a huge impact on the Latin America clergy. In 1968, the bishops of Latin America met in Medellín to apply Vatican II to Latin America. It was at Medellín that the Latin American Church took its option for the poor, condemning dictatorship, exploitation, the role of foreign capital and militarism. But, as Philip Berryman points out, more important than the statements emanating from Medellín was what he calls the 'Medellín method'.[6]

The bishops used a threefold structure for organizing their discussion: reality/reflection/pastoral consequences. The discussion of 'national reality' now became a common starting point for pastoral meetings. The material world and the fate of all souls in it was now a prime concern of Catholics.

Debates on the implications of Medellín became intense throughout the Churches of Latin America. Responses varied, from those who immediately launched the counter-attack, to those who agreed with some of its principles but wished to move gradually on them, and those who saw them as a call to political action. In El Salvador, a priest called José Alas began to implement the ideas in the late 1960s in Suchitoto parish, in the Archdiocese. Alas had studied with the influential Bishop of Riobamba in Quito, and he was anxious to implement the organizational methods of basic Christian communities he had learned there. He, indeed, established the first such communities in El Salvador. These brought together people from a village or district to discuss and interpret the Bible according to their social reality. As peasant unions were illegal in El Salvador, the peasants had remained isolated and atomized. The base communities were the first opportunity they had had to meet together, discuss their situation and work out collective solutions.

The political implications of this approach to pastoral work were evident in this early experiment. The local peasants were angry at the way two landowners were speculating with land in the area. Some 3,000 peasants marched to one of the landowner's estates and 400 later went to San Salvador, the first such demonstration since 1932. José Alas went with them and got the support of the Archbishop. The following year, Alas presented the Church's position at a conference on agrarian reform. Hours after his presentation he was abducted by men in civilian clothes, beaten, drugged and left naked on the edge of a cliff just outside San Salvador. This response of the authorities to the non-establishment Church was just the first, and in hindsight relatively restrained, sign of what was to come as his example was followed.

In 1970, the Archdiocese helped organize a national pastoral week. This would begin with a study of the socio-economic situation of the country, followed by theological reflection. The response of the hierarchy to the event showed the schism that was opening up within the Church. In the end, from the hierarchy, only Archbishop Chavez and his auxiliary, Bishop Rivera, participated in all five days of the event, together with 123 priests, clerical and lay workers from all over the country. Oscar Romero, appointed in 1970 as auxiliary Bishop to Archbishop Chavez, participated for some of the time. The final document caused great controversy with the bishops who had not attended, for it strongly criticized the existing work of the Church. It called for the establishment of base communities, and the formation of 'leaders who will be not only catechists but responsible individuals, dedicated to the integral development of the human person and the formation of communities'. These lay pastoral agents were to be of enormous importance to the future political life of the country. The declaration of the pastoral week was the first official recognition that lay people could participate in the spiritual work of the Salvadorean Church. It marked a complete rupture with the elitism of the traditional Church.

The involvement of lay people in Church functions was also a way of extending the Church's reach, given the small number of priests to people. But now many members of the religious orders went into the rural areas, where they had never worked, to implement the new pastoralism. Christian base communities were organized in many parts of the country, particularly in the parishes of the Archdiocese. One of the best documented experiences is that of the Jesuits in Aguilares. Rutilio Grande led the team. He had also spent some months with the Bishop of Riobamba in the Pastoral Institute in Ecuador. The work was carried out very methodically. The parish was divided up and two-week missions sent to each part during which the team lived and ate with the peasants and gathered data. It was not long before base communities were set up throughout the area, with lay leaders, or Delegates of the Word as they were also called, in each.

In May 1973, only eight months after the parish team had arrived, the 1,600 members of the local La Cabana sugar mill went on strike and refused to accept wages which they claimed were lower than they had been promised. The strike was spontaneous, it had nothing to do with the parish team, but most of its leading participants were Delegates of the Word. Shortly afterwards, the Association of Christian Peasants (FECCAS), which hitherto had been a docile grouping of peasants who mostly mobilized support for the Christian Democrat party, took on new life. It broke its ties with the party, mobilizing peasants around what, in the context of El Salvador, were radical demands for cheaper fertilizers, access to credit and higher wages on the plantation. In the neighbouring department of Chalatenango, where other priests had been active, the Union of Rural Workers (UTC) was formed in 1974. These peasant organizations heralded the emergence of a popular movement which in many respects has been unique in Latin America.

THE CHURCH AS CATALYST

The relationship between experience of God and witness to a life of justice is all the more clear in Latin America because structural injustice is given implicit or explicit theological sanction. The reigning structures – capitalism and national security in their many forms – operate as true deities because they claim characteristics and their own cult. They are deities because they claim characteristics that belong to God also: ultimateness, definitiveness, and untouchability, they have their own cult because they demand the daily sacrificing of those who oppose them.

. . . Since the reality of our continent makes it abundantly clear that there is no middle ground between life and death, grace and sin, justice and injustice, it is clear that in this matter the objective witness of the church cannot be any sort of third-way compromise.

Jon Sobrino, Salvadorean theologian

What made me first realize the path of our farmworkers union was when I compared the conditions we were living in with those that I saw in the Scriptures; the situation of the Israelites for example . . . where Moses had to struggle to take them out of Egypt to the Promised Land . . . then I compared it with the situation of slavery in which we were living. For example, when we asked for changes in work rates on the plantations, instead of reducing them for us, the following day they increased it, just like the Pharaoh did with the Hebrew people making bricks, right? . . . Our struggle is the same; Moses and his people had to cross the desert, as we are crossing one right now; and for me, I find that we are crossing a desert full of a thousand hardships, of hunger, misery and of exploitation.

Vidal, Salvadorean peasant[7]

The church people who conveyed the message of the new pastoralism to the poor did not set out with a clear political objective. A radical group did emerge within the Church, who came to believe that the Church should not just support the right to organize but should actively participate in the organizations the people built. These radicals were an important force in maintaining the momentum of the Church's commitment to the poor, but most of the clergy were more cautious. Many accepted Archbishop Chavez's view that the Church's role was to 'accompany' the people, not to take its own political stance, and they found it very problematic when the people demanded greater involvement. But whatever its objectives, there was no denying that the willingness of the popular Church to 'give the Bible back to the people' had revolutionary political implications.

The ideological universe which had governed the lives of the people for centuries, that mixture of Indian mysticism and ritualized Catholicism, gradually broke down. The new message of the priests accorded with the experience and material reality of the people. It demanded action, not passivity. And it did not provide ready-made answers and stifle thought and creativity; it was aimed at assisting the peasants to take control of their lives for the first time. The educational methods adapted from Paulo Freire were about awareness-building, education for organization, 'empowering people'. The Delegates of the Word were elected by the people themselves, giving the people confidence and responsibility for their own destiny. The organizational method of the base communities brought people together in the rural parishes in a structured way as never before, and the experience was repeated among the urban poor of San Salvador.

The radical Church was only one of the catalysts operating in El Salvador, however. It could help break down the negative effect of the traditional Church and begin to bring people together, but it could not take the resulting movement very far politically. That was the work of the Marxist political–military organizations in El Salvador. It was they who channelled the new popular movement into a political challenge to the state. And just as the Church had gone through much debate and soul-searching about the relationship of Christianity to Marxism, so the Marxists had to come to terms with the role that radical Christianity played in the movement they aspired to lead. Indeed, the Popular Liberation Forces (FPL), the largest of the political–military organizations during the 1970s, wrote a letter to the progressive clergy in 1975, in which it acknowledged the role of Christians in the revolution.

The relationship between the popular or 'mass' organizations as they were called (peasant and worker unions, associations of student and shanty town dwellers), the guerrilla movements and the Church was never to be unproblematic.[8] But the early work of the Church in consciousness-raising, encouraging collective action and leadership training, contributed significantly to the unique character of the Salvadorean popular movement. It enabled a movement to grow up which, in the first instance, operated independently of the political–military organizations. It only turned to them after experience in organizing around very basic demands resulted in harsh repression of the peasant communities, forcing those communities into direct confrontation with the state. This was not a movement mobilized by outsiders in favour of a political project defined by urban intellectuals; it was a movement with traditions, experience and leaders of its own. One of the main contributions of the political–military organizations was to link the different sectors of the population engaged in struggle, forging a strong national movement out of local and sectoral interests. But the reaction of the Salvadorean state was ferocious and the radical Churchmen soon became victim to it.

THE CHURCH EMBATTLED

I am very afraid that, very soon, the Bible and the Gospel will not be able to enter our frontiers. Only the covers will reach us, as its pages are subversive – against sin, of course. . . . If Jesus of Nazareth was to return, as in that time, coming down from Galilee to Judea, that is, from Chalatenango to San Salvador, I dare say that he would not get as far as Apopa with his preachings and actions. . . . They would stop him in Guazapa and jail him there.
Rutilio Grande[9]

Archbishop Chavez was deeply distrusted by the oligarchy for his increasingly open support of the poor and their right to organize. A second pastoral week had been organized for the Archdiocese in 1976 which evaluated the new pastoral work in the pursuit of a more unified pastoral line. It was attended by representatives of the many Christian base communities now active in the urban and rural parishes of the Archdiocese. But the right-wing in the country was now organizing to halt the growth of what was seen as a subversive tide sweeping the countryside. Between November 1976 and May 1977 there was a press campaign against the Church which included sixty-three paid adverts and thirty-two editorials against the Church. A number of priests were arrested, tortured and expelled from the country in the same period. In 1977, the Archbishop retired, and the Right manoeuvred to ensure that his auxiliary, Bishop Rivera did not succeed him. The final choice, Oscar Romero was considered a safe conservative. It was not long, however, before the new Archbishop became a significant figure in the country's rapidly unfolding political crisis.

The murder of Rutilio Grande, whom Romero had known and deeply respected, just three weeks after the Archbishop had taken office, had a deep effect on him. He refused to participate in government functions until the killing was investigated. In the face of the mounting repression, the Archbishop gave increasing support to the cause of the poor. His Sunday sermon was broadcast on the Archdiocesan radio YSAX and attracted large audiences. It was a kind of 'oral newspaper' in a country where almost all the communications media were in the hands of the wealthy minority. They would begin with theological teaching on the scripture readings of the day, these would then be related to the reality of El Salvador and, finally, there would be Church announcements, including a reading of documented cases of persons who had been killed, tortured or 'disappeared'. If there was an important event, Romero would produce a pastoral position on it.

Right-wing death squads were now operating freely in the country, identifying and killing leaders of the popular movement and those Church people associated with them. Indeed, the Right held the Church responsible for the emergence of such a movement in the first place; one death squad circulated handbills which read 'Be a Patriot, Kill a Priest'. The Jesuits were told in 1977 that if they did not leave the country in thirty days, they would be systematically killed. The situation was so serious that the US Congress held hearings in 1977 on the persecution of the Church in the country.

The Salvadorean Church was now deeply divided, but the strength of the popular movement in the 1970s, the progressive stance of the two Archbishops, and the energy and creativity of the radical clergy, put the latter in the acendency during these years. The violent reaction of the ruling class, who promoted the death squads in an effort to break the momentum of the radical movement, was given added virulence by their belief that the Church had betrayed them. The Church which had once helped justify their existence, now gave legitimacy to those who wanted to destroy their power; the Church, in short, had deserted the state. Jon Sobrino writes:

Latin American governments and the economic powers that represent them maintain that these countries are officially or unofficially 'Catholic', even when other kinds of 'Christian' communities are allowed. It is often in the interest of people in government to put in an appearance at religious events in order to give public, symbolic expression to the 'Catholicism'. In these countries a great deal of emphasis is placed on strictly religious terms such as 'God', 'the Almighty', 'the Supreme Maker', or on symbols that are religious in origin, such as 'fatherland' and 'freedom'. The important thing is to get into people's minds a sense that there is a religious absolute because this same sense can subsequently be extended to other absolutes such as private property, the state, and so on. If the state is to maintain its unqualified power the people must have a sense of the absolute. For this reason the state values the use of religious symbols of the absolute, which it can manipulate; it also favours and promotes everything to do with religion. . .that will help maintain an uncritical sense of the absolute. . . .The purpose of all this is to defend special interests under the cloak of a defence of 'Western Christian civilization'. The Catholic religion is thus seen as providing religious justification for political institutions, while an appeal to the complete incompatibility of communism and religion makes it possible to defend any and every attack on real or supposed communists as a defence of religion. Something new has made its appearance in the Church of Latin America. . . . Ever since Medellín there has been a movement in which absolute realities and their symbols are expressed with increasing clarity through historical meditations, especially the human person and, more concretely, the oppressed. The absolute that is 'God' is translated into another absolute, 'the kingdom of God', which includes God but also includes and treats as an absolute the reign of justice.[10]

The country was heading towards civil war by the end of the 1970s. The violence of the government forces compelled the popular movement to defend itself. The Church was caught up in deep moral dilemmas of whether violence was justified, and how far the Church should get directly involved in the unfolding struggle. Archbishop Romero, at the centre of the debates, produced a pastoral letter in 1978 on the issue of the relationship of the Church to the popular movement, supporting the right of the poor peasants to organize.

The response from the conservative bishops illustrated that the polarization in the country as a whole was now matched by that in the Church. The four bishops condemned the peasant unions, FECCAS and the UTC, and Marxist–Leninist organizations, declaring that priests should not collaborate directly or indirectly with them.

In March 1980, Archbishop Romero was assassinated. He had become a truly subversive figure in the eyes of the state. His fourth and last pastoral letter of August 1979 had referred to Pope Paul VI's statement on the right to insurrection in the 'very exceptional case of evident and prolonged tyranny'. His death brought over 200,000 people onto the streets of San Salvador to mourn and protest. But his death was also to mark a perceptible shift in the balance of forces within the Church. The Right was now on the counter-attack, with the backing of the US Administration and, ultimately, the Vatican.

CONCLUSIONS

In being honest about reality in Latin America, in refusing to manipulate the truth about antilife on the continent, and in not closing its ears to the cry for life rising from the entrails of the continent and to the longing for liberation, the Church is refusing to manipulate God. It allows him to be God. In so doing the Church is able to make the great act of faith in a God of life and justice.[11]

If the 1970s was the decade of the popular movement and its allies in the popular Church, the 1980s saw the outbreak of civil war and a strong counter-offensive by the state and its allies in the traditional Church. By the beginning of the decade, the popular movement had a guerrilla army, the Farabundo Martí National Movement for Liberation. But it was formed very hastily, as the pace of events quickened during 1980 and the repression grew. Many of the cadres of the popular movement went into the military wing of the struggle, weakening the political organizations which had been such a powerful force for mobilizing people in the 1970s. The movement in the cities in particular was weakened, and the guerrillas found themselves forced into the most backward rural areas, where they developed a very effective military capacity with strong support from the local population. In these zones of control, the most radical wing of the popular Church collaborated with the guerrillas, working closely with the local structures of 'popular power'. But the Reagan administration's determination to halt their advance proved difficult to resist. The guerrillas were not defeated, but the prospect of taking power became a much longer term one than originally envisaged. Political work was resumed in the cities and attempts made to rebuild the popular movement. But conditions were very different, and over 50,000 Salvadoreans died in the first seven years of the civil war, most of them poor peasants and workers.

The new Archbishop, Rivera y Damas, though a progressive, was placed under great pressure by the authorities. More dioceses were created, and new bishops loyal to the position of the Vatican appointed. The Vatican was by now intent on reversing the influence of the popular, participatory Church in Latin America and reasserting its control. Rivera was never elected President of the Bishops' Conference and he lacks the power and influence of his predecessor. Priests and nuns who work with the base communities are under threat of expulsion, as many of them are foreign.[12] Although the work of the base communities cannot be reversed, their resilience is being severely tested. The support of pastoral agents has been vital to them, along with the protective umbrella of a supportive Archbishop.

The struggle, as Sobrino's remarks make clear, is over how to define what is the 'true Church'. The liberation theologians have no doubt that the 'true Church' is the one which 'learns what it means to become part of the world of the poor and to make their cause and lot its own'. The struggle clearly mirrors what is taking place in society as a whole, and its outcome will ultimately depend on the direction in which the social and political crisis of El Salvador, in particular, and Central America as a whole, is resolved.

NOTES

1 See O. Maduro (1982), *Religion and Social Conflicts*, trans. by R.R. Barr, New York: Orbis Books; see also M.G. Dunn (1986), 'Liberation theology and class analysis: A reassessment of religion and class', *Latin American Perspectives*, vol. 13, no. 3, pp.59–70.
2 D.H. Levine (1981), *Religion and Politics in Latin America: The Catholic Church in Venezuela and Colombia*, Princeton: Princeton University Press.
3 J.M. Barnadas (1984), 'The Catholic Church in colonial Spanish America', in L. Bethell (ed), *The Cambridge History of Latin America*, vol. 1, Cambridge: Cambridge University Press, p.513.

4   R. Cardenal (1980), *El Poder Eclesiastico en El Salvador*, S
     UCA Editores.
5   J. Pearce (1986), *Promised Land: Peasant Rebellion in Chalatena*
     Salvador, London: Latin America Bureau.
6   P. Berryman (1984), *The Religious Roots of Rebellion: Christians in the*
     Central American Revolutions, London: SCM Press.
7   Pearce, op. cit.
8   See debates in O.A. Romero (1979), *Iglesia de los Pobres y Orga-*
     nizaciones Populares, Universidad Centroamericana Jose Simeon Canas,
     San Salvador: UCA Editores.
9   *Rutilio Grande: martir de la Evangelízacion Rural en El Salvador* (1978), San
     Salvador: UCA Editores.
10   J. Sobrino (1985), *The True Church and the Poor*, trans. by M.J. O'Connell,
     London: SCM Press.
11   ibid.
12   In the FMLN (Frente Farabundo Marti para la Liberación Nacional)
     offensive of November–December, 1989, government military forces
     raided Lutheran, Baptist, Episcopal and Roman Catholic Church
     buildings, arresting Church workers and deporting those with foreign
     passports. Furthermore, in January 1990, five soldiers and four army
     officers were formally charged with the murder, the previous November,
     of six Jesuit priests and two servants. The charges resulted from a
     Government Commission of Inquiry, created by President Alfredo
     Christiani acting under international pressure.

Chapter 9

Social change and political response:
the silent religious cleavage in North America

Kenneth D. Wald

INTRODUCTION

For many observers of the United States, 'religion and politics' connotes interaction between the institutional forms of Church and state. The language of the first amendment to the constitution – 'Congress shall make no law respecting an establishment of religion or prohibiting the free exercise thereof' – appears to confine religious and political forces to separate spheres, divided by an impregnable wall of separation. If taken as a statement about empirical reality, the sharp constitutional demarcation between religious institutions and governmental agencies may raise doubt that religion and politics are strongly enough related in the United States to warrant examination. Even so, an otherwise perceptive observer such as James Bryce concluded that the constitutional formulation (among other factors) had rendered the United States largely immune to the 'debate and strife' associated with sectarian political controversies in Europe.[1]

From the perspective of the late twentieth century, Bryce's judgement seems inadequate. Contrary to the suggestion that the Church–state divide is firmly settled in the public mind, debate over the permissible limits of religious expression by public authority still ignites fierce and passionate conflict in the United States. Moreover, the notion of a rigid wall of separation between religion and politics is tenable only within the confines of the most restricted definition of the two spheres. The concept of 'religion' must be broadened beyond the Church to take in the numerous voluntary associations and informal networks of social interaction that bind a congregation of believers. Involvement in the life of a church may expose the congregant to behavioural norms with political implications. With a broadened definition that takes account of the encompassing nature of religious commitment, the prospects for religion's political relevance are greatly enlarged. Similarly, when the realm of 'politics' is taken not only to denote formal government institutions but also to cover the many processes involved in governance, there is ample room for religious motivation in public life. With an inclusive approach to the forces represented by the terms 'Church' and 'state', it becomes clear that no governing charter could completely rule religion off the political agenda.

Far from rendering religion largely irrelevant to politics, as Bryce supposed, the structure of government in the United States may actually encourage a high degree of interaction. First, as it did on other matters, the constitution elaborated a general principle of Church–state relations but left responsibility for implementation to political authorities. The founders provided little guidance about the types of activity prohibited under the establishment clause or defended under the free exercise provision. Because of the ambiguity inherent in the First Amendment, questions about the regulation of religion thus remain very much on the public agenda and are contested anew with each generation. Second, the decision to treat Churches as voluntary associations, subject neither to legal privileges nor disabilities, has left religious groups with considerable freedom of operation. Subject to a few limitations that have not been rigorously enforced, Churches are free to engage in a wide variety of activities that may include some forms of political action. The constraints on Church political activism are largely internal and cultural, not the result of state sanctions. Third and last, the 'complex, decentralized and fragmented' political system created under the constitution has provided persons committed to causes (religious or secular) with manifold openings for political action.[2] Federalism, weak party discipline and separation of powers combine to multiply the points of access to decision-making processes. The political culture encourages the exploitation of access by purposive groups formed on the principle of voluntary association. Like their secular counterparts, religious groups may take advantage of these openings to pursue policy goals through political activity.

The US political system has long presented a fertile environment for the expression of group differences in the public realm. The prospects for a specifically religious presence in public life, already high due to favourable structural conditions, have been magnified further by the intensity of religious feeling, the strong tie between religious affiliation and ethnic identity and the extraordinary diversity of religious opinion in the nation. The potent combination has made religion an important ingredient in defining the terms of political conflict throughout US history. The early battles for disestablishment in the states generated bitter political conflicts that affected political allegiance long after the precipitating issue had receded from consciousness. The evangelical war against slavery helped inflame opinion in the north and south alike, contributing to the sectional tension that culminated in a bloody civil war and continuing estrangement between the regions. Throughout the nineteenth and twentieth centuries, conflict about the religious identity of the nation marked public debates about immigration restriction, alcohol consumption, public education and sabbath observance. As these examples suggest, the historical pattern of US politics is incomprehensible without recognizing the centrality and divisive potential of religious faith.[3]

James Bryce was neither the first nor last observer to underestimate the salience of religion in US political life. Even those who recognize the historical significance of the religious factor often draw a sharp line of demarcation at the Second World War, thereafter consigning religious conflict to the category of obsolete political cleavages. The US political system of the post-1945 era is far removed in tone and temper from the religious wars and controversies of the eighteenth, nineteenth and early twentieth centuries, farther still from the contemporary passions of Warsaw, Khartoum, Beirut or Ulster. But one should not be misled by either the virtual disappearance of overt religious conflict or the growing acceptance of the norm of tolerance to imagine that religion has surrendered political relevance in North America. Because contemporary patterns of confessional politics are subtle, the analyst must work harder to find evidence of the intersection of faith with politics. That search requires a consideration of how religion retains political significance through such diverse paths as the impact of sacred values on political perceptions, growing interaction between complex religious organizations and state regulatory agencies, the role of congregational involvement in political mobilization or the functionality of Churches as a political resource for disadvantaged groups. The traces of religion must be sought out not only in the realm of public policy, where denominational conflict has historically been most visible, but also in the operational political code of society and, closer to the ground, in the electoral behaviour of ordinary citizens.

In this chapter, I hope to demonstrate that religious change has affected but not eliminated the formative role of religion in US political culture, the national political agenda and patterns of issue preferences. The first part of the chapter examines changes in the nature of religious commitment during the postwar era. Subsequent sections consider how changes in the condition of religion have affected the modes of religious expression in politics. The findings for the United States will be briefly compared and contrasted with developments in Canada.

MODERNITY AND RELIGIOUS CHANGE

If religion involves more than churches and formal institutions, the institutional form of religious commitment is none the less a useful starting point for a discussion of the place of religion in the contemporary United States. The discussion must be conducted in the context of modernization theory in general and the secularization hypothesis in particular.

Modernization theory comprises a set of assumptions about economic development, social change and the evolution of political institutions in societies undergoing the transition from traditionalism to modernity. The hallmark of traditional society is commitment to a 'historical order of life that presupposes religious sanctions'.[4] The central role of religion in such societies is evident in a view of the state as the embodiment of divine will and the source of religious authority; even the legal standing of inhabitants, their privileges and immunities, depends on religious warrant. While such societies recognize a distinction between Church and state, the two structures are conceived as complementary agencies sharing responsibility for governance in accord with sacred obligations.[5]

Modernization is commonly supposed to undercut the consciousness of supernaturalism and divine sanction that sustains the traditional order. As formulated in classic social theory, the modernization model asserted an inevitable decline in the strength of religious commitment under the counter-pressure exerted by rising educational levels, urbanization, industrialization, the spread of scientific values and technological complexity, bureaucratization and associated trends. The social developments associated with modernity were assumed to render religious sensibilities implausible, irrelevant and/or impractical in the conduct of daily life. In societies that had been fully exposed to the various trends that compose the modernity syndrome, religious values and institutions were expected to occupy a decidedly marginal role in social affairs. Religious decline in society is assumed to foreshadow the decay of a religious presence in politics.

Though modernization theory has most often been applied to societies in transit from an agricultural to an industrial base, it should serve just as well to explain developments in the United States. Does the secularization hypothesis actually fit the facts of the US case? Can one find evidence that religion has ceased to inform the culture and the political order? At the very least, it is clear that the United States is a secular state. The government apparatus is formally independent of religion and does not exist, officially, for the purpose of securing religious ends, a task left to individuals. The rights of citizenship are not reserved for the religious nor do Churches enjoy a favoured role in governance. Like other modern states, the United States uses law rather than religious norms to regulate conduct and does not normally take account of the religious beliefs of citizens in its operations. These are qualities normally exhibited by a secular state.[6]

But secularization may entail considerably more than the formal divorce of Church and state and the autonomy of the latter from the former. In some accounts, secularization promotes a 'full-blown modernistic consciousness that has all but cut its ties with the historical legacy of past centuries' – a legacy that includes strong religious commitment.[7] The characteristic attitudes towards religion in secular society range from indifference to outright antagonism. Has the United States experienced an 'upheaval in the structure of modern consciousness' relegating religion to the periphery? The answer depends largely on how one chooses to measure the hold of religious sensibilities in modern society. If the condition of religion is assessed by the breadth of commitment to religious institutions and the persistence of ritualized behaviour, then it appears that US experience falsifies modernization theory. Measured against the developed nations of the world and expectations about the disappearance of churches from the landscape, the condition of religion in the United States must be adjudged healthy and vigorous. But a more sophisticated version of the secularization hypothesis calls attention to the depth and quality of commitment as the appropriate index of religiosity. From this perspective, the impact

of modernization is apparent in the degree to which religion has
become a private matter for individuals, compartmentalized in the
form of conscience, rather than a vital force in public arenas. By that
standard – the central role many Americans *wish* religion to play in
their culture – the position of faith appears far more precarious. We
shall consider both these assessments.

By now it has become commonplace for observers to note the
inadequacies of the naive form of the secularization hypothesis as
applied to North America. Compared to populations in advanced
industrial societies and, indeed, even to citizens from the less
developed countries, Americans exhibit a striking commitment to
Churches and related institutions. The rate of Church membership,
attendance at worship, participation in Church-related activities,
enrolments in Church-affiliated educational institutions, financial
donations to religious causes and other available behavioural indicators all attest to the continuing hold of Churches upon the loyalties
of the population. The faith that undergirds that commitment, while
often instrumental and idiosyncratic, none the less remains grounded
in traditional assumptions about the existence and nature of the deity,
the prospects for an after-life and the efficacy of prayer. Americans
report strong loyalties to their faiths and experience religion as a
significant force in their lives.[8]

Owing to the development of mass surveys of religiosity, it is
possible to provide some gross statistical comparisons of postwar
patterns and prewar tendencies. By and large, temporal comparisons
attest to continuity rather than change in the level of religious
commitment. Statistics of Church membership which span the
divide suggest no significant attenuation in overall attachment to
religious institutions during the modern period. Based on admittedly
incomplete figures reported by denominational bodies, the rate of
Church membership in the population has actually risen from a
prewar figure of 50 per cent to the most recent estimate of 60 per
cent.[9] Self-reported Church membership rates among adults, which
probably err in the direction of overstatement, have varied minimally
around a 70 per cent baseline. Similar stability has been evident in
the proportion of adults reporting weekly church attendance (from
41 per cent in 1939 to 40 per cent in 1984); belief in a supreme
being (90 per cent in 1948 to 87 per cent in 1985); belief in
an after-life (68 per cent in 1948 to 71 per cent in 1981); and
performance of prayers to God (90 per cent in 1948 to 87 per cent
in 1985).[10] On some biblical information items periodically included

in postwar surveys, Gallup pollsters have even reported measurable increases in correct responses. The stability in core theological values and ritual observance, coupled with undeniable evidence of rapid growth in Orthodox Churches, has persuaded some observers of a postwar religious revival like the great awakenings of centuries past.

The durability of traditional religious attachments was also established by a replication in the 1970s of a classic prewar study of social processes in the small industrial city of Muncie, Indiana.[11] Researchers who returned to the site of the Lynd's 'Middletown' studies after a half-century found little evidence of irreligion or religious indifference despite the increased exposure of contemporary residents to various modernizing influences. The Churches remained strong and maintained their traditional emphasis upon pastoral care and the propagation of faith. According to the evidence from both self-reports and intensive observation, religious enthusiasm in the United States may ebb and flow but it has *not* followed the steady downward spiral predicted by the naive version of the modernization model.

Observers who look for different signs of religiosity have pointed to tendencies suggesting that the institutional strength of religion belies the weakened state of faith in the contemporary period. For such observers, secularization has been a subtle process which has greatly transformed the character and scope of religious sensibility despite the appearance of stability. The same polls that document widespread commitment to traditional religious groups reveal a pervasive sense that religion no longer plays the central role that it formerly did.[12] During the last thirty years, Americans by fractions ranging from one-third to three-quarters have reported a sense that religion was losing influence in their society. Asked to describe the importance of religion in their own lives, the percentage of adults picking the 'very important' option declined from 75 per cent in 1952 to 56 per cent in 1984; the decline was most precipitous among young people who best indicate the future course of religious attachment. In 1985, the Gallup organization undertook an interesting attempt to assess the depth of 'spiritual commitment' using attitudinal and behavioural items independent of Church involvement or participation. That study revealed that only one-tenth of the population could be regarded by their own answers as deeply committed to, or influenced by, religious faith. Without comparable data from an earlier period, it is hazardous to interpret this figure as an indicator of decline but it suggests that formalized religious commitment vastly overstates religious consciousness in the American mind.

As further evidence for the diminished status of religion, social critics have cited the spread of secularism among the emerging technocratic elite known variously as the New Class or Knowledge Class. According to this perspective, the evolution of the industrial economy has shifted the basis of social power from traditional elites who control production of goods to the sectors that create and disseminate knowledge and services. Research on elites in the newly-ascendant sectors suggests that religious sentiments are far weaker among them than was the case for traditional elites. Indeed, the growing share of the population that denies identification with any religious group is preponderantly composed of well-educated professionals and service workers who occupy strategic positions in the emerging post-industrial economy and who are thus well-placed to propagate a secularist vision in critical institutions such as schools, the media and various interest groups. To some observers, the polarization between traditional and emerging elites signals the emergence of a fundamental generational cleavage involving divergent world-views and cultural norms.[13]

The main religious communities have undergone changes that strike some observers as indicative of secularization. The Protestant tradition, which stresses the capacity of every believer to confront God directly and without mediation, has worked its way into all US faiths. For Catholics, this has meant the development of a popular consciousness fundamentally at odds with Rome on a wide range of doctrinal, sacramental and social issues. The result has been the development of a mentality that some critics decry as 'cafeteria-style' Catholicism, a metaphor suggesting the triumph of a quintessentially American style stressing choice over the historical authority of a universal Church. Among some Jews, commitment to the Jewish community has come to mean an assertion of ethnic identity which downplays faith and affiliation with the synagogue. The mainline Protestant clergy have been accused of denuding their theological inheritance by reducing it to little more than a gloss upon the liberal political agenda. The evangelical and fundamentalist wings of Protestantism have similarly been charged with trivializing Christian doctrine by their proclivity to approach faith from an instrumental perspective. Critics look askance at the determined promotion of religion as a means to foster economic success, good physical and mental health, strong families, stable marriages and other therapeutic ends.

To those who suspect a loss of traditional faith, all these tendencies bespeak a fundamental transformation in the terms of religious attachment. Without an anchoring in tradition, it is argued, religious faith has degenerated into a justification of self-interest that bears little relationship to a communal ethic. The extent to which the character of religious faith has shifted under the onslaught of individualism is documented most vividly in work by Robert Bellah and his associates. Their influential cultural critique of contemporary US society, *Habits of the Heart*, reports the extreme but not unrepresentative case of a respondent who had developed a personal religion of 'Shellahism' expressed in a personal voice that counselled her 'to love yourself and be gentle to yourself' and 'to take care of each other'.[14] Individualized religion of a deist cast is not new in the United States, as Bellah noted, but neither Jefferson nor the transcendentalists quite so baldly elevated themselves to the centre of the universe or disconnected faith from the holy.

With divergent understandings of religion and uncertainty about how faith is manifested by contemporary Americans, it remains unclear whether modernity has in fact strengthened or weakened religious commitment. Those who index religion by looking at Church affiliation, agreement with traditional verities and participation in rituals, conclude that religion retains a primary role while observers who examine the texture of faith are prone to interpret the contemporary religious situation far more sceptically. Because there is no definite standard by which to determine if a culture has become secular, it is more fruitful to identify the changes in contemporary religion associated with modernity than to debate whether these changes constitute the inevitable fate of religion under secularity. When the focus is shifted in that manner, it is clear that modernity has affected the *pattern* of religious commitment. In particular, the modern age has encouraged tendencies towards differentiation and voluntarism.

'Differentiation' refers to the fragmentation of large religious traditions into smaller, competitive denominations and the development of new religious traditions. While the postwar period has witnessed some mergers among cognate religious bodies and the re-unification of confessions whose divisions could be traced back to the mid-nineteenth century rupture over slavery, the more prevalent tendency has been towards even finer divisions within the dominant Christian tradition. At the same time, the range of religious choice has broadened through the proliferation of what are collectively called the 'New Religious Movements'. This pot pourri of eastern religions, folk religions from Africa and the Caribbean, new faiths such as Scientology and the Unification Church and various cults and sects has resulted from immigration – long a source of revitalization – as well as conversion from older faiths and the mobilization of the previously irreligious. Attesting to the magnitude of both types of diversification, the most comprehensive religious directory lists nearly 1,300 discrete religious bodies – Churches, sects, denominations and cults – in the United States.[15] The pattern of contemporary religious affiliation has aptly been described as a mosaic and few commentators can avoid involving the spirit of pluralism when attempting to characterize mass loyalties.

In attempting to make sense of the contours of faith, it has been customary for scholars to divide the US population into three groups defined by affinities of theology, Church polity and historical development: Roman Catholic, 'mainline' or 'moderate' Protestantism and 'evangelical' or 'conservative' Protestantism.[16] The Roman Catholic Church, the single largest denomination, claims approximately 25 per cent of all Church identifiers. The mainline Protestant Churches – a label that conventionally includes at least the Episcopalian, Presbyterian, Methodist, Congregational and Unitarian denominations plus wings of the Lutheran and Baptist Churches – once harboured the nation's social, political and economic elite. The share of the population affiliated with mainline Protestant Churches has declined over the postwar period to approximately 33 per cent today. Evangelical Protestants have emerged to claim an increasing share of the Christian community, perhaps as much as 25 per cent of the entire population. Despite the habit of some commentators to force all evangelicals into a common mould, the tendency represented by the label defies easy description. Theologically, the essence of evangelicalism involves respect for biblical authority, insistence on personal commitment to Jesus Christ and a willingness to evangelize. The term has been applied to some denominations which emerged from the Reformation era, such as most Lutherans and various branches of the Reformed Church, to the Baptists and other denominations that grew rapidly following the Great Awakenings of the late eighteenth and early nineteenth centuries, to the practitioners of Pentecostalism, as well as to the smaller Churches and sects which split off in schisms from established Churches.

The remainder of the population is allocated among a variety of small religious groups. Though only 2 to 3 per cent of the entire adult population, the Jewish community remains a force to be reckoned with in the cultural, political and social life of the United States. Mormonism, concentrated in the western states, has similarly overcome a small population share (1 per cent) to constitute an increasingly important community. The broadening of the US religious mosaic beyond the Judaeo–Christian ambit has been evident in the growth of small communities committed to Islam and eastern religions. Some analysts would also reserve a separate heading for the 'alternative' religions or cults that are built around charismatic founders. That enumeration leaves about 6 per cent of the population in other faiths and 7 per cent which disclaims identification with any formally constituted religious group.

Differentiation has also manifested itself *within* religious traditions. The denominational label or the broader classification of denominations into confessional 'families' can be no more than a rough approximation of reality in a culture that prizes individualism and respects congregational autonomy. The existence of hybrids like 'Jews for Jesus', charismatic Catholics and the Black Israelites all illustrate the difficulty of neatly separating Americans by traditional religious categories. The process also affects the mainstream. Once primarily the Church of European peasants who migrated to US cities, Catholicism now comprises suburbanites many generations removed from the immigrant experience, an urban working class still bound by strong affective ties to the parish church and the new immigrants from Spanish-speaking countries and Asia. Each subculture approaches the Catholic heritage from a distinctive perspective. The extremes in the Jewish community range from thoroughly assimilated native-born elites of distant European ancestry to Orthodox refugees freshly arrived from virtually every continent. Evangelical Protestantism was once portrayed as an exclusively rural phenomenon whose adherents were marked by poverty, poor education, cultural estrangement and alienation from the institutions and practices associated with modernity. Though the evangelical population as a whole still lags behind other religious communities on most indicators of socio-economic attainment, the distances are much smaller today as the community boasts a substantial urban presence, an impressive educational network, an indigenous middle class and other traits that signal adaptation to modernity. As US religion sheds it tribal character, the cultural stereotypes of the prewar period – the inner city priest with his Irish brogue, the Yiddish momma from the tenements, the Bible-thumping evangelical from the hinterlands – have less and less anchoring in reality.

The voluntary tradition in US religion has meant that religious identity was less an ascriptive trait conferred by birth than a matter of choice and discretionary involvement. The possibility of voluntary religion was present before 1945, of course, but Americans have made more frequent use of it in the postwar period. This has been evident, for example, in the growth of the non-religious segment of the population from 2 per cent to around 7 or 8 per cent in contemporary surveys of religious self-identification.[17] Voluntarism has also meant the loosening of the ties that hold individuals to inherited religious identity. The main religious groups co-exist across highly permeable boundaries broached repeatedly by intermarriage, conversion and Church-switching, processes which blur identity and ease inter-group tensions. Religious affiliation is such a private matter that it has become a suspect classification in polite society. Within the Churches, too, individuals now face an unprecedented choice about how intensely they will associate with their religious communities. Affiliation with a denomination may mean only nominal attachment to the Church, perhaps merely the residue of childhood loyalties and nostalgia, or constitute thorough immersion in an encapsulating subculture.

The postwar period presents the secularization hypothesis with a mixed set of results. The persistence of strong Churches, widely diffused religious identity and respect for religious institutions undercut the claim that formal religion could not withstand the onslaught of modernity. But modernity has left a mark upon religion in several ways. Religious commitment may mean less in the eyes of contemporary adherents than it did for their forebears – or it may mean something else that has more to do with secular goals than matters of transcendence. The objects of attraction, the Churches, are clearly less monolithic and may make smaller and less tenable claims upon the consciousness of believers. It remains to be seen how the various, disputed and occasionally contradictory trends in the condition of US religion bear upon the political realm. In undertaking that investigation, I plan to ask not whether US politics has become 'desacralized' but rather how the changes in religion associated with modernity have affected the political expression of faith.

RELIGION IN THE POLITICAL CULTURE OF THE UNITED STATES

Assessing the political impact of religion depends greatly on what facet of religion is being considered and which specific political arena is under investigation. For purposes of social analysis, religion may be approached as a body of ideas and outlooks (theology and ethical code), a species of formal organization (the ecclesiastical Church) or a human collectivity (social group). While the distinctions among these facets of religion are not exact, each form of religious presence is characteristically associated with a particular form of political conflict. The political importance of religious ideas shows up most clearly in the realm of political culture, core assumptions about governance. Religious institutions are most commonly the focus of political conflict in the constitutional sphere. Treated as communities of believers, religion has special relevance to the study of group conflict and electoral cleavages. Religion has remained politically important in all these guises since 1945 even as the form of expression has shifted in response to the religious dynamics identified in the previous section.

The cultural significance of US religion has been discussed under the rubric of 'civil religion', a term given wide currency by the publication of Robert Bellah's seminal essay in 1967.[18] Alongside the many religious denominations in the United States, Bellah identified a collective faith that the nation served a transcendant purpose in history. Americans have been particularly prone to the conception of their nation as 'God's New Israel' bound to the creator by a covenant of obligation. Because this consensus cannot be given official expression in a constitutional system that forbids establishment of religion, it is best discerned in the rhetoric of political leaders, the religious nature of public ceremonies and the yearning to require godly qualities of public officials. The closest the formulation has come to institutionalization was the decision in the 1950s to amend the Pledge of Allegiance to refer to the United States as 'one nation under God'. The approach to the nation as a 'city on a hill' originated with the Puritan founders but survived the formal secularization of the state in the early nineteenth century to remain the *de facto* establishment of the twentieth century.

Bellah treated civil religion as a functional requisite for stable democracy in a pluralistic and individualistic culture. While the sense of the United States as a 'light unto the nations' could degenerate into chauvinism, Bellah thought civil religion made a positive contribution to societal integration by binding a fractious people around a common goal and imparting a sacred character to civic obligation. That quality was important because it countered the US reflex to subordinate the common good to the single-minded pursuit of material self-interest – a cultural tendency that foreign observers from Tocqueville onwards have regarded as worrisome if not potentially destructive of communal cohesion. More broadly, civil religion served to legitimate the political order by providing it with at least a tenuous tie to divinity.

In the context of modernization theory, we can recognize civil religion as a response to the perennial problem posed by the secular state which forfeits an important bond of allegiance by disclaiming the mantle of religious authority.[19] When civic obligation is no longer buttressed by sacred norms, members of a society have little incentive to forego self-interest 'in deference to corporate demands that are real and imperative'.[20] Without some strongly felt sense of responsibility to a higher good, citizens cannot easily be persuaded to adopt restraint, to exhibit generosity, to honour the norm of mutual obligation. Civil religion is a solution, Bellah argued, because it provides a sense of ultimate purpose that can motivate citizens to perform actions necessary for collective survival – obedience to law, payment of taxes, participation in community affairs and sacrifice in war. Moreover, religious sensibility is an important source of standards and restraints that guard against debasement of the human spirit through tyranny and fanaticism.

The appeal of this vision probably owes much to the religious changes identified in the preceding section of the chapter. The continuing differentiation of religious identity – the fracturing of traditional Churches and the emergence of 'alien' faiths – seems to threaten the ideological basis for unity of the culture. Voluntarism and the consignment of faith to private conscience further undermine communal cohesion. In these circumstances, it is not surprising to hear calls for religious renewal in the public sphere. Bellah's theme has been seized upon by commentators who urge greater respect for religion and other traditional institutions as a means to instil patriotism and to prevent the development of a mass society composed of rootless, atomized individuals. The urgency of the call to restore civic faith reflects concern about the perceived success of secular elites in purging the state apparatus (specifically) and public life (generally) of religious influence and purpose.

Unlike Bellah, who emphasized the integrative contribution of civil religion, its capacity to provide an antidote to the excesses of liberal individualism, other commentators regard the phenomenon as a thinly disguised mechanism of social control.[21] Bellah's critics have worried less about the decline of social cohesion and more about the potentially restrictive consequences inherent in the political uses of religion. For such critics, it is a small step from the assumption that the United States should embody a divine purpose to the conclusion that the state is divinely sanctioned and should be above the rough and tumble of democratic discourse. Giving the actions of the government a religious warrant, they charge, will inhibit the scope of political debate by branding dissenters as blasphemous and disloyal. Rather than sustaining democracy as Bellah supposed, the critics insist that any tendency to endow policy proposals with a transcendent aura or even to promote religious values through public policy breeds fanaticism and conflict that undermines the democratic principle of respect for the individual and the law. The attribution of divine virtue to the United States, treating it as the carrier of God's redeeming plan for humankind, poses the further danger of unbearable hubris in the conduct of foreign policy.

While Bellah recognized the possibility that civil religion could degenerate in this fashion, he valued it principally as a source of 'prophetic' awareness in politics. The prophetic power of civic faith, illustrated by Abraham Lincoln's harsh judgement on the nation during the Civil War, was demonstrated anew in the postwar era when the Reverend Martin Luther King, Jr called on American Christians to repent of segregation, and other clergy assessed the morality and legitimacy of the Vietnam War. Yet Bellah himself admitted that civil religion was eroding at just the moment when he had first called attention to it. The title of his 1975 book, *The Broken Covenant*, reflects his belief that social changes in the mid-1960s destroyed confidence in US intentions and weakened the religious tradition that had sustained faith in the republic.

Bellah did not invent civil religion (or claim to have done so) but rather found a pithy phrase to label a phenomenon which had frequently been observed, the tendency of citizens to seek and discover supernatural purpose in the existence of the United States. In the first blush of enthusiasm following publication of his 1967 essay, the civil religion hypothesis was widely accepted as an important key to US political development. In time sceptics began to wonder if Bellah had discovered anything more than a superficial and sporadic religious nationalism, merely a gloss upon public rhetoric rather than an operational code in political behaviour.[22] To what extent has civil religion really existed as a differentiated cultural strain in the United States and does it now, if ever, exert genuine influence over the conduct of political life? Because civil religion is often portrayed as an indirect cultural influence, it is difficult to assess its presence or strength in the postwar United States. Most of the initial evidence regarding civil religion was literary and anecdotal. As interest in civil religion grew in tandem with the behavioural approach to politics, research utilizing more sophisticated techniques confronted the civil religion hypothesis with mixed results. The rhetoric of US presidents, especially the inaugural address, resonated with references to divine or transcendent influences but that language was not used on the occasion of other public celebrations. Large numbers of Americans assented to abstract propositions consistent with the civil religion motif but similar statements drew only limited support from members of the national legislature.

If the civil religion proposition has been overstated, as I believe it has, it nevertheless points to an important moralistic strain in US public life. That tendency has frequently been visible in the definition of 'crisis' situations. Some of the most important political turning points in postwar US politics have been associated with events that partake of individual moral failings and betrayal. Not to diminish the importance of these scandals, it is none the less worth observing that public concern with discrete episodes of unethical behaviour by public officials tends to overshadow the serious debates about public purpose which the scandals might otherwise occasion.

There is no better example of political moralism than the Watergate affair of 1973 to 1974. Left-wing critics had been unable to incite mass resistance to Richard Nixon's hold on national power by calling attention to the illegal and systematic bombing campaign of Cambodia mounted by his administration. Yet to the 'mingled astonishment and laughter' of sophisticated Europeans and the chagrin of some domestic critics, Nixon was first discredited, then rendered politically impotent and finally driven from office in disgrace by accusations of personal dishonesty, financial improprieties and conspiracy to hide evidence of collusion with his associates.[23] The event left the population with a pronounced distaste for political impurity that soon bore political dividends for the opposition party. Republicans were routed in the 1974 mid-term elections and Nixon's chosen successor, stained by the issuance of a pardon to Nixon, was replaced in 1976 by a largely unknown former governor who emphasized personal piety and made a virtue of his lack of experience in the ways of national politics. Ten years later, President Ronald Reagan saw his seemingly invincible public standing founder in a scandal that similarly involved charges of untruthfulness against the President and fraud by his subordinates. That crisis, too, was defined largely in terms of the moral failings of individuals; the fascination with illegality seemed far more salient than the larger issues of foreign policy and democratic accountability that investigations had revealed.

The apparent fascination with moral rectitude in public life has been demonstrated anew by the rise of the 'character' issue in recent presidential politics. While divorce has largely disappeared as a political handicap, new types of moral evaluation have been applied to the behaviour of aspirants for the presidency. The campaign for the 1988 Democratic nomination was thrown into disarray by the revelation that the leading candidate had apparently had an extra-marital affair with an attractive young model. Gary Hart's campaign collapsed in upon itself with breathtaking suddenness not just because most Americans disapproved of extra-marital affairs – they did – but because the episode seemed to impugn his character and his moral fitness to guide the republic. A similar outburst followed the revelation that another Democratic contender, Senator Joseph Biden, had quoted without attribution from the speeches of other political leaders, exaggerated his modest educational attainments and had been accused of plagiarism as a law school student. Similar charges of moral transgression were levelled against Pat Robertson, a candidate for the Republican nomination. Revelations that Robertson's son was conceived out of wedlock and that the candidate has not always been truthful in claims about his background damaged what otherwise was a surprisingly strong candidacy.

For these candidates, the issues of fitness or character have received far more attention and scrutiny than their positions on the paramount issues in the campaign or previous record in public life. A concern for the purity of purpose is a sign that moralistic tendencies have not disappeared from US political consciousness. It has been suggested that only a nation 'with the soul of a church' or a Puritan culture would care so deeply about the personal morality of candidates or treat that quality as the paramount basis to judge aspirants for national office. While no systematic studies have yet been reported, populations in other countries seem to accord politicians rather wider latitude in matters of personal conduct.[24]

Judged by these events, Bellah's forecast about the imminent disappearance of civil religion may be premature. Indeed, if we accept as the core of the concept the tendency to hold the nation accountable to divine standards, then the case can be made that US political culture has actually been revitalized by the rise of the 'New Christian Right' in the 1980s. The theme of repentance that has sounded loudest in recent political rhetoric has been the voice of theologically-conservative Christians who regard America's travails as punishment for its departure from what is styled as 'traditional Judaeo–Christian morality'. The evangelical critique, which echoed powerfully in Ronald Reagan's public statements, focuses on the degree to which the United States has fallen away from its original commitment to high moral standards by tolerating, if not glorifying, sinful behaviour. These critics have been particularly exercised about the development of public policies that have pushed religion out of the public square – such as limits on religious expression in public schools – and have given free reign to licentiousness – a charge applied to policies as diverse as decriminalization of marijuana, prohibitions on gender-based discrimination, liberalization of abortion, increased rates of cohabitation, permissiveness towards sexual expression in art and literature and reduced sanctions regarding homosexuality. Americans are once again being called home to a high purpose and threatened with severe tribulations if they fail to heed the call.

RELIGION IN THE JUDICIAL REALM

The 'official' status of churches in US society is probably the realm where religion has undergone the greatest change in the postwar period. The basic constitutional framework governing Church–state relations was set in 1791 when the addition of the First Amendment prohibited 'establishment' of religion or interference with the 'free exercise' of religious liberty by the Congress. At the time of the American Revolution, most colonies conferred a preferred position on certain religions and simultaneously restricted the practice of other faiths. The privileges of establishment might include public compulsion for attendance at prayer services, tax support for clergy, prohibitions against heresy, a privileged position for Church members in government and prosecution for unauthorized worship. This was not an exclusive establishment along European lines, as Leonard Levy has reminded us, but a plural system that frequently included several Churches within its ambit.[25] None the less, the constitution as amended by the First Congress prohibited such official favouritism to one Church or multiple Churches at the national level but left the state establishments undisturbed. Despite this favourable legal environment, the last state establishment disappeared by the early nineteenth century, the victim of the rapid growth of new sects that chafed under the favouritism granted to established Churches.

In the subsequent development of constitutional law up until the Second World War, the formal status of religion was not seriously contested.[26] In a few landmark decisions, the Supreme Court upheld the right of Congress to insist that Mormons in Utah Territory give up the practice of polygamy as a condition for statehood and the Court also forbid the state of Oregon from insisting that all elementary school students attend secular state schools. Apart from these cases, the pre-1945 judicial record of significant litigation on Church–state issues is rather thin. For its part, the US Congress demurred from formal declarations of support for Christianity as an official faith or from implementing policies that favoured religion in the public realm. Far more active support of religion was still permitted at the state and local levels of government owing to the language of the First Amendment.

This state of affairs came to an abrupt end in the period following (or, in a few instances, during) the Second World War. The source of transformation was a set of developments that together altered fundamental understandings of the place of religion in US life. The first element was the decision of the Supreme Court to apply to religious expression the First Amendment guarantees of free speech, assembly and petition. These guarantees had previously been limited to explicitly 'political' speech but were now broadened to include the type of activity associated with religion. This development was accompanied by another, the decision or discovery that the rights enumerated in the constitution enjoined the states and localities as well as the national government. The application of the religion clauses to the states and local governments was the product of a general decision to bind all governments to the strictures of the First Amendment. Constitutional jurisprudence was also revolutionized after 1945 by new understandings of what was meant by 'establishment' and 'free exercise'. Under the decisions, government agencies could do less to aid religion or to inhibit individuals from acting true to their faiths.

What began as a trickle of cases eventually turned into a torrent of litigation, much of it initiated by groups that stressed the value of keeping religious advocacy to a minimum in public life. The growth of the establishment concept can best be described by listing the kinds of activities that Supreme Court decisions have rendered impermissible forms of state support for religion:

- mandatory prayer, Bible reading or other types of worship before, during or after classes in state schools;
- religious instruction on the premises in state schools;
- limiting exemption from conscription to persons professing faith in God;
- posting the Ten Commandments in public school classrooms;
- giving Churches veto power over the issuance of liquor licences within a specified distance from Church property;
- mandating the teaching of biblical accounts of the creation of the universe;
- providing subsidies to teachers in religious schools;
- providing tax subsidies exclusively to parents with children in religious schools;
- requiring employers to grant employees the day off on their sabbath.

As a rule, the courts upheld state support for religion only when the behavioural standard in question was similarly applied to secular individuals and institutions. Thus, the Court upheld tax exemption for Church property as part of a broad policy to exempt from taxation all types of non-profit institutions. Similarly, tax exemptions granted to religious school tuition payments was held acceptable under the establishment clause if, and only if, the educational expenses incurred by children in state schools were similarly available to parents. In some of these cases, the Court expressly followed a rule formulated in a 1971 decision: actions that favoured religion were permissible only if they were primarily secular in purpose and effect and did not too closely entangle Churches with the state or *vice versa*.

As the scope for official recognition of religion narrowed, so the Court expanded the rights of individuals for exemption from state laws that hindered their expression of religious conscience. Once again, a listing of precedents is instructive. The free exercise clause was expanded to require that prisons allow adherents of minority faiths access to religious materials and the right to conduct prayer services; to force states to pay unemployment compensation to workers with religious objections to weapons construction; and to forbid schools from requiring students to declare support for the government by saluting the flag. The government is allowed to restrict religious expression only when it serves an overriding public policy purpose and no reasonable alternative is available. Thus, religious scruples have *not* been accepted as a legitimate reason for parents to withhold needed medical treatment from children or to earn exemption from compulsory vaccination laws. In both cases, courts have accepted a valid public health purpose as sufficient to override conflicting religious beliefs. The same standard that binds individuals has been applied to corporate religious organizations. Churches may not deny social security coverage to secular employees, whatever the doctrinal position on that issue, because state pensions are deemed a legitimate and necessary element of public policy.

It is tempting to treat the two religious components of the First Amendment as distinct, serving different but related purposes. On this reading, the establishment clause regulates what government can do to advance religion while the free exercise clause limits what government may do to restrict religious observance. As such, the two clauses seem to fit together nicely and work towards a common purpose of neither advancing nor retarding religion by state action. While some of the cases decided by the Court may work that way, the two clauses can also work against each other.

Consider the consequences when the Supreme Court ruled on 'free exercise' grounds that members of the Amish sect could legitimately withdraw their children from the final year of secondary education mandated by the state of Wisconsin. The decision was predicated on the assumption that an additional year of schooling counted less than the Amish fear that advanced secular education would undermine a culture based on simplicity and faith. By exempting the Amish from a requirement applied to every other child in Wisconsin, the Court seemingly granted the Amish faith a privileged position – the type of action that smacks of establishment. Or to take the opposite tack, some parents have argued that prohibiting organized prayers in the schools effectively denies their children the right of religious free expression. Under lawsuits filed by fundamentalist organizations, federal judges have ruled that requiring children to read and discuss certain material – stories about witchcraft and myth or materials that challenge traditional sex roles by having girls perform actions traditionally reserved for males – has the effect of compelling fundamentalists to accept doctrine offensive to their beliefs. Thus the religious guarantees against establishment or infringement on religious expression may exist in tension rather than harmony.

The Court's changing conception of the religious clauses has not met with unanimous support. Advocates of greater 'accommodation' to religion in the public sphere insist that the justices have misread the intentions of the framers of the First Amendment.[27] All that was prohibited by 'establishment', the critics contend, was state support for a particular faith or religion. The Court has broadened the meaning of establishment beyond that circumscribed idea to include virtually any state support for religion in general or promotion of compulsory religious observance in public places. Critics of this extended view have called for a return to 'non-preferentialism', the doctrine that the state is permitted to assist religion so long as it does not favour any one faith. There have also been challenges to the enlargement of the free exercise clause. Some scholars have insisted on a narrow reading which would guarantee to individuals only the right to express freely their religious ideas and to worship without restraint. But under this standard, which takes the concept of 'expression' rather literally to designate speech and thought, religious beliefs would not entitle individuals to exemption from laws governing behaviour.

When legal precedent is driven by case law, as it is in the common law system of the United States, judicial doctrine evolves in fits and starts. Thus the broadening that I have detected in postwar jurisprudence has admitted of frequent exceptions and qualifications. Similarly, though some observers have professed to note a return to prewar concepts of the religion clauses in recent decisions, the counter-revolution has not been smooth or linear. Indeed, the preponderance of decisions suggests continuity with the broadened interpretations of the First Amendment rather than repudiation. As late as 1985, the Supreme Court struck down a state law that mandated a 'moment of silence' for reflection or private prayer during the day in state schools. Though it was surely less directive than the practices outlawed in the early 1960s, the Court continued to hold firm against what it perceived as inappropriate public endorsement of religious practices in the context of compulsory school attendance. Similarly, the Court has continued to honour many claims of conscience where individuals allege that actions by governmental or private organizations abridge their religious liberty.

It is clear that the terms of the Church–state debate have shifted in ways that could barely have been imagined in the 1940s. Where once the burden of proof for establishment clause cases rested on those who challenged state policies, now those who wish to grant the state some latitude in recognizing religion must justify their favoured policies as primarily secular and unlikely to promote excessive interaction between Church and state. Similarly, it was once taken for granted that dominant religious groups could enact policies which coincided with their version of public rectitude but conflicted with the presuppositions of minority faiths or the non-religious. This privileged position has been eroded by court decisions mandating respect for the consciences of dissenters. The burden is on the state to indicate that it has no reasonable alternative but to require behaviour that some persons of faith might find repugnant.

The most salient form of religious conflict that remains on the public agenda is not Church–state issues *per se* but a new type of dispute that has been encapsulated as the 'social issue'. The Supreme Court has increasingly embraced a libertarian stance towards forms of behaviour that were historically proscribed by religious traditions. The courts have rolled back limitations on sexual expression in art, literature and mass media, cited a right to privacy as grounds to strike down restrictions on access to abortion and otherwise seem to take a more permissive stance towards behaviour once punishable as deviance. States and localities have followed the trend by reducing penalties for some categories of drug and alcohol offences, permitting legalized gambling, allowing private businesses to function on the Christian sabbath and repealing laws and ordinances which discriminate against homosexuals or proscribe certain types of sexual activity.

To traditionalists, these decisions in combination with structures against Church–state collusion have amounted to nothing less than the denial of morality in the public sphere. The issue was joined during the 1984 presidential campaign when Ronald Reagan took a strong public position favouring accommodation to religion and moral traditionalism in public policy while the Democratic candidate, Walter Mondale, called forcefully for the state to refrain from promoting religion or insisting on traditional standards in personal behaviour. While Reagan won the election, commentators have suggested he did so despite a growing public consensus which favours the more libertarian approach and deregulation of private behaviour.[28]

The conflict has been most intense on the issue of abortion which was rendered justifiable by the Court's *Roe* v. *Wade* decision of 1972. In that case, the Court ruled that governments had no warrant to prohibit elective abortion during the first three months of pregnancy and only a limited basis to regulate abortion in the middle trimester. While not strictly a Church–state issue, the decision quickly took on a religious dimension when it was portrayed as a struggle between a religious view about the sanctity of life versus a secular morality that stressed supremacy of private conscience. Research on mass attitudes and elite behaviour has demonstrated conclusively that support for restrictive abortion legislation is most concentrated among persons who are intensely committed to religious orthodoxy while the supporters of the post-Wade policy are found disproportionately among the population groups least attached to traditionalist Churches and faiths.[29] The former group has pressed repeatedly for constitutional amendments designed to restore a more restrictive policy and, where traditionalist groups are heavily found, has succeeded in passing legislation that attempts to qualify the Roe policy of unfettered access to abortion. The Court has held firm to the Roe decision despite requests to overturn it but has allowed some restrictions and may yet return the issue to the jurisdiction of states and local communities.

The constitutional trends of the postwar period demonstrate that the political system has responded to religious changes and contributed to religious evolution by legitimating further departures from tradition. The court decisions have collectively reaffirmed the secular character of the state, instructing the government to refrain from promoting religious observance in its official capacity or from using its coercive power to punish religious dissidents. Divisions and fragmentation within the religious community prevented the drive for disestablishment from becoming simply a conflict between the religious and the secular. Groups as diverse as Lutherans, Baptists and Jews coalesced to attack mandatory school prayer and manifestations of official religion were similarly repudiated by sizable segments of many religious communities.[30] The supporters of discretionary abortion include a number of mainstream religious organizations as well as the unchurched. Growing acceptance for the voluntary principle has also contributed to religious change by undermining mass support for compulsory religious observance and promoting greater respect and sensitivity towards minority faiths. State neutrality towards religion undoubtedly sends a message that faith is a private matter neither to be demanded of nor forbidden to citizens.

The spread of a secular mentality has even been apparent where it might at first glance seem to have encountered its stiffest resistance – among the opponents of abortion. Response to abortion questions in mass surveys has generally depended upon the precise circumstances that surround the decision of the pregnant woman. Public opinion experts have presented respondents with hypothetical scenarios in which abortion might be contemplated. When the mother-to-be was portrayed as the victim of rape, a person whose health was threatened by the delivery or the fetus was known to be afflicted with serious birth defects, the public generally supported liberalized abortion laws. On the other hand, if the abortion was considered for economic reasons, because the mother already had a family or was single, then public opinion grew far more restrictive.[31] This suggests the development of a situational approach to moral judgement rather than a global view that abortion 'always' is good or bad. The development of such relativism might be taken to indicate the triumph of secular perspectives about public policy issues. Similarly, the prevailing strategy of anti-abortion organizations now appears to be support for a return to state and local option. In pressing for discretion rather than flat prohibition, the opponents of Roe appear to have come to terms with the potency of the 'freedom of choice' theme associated with the secular outlook. That is a further testament to the impact of religious change upon public legislation.

RELIGION AND MASS POLITICS

The contribution of religion to political culture and the judicial sphere has undergone significant change during the postwar era. At the level of social groups, too, it is apparent that religion has assumed a new role. Religious cleavages have not disappeared, as some modernization theorists predicted, but rather the alignments have been redefined and group differences extended to new political issues. The traditional Catholic versus Protestant cleavage has largely been displaced by a new alignment that divides most denominations internally and forges a divide between religious leaders and ordinary congregants.

In the period prior to the Second World War, the Protestant versus non-Protestant cleavage was a major dimension of American political conflict. The political fault-line ran between one segment of the country – the numerically dominant segment of the population which was rural, agrarian, self-employed, 'dry' (alcohol policy), native and Protestant – and an opposition which was largely urban, industrial, unionized, 'wet', immigrant and predominantly non-Protestant. During the first third of the twentieth century, the cleavage was largely fought out within the Democratic party which suffered consistent defeat in presidential elections. In time, the urban industrial wing seized control of the Democratic party and the party, in turn, achieved dominance in the national electorate. Democratic supremacy rested on the ability of Franklin Roosevelt and his successors to appeal simultaneously to the urban industrial bloc (including religious minorities), blacks and white southerners. The religious dimension to this partisan equation featured competition between mainline Protestants, predominantly rural, self-employed natives who favoured sumptuary legislation and the Catholic and Jewish immigrants who were clustered in urban-industrial environments, supported labour unions and favoured more lenient policies towards alcohol consumption and sabbath observance.[32]

The claim that voter loyalties reflected religious sympathies must not be construed to convey the impression that party conflict was fundamentally about religion. For the most part, that was not the case. From time to time, religious-based issues such as prohibition or issues with religious overtones such as immigration restriction did intrude on the national agenda. But for the most part, overt political conflict prior to 1945 focused largely on questions about social welfare and labour policy rather than religious doctrine. As Samuel Lubell so accurately described it, the lines of electoral conflict during the interwar period represented at base the clash between the ins and the outs.[33] The Democrats had managed to unite under one banner a set of groups struggling against the economic and social establishment for a share of power and social respect. While each component of the coalition had its own particular needs, interests and agenda, religion was one of the elements that bound Catholics, Jews and evangelical Protestants (white and black alike) together as outsiders and prompted them to contend against mainline Protestants for political power.

The religious dimension in mass political behaviour persisted into the postwar era and reached its peak in the presidential election of 1960. As in 1928, the Democrats chose a Catholic of Irish descent to represent the party while the Republicans nominated a Protestant. But unlike 1928, when the campaign was dominated by anti-Catholic rhetoric, the Republican campaign of 1960 largely refrained from waving the banner of Protestant supremacy, and overt religious appeals were generally muted. In comparison with the three preceding elections, the electorate of 1960 was strongly polarized by religion. The Kennedy candidacy brought in very high levels of support from Roman Catholic and Jewish voters but the Democratic ticket suffered substantial defections among Protestants with the most severe losses coming from regular Churchgoers in the South. When compared to 1928, however, the religious differences in voting were markedly less intense. Al Smith's Catholicism cost the Democrats six southern states carried in the previous elections but Kennedy and his running-mate managed to hold all but one of the southern states won four years previously and to win two additional states in the region. The largest difference between the contests of 1928 and 1960 was of course Kennedy's national victory versus Smith's landslide defeat in 1928.

Whatever the short-term outcome of the 1960 campaign, it challenged a tradition reserving national office for Protestants from high-status mainline denominations. In subsequent elections, affiliation with a 'minority' religion no longer posed a decisive electoral handicap. Since 1960 the Democrats have three times accorded the vice-presidential nomination to a Roman Catholic (1968, 1972, 1984) and the Republicans did so in 1964. It is no longer considered newsworthy when Catholics enter the competition for either the Republican or Democratic presidential nomination. In the campaign for the 1988 presidential election, for example, one Catholic (Alexander Haig) competed for the Republican nomination, a second (Jeanne Kirkpatrick) was strongly encouraged to enter the race by some conservative strategists and another member of the faith (Patrick Buchanan) seriously considered seeking the nomination. Prior to 1960, it would have been difficult to identify even a single Roman Catholic who commanded substantial influence in Republican ranks. Members of evangelical Protestant denominations have also competed seriously in nomination contests for both parties and adherents of the Greek Orthodox tradition have similarly entered the partisan fray with impressive results. While no member of the Jewish faith has yet emerged as a serious contender for the presidency, Jewish candidates have achieved success in areas with predominantly non-Jewish constituencies. By 1981, six Jews served in the United States Senate, most were Republicans and from states without substantial Jewish populations.

The apparent decline in the salience of religion for candidacies has persuaded some students of US politics that religion is similarly growing irrelevant to voter choice. Since 1960, Protestant–Catholic differences in presidential voting have dropped precipitously. From a postwar high of 46 per cent in 1960, the average difference between Catholic and Protestant electors has been less than 8 per cent in the last four presidential contests.[34] The virtual elimination of Protestant versus Catholic differences in presidential elections has not yet worked its way fully into voting patterns below the presidential contest. In congressional elections, for example, Jews, Catholics, black Protestants and white southern Protestants still demonstrate a marked affinity for Democratic candidates while Republicans enjoy a preponderance of support from mainline Protestants.[35] That pattern replicates the prewar New Deal coalition and explains why the Democrats have maintained their supremacy in Congress. Similarly, the nature of partisan identification has continued to bear the imprint of the traditional New Deal era cleavages and attitudes on issues which defined the political agenda for the New Deal era – government support for the economically disadvantaged through welfare state policies – continue to produce the traditional pattern of religious group differences.

Despite these residues, it is none the less clear that the Protestant versus Catholic division has declining relevance for partisan competition in the United States. Rather than conclude that this obsolescence of the old duality signals the end of religious distinctiveness in politics, it is more accurate to talk about the fragmentation of religious–political alignments. New patterns of group affiliation have emerged to replace the Protestant/non-Protestant divide. These contemporary alignments are highly issue-specific. As I noted in the preceding section, social issues revolving around restraints on personal behaviour have gained a new level of prominence in the postwar era. On issues such as drug use, pornography, homosexuality and marital fidelity, there is a pronounced attitudinal gap between Christians and non-Christians. The abortion issue has produced its own distinctive alignment in which evangelical Protestants and Catholics generally support restrictive policies while Jews, mainline Protestants and the 'unchurched' favour the liberalized practice that developed after the *Roe* v. *Wade* decision. The coalition patterns are different still on racial issues in which black Protestants, Jews and the unchurched support greater state action while other blocs call for retention of the status quo. Limited research on environmental attitudes, feminist issues and political tolerance reveals distinctive religious preferences which do not conform to the historical dimension that previously defined religious conflict on public issues. Such patterns are no longer as simple as the divisions previously noted in presidential politics and they tend to be overlooked when analysts speak in more global terms about the decline of religious polarization in politics.

Fragmentation has also appeared in the form of dramatic increases in mass-elite tensions within the major religious communities.[36] Like religious leaders throughout the industrial west, US religious elites have increasingly come to differ from their congregants on a host of social and political issues. The conflict was first apparent in the mainline Protestant community during the 1960s when pastors proved decidedly more receptive than their congregants to the appeals of the civil rights movement. The division widened as the political agenda encompassed the Vietnam War and a series of disputes over questions of social justice. By now, the cleavage has virtually been institutionalized as Protestant elites in seminaries, denominational bureaucracies, interchurch coalitions and the pulpit face resistance from ordinary Church members on a wide range of public policy issues. The voting behaviour of mainline clergy more closely resembles that of other elites than their co-religionists. The same tendency surfaced in the US Catholic community when members of the hierarchy supported mandatory bussing to achieve racial integration of state schools over the vociferous objections of their urban working-class parishioners on questions of economic policy, military assistance and nuclear strategy have not met with conspicuous success. On each of these issues, the position favoured by the bishops has been associated with the liberal side of the spectrum, a dramatic shift from the traditional conservatism of the hierarchy. This liberalizing tendency has been ascribed to such factors as the recruitment of bishops with more cosmopolitan backgrounds, the development and staffing of Church agencies by secular elites and the general opening up of Catholic social thought in the wake of the Second Vatican Council. Whatever the source, the contemporary Catholic episcopate no longer resembles the insular, nationalistic and censorious hierarchy that was symbolized by the late Cardinal of New York, Francis Spellman.

We have recently seen the possible beginnings of such a split within evangelical Protestantism.[37] In this case, however, the elite appears to have moved to the right of the mass. We know from the research of James Guth that conservative Protestantism, has undergone a wholesale conversion in party loyalties towards a strong identification with the Republican party and adoption of conservative domestic and foreign policy preferences. Like evangelicals in general, the SBC (Southern Baptist Convention) laity have been slower to move to the right. The attitudinal gap is stronger yet within the so-called 'electronic church' of independent fundamentalist ministers. 'Televangelists' part company with evangelical opinion on issues such as dissemination of birth control information in schools, passage of a constitutional amendment mandating legal equality of the sexes, AIDS policy, the nuclear freeze and defence spending. The members of evangelical denominations have not fallen into lock step with their erstwhile spokesmen who call for the implementation of strict policies of social regulation in these areas. It remains to be seen whether this gap will be closed or whether mass-elite estrangement on politics becomes the rule among evangelicals as it has been for Catholics and mainline Protestants.

The trend towards voluntarism in US religion has also borne political consequences. To borrow a phrase used in another context, it matters less for political behaviour *whether* a person is religious than *how* they are religious. The principal political cleavages associated with religion are increasingly found to depend upon the intensity of affiliation rather than the choice of denomination.[38] Surveys conducted in 1986 have revealed massive partisan differences between non-Churchgoers, occasional Church attenders and regular Churchgoers. The attempt of the Reagan administration to communicate moral traditionalism resonated with those most strongly attached to religious observance, somewhat less so with occasional worshippers and not at all with the nominally religious. These differences transcend denominational boundaries. The Republican advantage over the Democrats rises from −9 per cent among the least religiously-involved white northern Protestants to an overwhelming 43 per cent among regular Churchgoers; conversely, the Democrat's lead of 42 per cent among non-attending Catholics actually becomes a Republican margin of 10 per cent among the most devout Roman Catholics. The pattern also holds among white southerners, who are mostly committed to the evangelical Protestant tradition. The Republican advantage rises from −7¼ per cent to 19 per cent and then to 25 per cent across the three categories representing increases in religiosity. The gap between the least and most involved members within the major denominations equals or exceeds the average partisan differences between denominations.

The development of political cleavages within religious groups has also been noted in studies of political elites. Research about the impact of denominational affiliation on congressional voting decisions has traditionally yielded modest effects at best. Except for the sole issue of abortion, voting differences between representatives from different religious communities can usually be attributed to the impact of constituency forces rather than the personal religious convictions of officials. That view has been challenged by recent work involving detailed interviews about the religious outlooks of members of Congress.[39] Researchers have discovered that style of religiosity is an important variable affecting a wide range of decisions by elected officials. Those congressmen and congresswomen who perceive a communitarian ethic in religion are disposed to support policies on the liberal agenda while those representatives who perceive religion rather more hierarchically incline to the conservative side of the political spectrum. These differences operate within religious traditions and stand athwart traditional cleavages associated with party, social class and other important variables.

The enquiry into the political impact of religious imagery has now been extended to samples of congregants.[40] Early studies suggest that members of the same religious denomination may partake of radically different understandings about the cosmos and then connect the divergent perceptions to political objects. A traditional view of the deity as a stern ruler who holds individuals to exacting standards of personal conduct comports with a conservative emphasis on order and support for political authority. Yet that harsh image of the vengeful Old Testament deity competes with another view of God as warm, supportive and loving – an image most compatible with a political ethic emphasizing social justice and mutual obligation. This line of research recalls early work on the 'intrinsic' and 'extrinsic' dimensions of religious commitment. Congregants who accepted religious values as a source of personal guidance, who internalized the gospel, were shown to differ politically from Church members who were attracted to religion by instrumental considerations. The intrinsically religious showed a stronger disposition to racial, religious and political tolerance.

Such conflicting religious visions – with their associated messages for political conduct – are a test to the strength of voluntarism in contemporary US religion. The principle that individuals should be free to choose their own denomination (or none, for that matter) has broadened to the belief that the definition of proper faith within a religious tradition is also the prerogative of the individual believer.[41] It is hard to imagine such an individualized perspective in an age when religion was inculcated as part of a tribal inheritance in ethnic enclaves. But as geographic mobility and social development have undermined the homogeneity of 'urban villages', individuals have acquired a new freedom to select religious identity and to define a personal moral universe. Researchers have just begun to explore the genesis and significance of individualized religious outlooks for the political system. While a great deal remains to be examined, it seems clear that traditions like Protestantism, Catholicism and Judaism exert less political relevance while the more immediate religious perspective – the product of personal values, the congregation and social networks within the religious community – count for more. These cleavages represent a change in the form of linkage between religion and politics rather than a desacralization of the mass political realm.

Both fragmentation and voluntarism have thus shaped the manner in which religion intersects mass political life. If modernization theory can be forgiven for failing to anticipate these trends, that perspective is called even more thoroughly into question by the political emergence of evangelical Christians in the late 1970s. Largely quiescent during the twentieth century, fundamentalists emerged from their internal exile to spearhead resistance to many of the liberalizing trends unleashed by the 1960s. Local and state movements blossomed in opposition to initiatives involving gay rights, critical school textbooks, educational innovation and sexual equality. These local movements were eventually linked by national organizations such as Moral Majority, Christian Voice, Religious Roundtable and the American Coalition for Traditional Values which pursued all the avenues of interest group activity – public demonstrations, lobbying, campaign contributions, patronage and so forth – and achieved some notable successes. To the satisfaction of many political conservatives and the dismay of liberals, the political resurgence of evangelical Protestants has reinvigorated the religious dimension to US mass politics. The mobilization confounded social theorists who had written off evangelicalism as a declining force in the society.

Far from disappearing or withdrawing into enclaves on the margins of modern society, evangelicals have gathered strength from modernization and emerged to contest for national power.[42] In at least two respects, the modernizing processes that were supposed to eliminate conservative Christianity have, instead, propelled it to new political strength. The evangelical migration from the periphery to the centre has brought about greater contact between traditional populations and ways of life associated with modernity. While the interaction has affected both communities, the common reaction of fundamentalists has been to redouble their efforts against 'deviance'. Modernization has also equipped traditionalist populations with substantial resources for political combat. Compared to their parents, today's evangelicals and fundamentalists possess greater education, more free time, a higher level of affluence and closer familiarity with bureaucratic skills. Evangelical communities have acquired important organizational networks that provide a base for mass mobilization. Fundamentalist Churches have evolved into sophisticated administrative structures with links to other congregations. The 'electronic church' provides an important source of communication that counters the tradition of political passivity and isolation. Taken together, these trends provide channels for political action which earlier generations of evangelicals lacked. The need for political action seems more urgent to contemporary fundamentalists and they increasingly possess the resources necessary to convert moral outrage into effective political mobilization.

CANADA

The Canadian religious situation presents a number of instructive parallels and contrasts with the US pattern. The similarities between the two nations involve strong adherence to the traditional pillars of faith and the overwhelming numerical predominance of Christianity. Yet the two societies differ in other respects: compared to the United States, Canadian religion is less orthodox in content, less inclined to a fundamentalist outlook, more hierarchical in structure and more closely tied to distinctive ethnic communities. These differences in religion, coupled with contrasting patterns of national development and political authority, have produced divergent traditions in the encounter between faith and politics.

Like the United States, Canadian society is distinguished by a high level of formal commitment to religious institutions and the core values of Christianity.[43] Sixty-five per cent of the population maintain membership in Churches and roughly one-third of Canadians are likely to be found attending worship services in any week. Almost 90 per cent of Canadians evince a belief in God and 70 per cent or more assent to the existence of heaven. These figures are well above the levels of orthodoxy reported in comparably developed societies. The distribution of religious preferences in Canada also bears comparison with the US pattern of affiliation. In Canada, as in the United States, Roman Catholics constitute the single largest religious body but fall short of majority status. Protestantism in a variety of denominational forms is the faith of the majority in both societies. Most high-status Canadian Protestants, roughly one-third of all the Church-affiliated, belong either to the Anglican Church or the ecumenical United Church, the product of a merger of Methodists, Congregationalists, Presbyterians and Evangelical United Brethren. The remainder of the Canadian religious population is associated with evangelical Protestant Churches or scattered among a number of minority religions.

These superficial similarities aside, religious patterns in the two nations diverge at several points. To begin with, there is seemingly less religious intensity and orthodoxy in Canada. Notwithstanding that, Canadians match the level of US belief in the existence of a deity and heaven, they exhibit less commitment than Americans to other traditional Christian beliefs, report falling levels of Church attendance and regard religion as a smaller factor in their lives. This religious detachment – 'detachment' relative only to the very high degree of formal religiosity in the United States – may be the product of another important distinction between the two countries. Evangelical and fundamentalist Christianity, which lends urgency and intensity to religious feeling, is a less significant force in Canadian Protestantism. Canadian fundamentalist denominations are substantially smaller than their US counterparts and the fundamentalist outlook has not penetrated very deeply among mainline Canadian Protestants.

The Churches in Canada also differ in ecclesiastical organization. Unlike the US congregational polity which stresses organizational autonomy, self-government and the supremacy of the laity, the Protestant Churches in Canada are organized as units of centralized, hierarchical bodies. Though derived from the Protestant model, the spirit of religious independence has also imbued Catholicism in the United States with an independent cast. The Roman Catholic

Church in Canada has shown less tendency than its US counterpart to dissent from papal teaching, foster lay authority and otherwise to impart a distinctly national tone to the universal Church.

Finally, to a much greater extent than recently in the United States, Canadian religious divisions are reinforced by ethnic differences. The ethno-religious dimension in Canada pits Catholicism, principally the faith of the francophone population in Quebec, against the largely Protestant English-speaking community – a situation which conflates religious divisions with territorial, linguistic, and ethnic distinctiveness. 'This fact' of insular religious communities, commented Andre Siegfried in 1907, 'contains the key to the entire political situation in the Dominion'.[44]

These differences seem to bear heavily on the characteristic role of religion in political life. We shall consider with reference to the same three themes examined in the United States – the contribution of religion to political culture, constitutional debate and partisan competition. As discussed earlier in the chapter, students of US development attribute to religious faith an important role in shaping basic political attitudes and orientations. Specifically, the 'civil religion' hypothesis suggests that religion has contributed to the maintenance of political stability by providing an antidote to the extreme individualism of US culture, sanctifying transcendant standards of political judgement and promoting the national integration of a heterogeneous population. It has also been suggested that the high level of religiosity in the United States has bred a moralistic political style.

According to many distinguished observers, religion does not fulfil the same function in Canadian life.[45] For a variety of reasons associated with Canada's developmental experience, there is less emphasis on individual autonomy and correspondingly greater collective consciousness in Canadian life. In a sense, the culture has less need for religious sensibilities to counter the threat of extreme individualism. It is also difficult to find evidence that religion plays the prophetic role of speaking truth to power in Canada. That may reflect the emphasis on obedience and respect for authority that characterizes ecclesiastical Churches and the traditional association between such religion and state power. Few observers would suggest that religious attachment effectively serves to promote national unity in Canada as it is supposed to do in the United States. Quite the contrary, the presence of two segmented religious communities is regarded as the paramount problem of Canadian identity rather than a contribution to its solution. Finally, the strident moral tone that frequently erupts in US politics is rarely heard north of the border. The Puritan influence that dominated US religion made itself felt with much less force in Canada and, in consequence, has not bequeathed the moralistic style to politics.

The formal place of religion in Canadian public life has also undergone less challenge than in the US experience. One finds in Canada less sensitivity to governmental accommodation of religious groups and, by the same token, less resistance to political initiatives by the clergy. The majority of Canadians are affiliated with Churches that have historically smiled on close relationships with the state. Catholicism has traditionally sought and received provincial support for its educational system and has not been reluctant to press upon the state its philosophy regarding the family and other social issues. The Catholic accommodation to religious pluralism in America was strategic rather than wholehearted and did not take root in Canadian soil. Hostility to the public claims of Catholicism might have fuelled reactive calls for rigid Church–state separation by Protestants – as happened in the United States – had it not been for the predominance of Anglicanism, a faith accustomed by English heritage to a privileged position. The relative religious homogeneity within the Canadian provinces and the confinement of many religious issues to that level of government have also made it seem less urgent for government to avoid any sign of favouring religion. Hence in Canada, the call for a secular public arena does not resonate with the same force as in the United States.

In the realm of mass politics, Canada resembles the United States in one sense yet differs fundamentally in another. Canada possesses the same puzzling combination of low overt religious conflict – which manifests itself in a party system which rarely issues confessional appeals – yet simultaneously exhibits a durable religious cleavage in political choice. Throughout their history, Canadians have confronted a number of divisive political issues rooted in religious conflict.[46] Inter-group differences have not disappeared during the postwar era but religious conflicts have hardly constituted the essence of political controversy. Thus it is surprising to find that religious affiliation remains the single best predictor of party choice in national and provincial elections.[47] This pattern has been observed too often to constitute a fluke and has survived multivariate application of controls for social factors correlated with religious affiliation – ethnicity and language in particular.

According to both survey data and ecological analysis of national elections, Catholicism is a strong and significant predictor of liberal support while Protestantism correlates highly with conservatism. The relationship has survived at the mass base despite elite recruitment strategies that cross communal lines. The provincial pattern is more complex but the broad outlines of national elections are reproduced. Religious cleavages in Canadian politics appear to have outlasted the issues that first precipitated confessional voting patterns.

While religion remains electorally salient in Canada, the configuration of religious identity accounts for some contrasts with the United States in the manner faith is linked to politics. The postwar US political system has witnessed the displacement of Catholic versus Protestant competition by new cleavages that array religious conservatives and fundamentalists against those of a more ecumenical perspective. These new lines of conflict, which straddle traditional denominational loyalties, surface in the context of the contemporary social issues such as abortion, drug use, pornography and the like. No such development is apparent in Canada where the Protestant–Catholic duality retains political primacy and the fundamentalist challenge to modernity has failed to achieve potency. Attempts to mobilize Canadian Catholics on behalf of resistance to liberalized abortion law have failed to dislodge Catholic parishioners from traditional liberal partisanship. Voters from all denominations have resisted internal divisions tied to levels of religious adherence.

There are really two important patterns that require explanation – the continuing political relevance of Protestant–Catholic differences and, what is perhaps more puzzling, the absence of the emerging US cleavage between moralists and modernists. One promising attempt to account for the persistence of the traditional religious cleavage in Canada, W.P. Irvine's socialization model, suggested that the conflict continued due to the effectiveness of inter-generational transmission of partisanship within religious communities.[48] Catholics in particular inherit liberal partisanship with enough efficiency to maintain political distinctiveness. But as R.J. Johnston has properly noted, even if that explanation were technically accurate it would not explain *why* religious groups continued to transmit political cues and why subsequent generations accepted them in the absence of some external reinforcement. Johnston suggests that religious differences have not disappeared or diminished appreciably because 'the Catholic/non-Catholic cleavage corresponds to a major divide in Canadian life'.[49] He traces the divide, first, to the maintenance of a Catholic school system in the provinces, which has the consequence of keeping alive group norms, traditions and consciousness. There are also real value differences between the two communities which extend beyond moral conflicts to national policy debates over language and Canadian identity. Finally, Johnston points to the significance of geographical segregation in sustaining Protestant–Catholic political differences. To an extent unmatched in the US setting, Catholicism is geographically concentrated in selected provinces and confined to small areas in provinces with a Catholic minority. Subcommunal political differences, rooted in the first instance in historical conflicts over power and recognition, have been prolonged by the continuing salience of group identity. The contrasting decline in the political distinctiveness of US Catholics may be traced to the lowering of social barriers between religious communities. To the degree that Catholics remain socially insulated in Canadian society, the traditional cleavage is likely to remain strong even in the absence of overt religious conflict.

The failure of social issues to develop more fully on the Canadian political agenda may be explained partly by the relatively small size of the evangelical and fundamentalist community which has been the carrier of such politics in most societies. Structural factors are commonly invoked to account for the absence of strong 'moral' controversies in a society like Canada with such a high degree of religiosity. Noting the lack of a populist tradition and the persistent insulation of elites from mass politics, social scientists have argued that Canadian moral traditionalists are effectively denied access to the political agenda.[50] As noted at the outset of this chapter, the decentralized political system and the norm of popular sovereignty encourage 'issue entrepreneurship' by organized groups in the United States. Advocates of popular causes may find ready acceptance by ambitious elites who perceive the issues as a means to displace established leaders. Such expectations are realistic given the repeated penetration of the political system by outsiders during the course of US history. But a would-be issue entrepreneur in Canada faces formidable obstacles should he or she attempt to convert moral outrage in the periphery to governing authority in the centre. A parliamentary system deprives petitioners of venues that are open to advocates in nations with separation of governmental powers. Strong party discipline further restrains those who would attempt to seize power by storming the party from outside the establishment. In short, the structure of government in Canada is generally inhospitable to the type of single-issue politics which has been practised to such effect by religiously-motivated groups in the United States.

CONCLUSION

From this survey of religious–political interactions in postwar North America, it is possible to draw several conclusions. In both societies investigated in this chapter, religion emerged as a political factor of significance. At the most general level, the importance of religion in postwar North American politics runs counter to the widespread impression that confessional politics somehow requires religiously distinct political parties and overt religious controversy. Neither country has had a confessional political party of significance during the twentieth century. While parties have acquired the ethos of religious traditions and have tended to recruit elites and the bulk of mass support from particular communities, none has appealed for support as a religious party nor broadcast its appeal solely to members of a denomination. In both the United States and Canada, particularistic political rhetoric by religious or political leaders is rare and more likely to engender backlash than support. Thus, religion functions as something of a 'silent cleavage' with an existence that is rarely acknowledged openly and constitutes something of an embarrassment to sophisticated observers.

I comment on this seemingly obvious characteristic because it has not been fully recognized in research on politics and religion. Most research on the topic has been conducted with an implicit interest group model. That is, we recognize as 'confessional' politics the pursuit of some immediate and tangible state benefits by corporate religious organizations. The paradigmatic model of a religiously based party system takes the form of competition between a party representing the monopoly of a state Church and a party of minority religious defence which embraces secularism or at least neutrality in public policy. The essence of conflict in such systems is to be found in attempts by the dominant religious community to maintain religious authority over education, family law, sabbath observance, access to political authority and the means of social advancement. The hegemony of the dominant religion engenders reactive demands by subordinate communities for equity and recognition.[51] Where such religious conflict is modulated and political parties follow a 'catch-all' electoral strategy, the political system is said to be desacralized.

This model does not fit the US or Canadian political systems, neither of which has ever granted a religion official status at the national level, yet both societies have been marked by the political salience of religion. It is important to recognize that the source of political differences between religious groups does not rest solely upon considerations of narrow group advantage. Religious communities may follow unique political directions because of value commitments and sociological commonalities as well as group interest. Religious differences in politics may also be manifested in ways that escape detection by a narrow focus on public policy formation. Fundamental political assumptions and the tone of political discourse may be affected by religious suppositions and traditions. It does not require a confessional party in order for these religious themes to be expressed. Political scientists need to look beyond interest group activity to different facts of religious commitment as motivation for political involvement and to consider a broader range of political objects for evidence of religious impact. That advice is particularly appropriate in developed societies with government charters that disclaim religious authority.

The North American experience in the sphere of religion and politics also bears on the issue of social change and political response. Political development researchers have usually subscribed to 'the paradigmatic expectation that modernisation and mass participation in industrial societies would tend to eliminate ascriptive solidarities as the basis of political cleavage in favor of class or interest group activity.'[52] Both the Canadian and US examples falsify this prediction. The Canadian experience demonstrates remarkable stability of religious cleavages during a period of rapid social development. Despite rapid modernization as indexed by traditional indicators, the Canadian party system seems 'frozen' in a mould which elevates to primacy ethnocultural differences such as religion and relegates to secondary importance class differences, rooted though they are in the functional organization of modern society. The US political system has known class differences in politics but they have seldom been able to compete in scope or intensity with conflicts rooted in ethnocultural competition. Other developed societies have produced the same counter-intuitive hierarchies of cleavage in which cultural differences outweigh material interests.[53]

Why should religion remain so politically potent in societies where 'opportunities in life' are much more determined by socio-economic stratification than by religious affiliation? To pose the question in that manner is to ask why cleavages, i.e. group differences become politicized. A growing body of evidence suggests that potential cleavages stand the best chance of gaining political expression when the 'members' of a cleavage group constitute a segmented subculture isolated from competing influences by a dense network of interlocking organizations.[54] Lee Benson's general explanation for the superior role of ethnocultural forces stresses the capacity of religious affiliation, more so than class relations, to provide citizens with a cognitive basis to develop a reference group framework:

> identity, communality, protection from hostile others, solidarity and strength in pursuit of material interest, a sense of worthiness, value-systems to help orient their lives, life-styles to practise, a living space in which they can try to escape from alienation and feel at home.[55]

As long as religious communities command the resources to encapsulate and socialize the group member, they retain the capacity to structure political perspectives.

In Canada, the reinforcement of religious differences by other social divisions has perpetuated the political capacity of religious communities. Catholics remain segmented in a manner that keeps alive an independent political consciousness and prompts them to retain loyalty to the party that has traditionally respected Catholic interests and values. The US experience has been somewhat different. Social change and development have diminished the subcultural nature of the major religious groupings – Protestant and Catholic. Rather than all-encompassing environments, these traditions signify voluntary allegiance to secondary groups. A significant share of the Catholic population has moved out of psychological, economic and geographical ghettos and simultaneously discarded the norm of loyalty to the Democratic party. Mainline Protestantism has similarly lost its hold as a source of socialization values. Not surprisingly, these trends have coincided with a diminution in the traditional political cleavage between Catholics and Protestants.

Some observers have moved from this finding to the premature conclusion that religion has ceased to count politically in the United States. What such forecasts fail to discern is the replacement of one alignment by new configurations of ethno-religious party support.

The political lines have increasingly been drawn between those
in all major religious communities who remain deeply enmeshed
in religious cultures and persons who wear their religious loyalty
rather more lightly. The former inhabit subcultures that stress
moral traditionalism and encourage its application to public policy
while the latter, freed of exposure to traditional rules of conduct,
are more disposed to accept a libertarian ethic in what is called
'lifestyle choice'. By virtue of their encapsulation in organizations
which transmit political norms, the strongly religious exhibit greater
political cohesion than the unchurched who divide according to other
criteria. In sum, this enquiry reveals that religious conflicts have
not disappeared from postwar political conflict in North America.
Ethnoreligious political conflict has remained essentially unchanged
in one society and persisted in a different idiom in the other.

NOTES

1. J. Bryce (1905), *The American Commonwealth*, 2 vols, New York: Macmillan, vol. 2, p.695.
2. A. Ranney and W. Kendall (1956), *Democracy and the American Party System*, New York: Harcourt, Brace and Co., p.486.
3. R. A. Billington (1965), *The Protestant Crusade, 1900–1960*, Chicago: Quadrangle; S. M. Lipset (1964), 'Religion and politics in the American past and present', in R. Lee and M. E. Marty (eds), *Religion and Social Conflict*, New York: Oxford University Press, pp.69–126; R. T. Handy (1984), *A Christian America: Protestant Hopes and Historical Realities*, 2nd edn, New York: Oxford University Press.
4. B. E. Meland (1966), *The secularization of Modern Cultures*, New York: Oxford University Press, p.1.
5. D. Apter (1968), 'Government' in D.L. Sills (ed.), *International Encyclopedia of the Social Sciences*, New York: Macmillan, vol. 6, pp.218–24.
6. D. E. Smith (1963), *India as a Secular State*, Princeton: Princeton University Press, pp.3–8.
7. Meland, op. cit., p.16.
8. For documentation of these trends, see K. D. Wald (1987), *Religion and politics in the United States*, New York: St. Martin's Press, Ch. 1.
9. C. H. Jacquet, Jr (ed) (1983), *Yearbook of American and Canadian churches 1983*, Nashville, TN: Abingdon Press, p.21.
10. 'Religion in America: 30 years: 1935–1965' (1985), *Gallup Report*, no. 236.
11. T. Caplow, H. M. Bahr, B. A. Chadwick and associates (1983), *All Faithful People: Change and Continuity in Middletown's Religion*, Minneapolis: University of Minnesota Press.
12. 'Religion in America', op. cit., pp.16, 22, 24.

13   J. D. Hunter (1983), *American Evangelicalism: Conservative Religion and the Quandary of Modernity*, New Brunswick, NJ: Rutgers University Press, pp.107–12; E. C. Ladd (1982), *Where have all the Voters Gone?*, 2nd edn, New York: W.W. Norton, Ch. 2; B. E. Shafer (1985), 'The new cultural politics', *PS*, vol. 18, no. 2, pp.221–31. The secular perspectives of the New Class have been chronicled in a number of studies by Stanley Rothman and S. Robert Lichter. For an example, see their 'What are moviemakers made of?' (1984), *Public Opinion*, vol. 6, no. 6, pp.14–18.

14   R. N. Bellah, R. Madsen, W. M. Sullivan, A. Swidler and S. M. Tipton (1985), *Habits of the heart: Individualism in American Life*, Berkeley: University of California Press, p.221.

15   J. G. Melton (1977), *A Directory of Religious Bodies in the United States*, New York: Garland.

16   Percentages are based on data from the eleven General Social Surveys conducted between 1972 and 1984 as reported in W. C. Roof and W. McKinney (1987), *American Mainline Religion: Its Changing Shape and Future*, New Brunswick, NJ: Rutgers University Press, p.255. I have combined their 'liberal' and 'moderate' Protestants into the 'mainline' category and added black Protestants to the 'evangelical' total. Using a decision rule that apportioned members of 'moderate' Churches into either the 'mainline' or 'evangelical' category depending upon region where the respondent was raised, I have come up with the figure of 23 per cent for mainline Protestantism and 33 per cent for the evangelicals (Wald, op. cit., p.65).

17   N. D. Glenn (1987), 'The trend in "no religion" respondents to U.S. national surveys, late 1950s to early 1980s', *Public Opinion Quarterly*, vol. 51, no. 3, pp.293–314.

18   R. N. Bellah (1967), 'Civil religion in America', in W. G. McLoughlin and R. N. Bellah (eds), *Religion in America*, Boston, MA: Beacon Press, pp.3–23.

19   R. K. Fenn (1977), 'The relevance of Bellah's "civil religion" thesis to a theory of secularization', *Social Science History*, vol. 1, no. 4, pp.502–17.

20   Meland, op. cit., p.46.

21   L. Lipsitz (1968), 'If, as Verba says, the state functions as a religion, what are we to do then to save our souls?', *American Political Science Review*, vol. 62, no. 2, pp.527–96.

22   J. F. Wilson (1979), *Public Religion in American Culture*, Philadelphia, PA: Temple University Press.

23   R. Nisbet (1987), 'America as Utopia', *Reason*, vol. 18, no. 10, p.39.

24   R. Sennett (1987), 'A republic of souls: puritanism and the American Presidency' *Harper's Magazine*, pp.41–6; P. Revzin (1987), 'A politician's past isn't a drawback in Italy's parliament', *Wall Street Journal*, 14 October.

25   L. W. Levy (1986), *The Establishment Clause: Religion and the First Amendment*, New York: Macmillan.

26   The best collection of case law is R. T. Miller and R. B. Flowers (1987), *Toward Benevolent Neutrality: Church, State and the Supreme Court*, 3rd edn, Waco, TX: Baylor University Press.

27   M. J. Malbin (1978), *Religion and Politics: The Intentions of the Authors of*

the First Amendment, Studies in Legal Policy Series, Washington, DC: American Enterprise Institute.

28   T. W. Smith (1980), 'General liberalism and social change in post World War II America: a summary of trends', *Social Indicators Research*, vol. 10, no. 1, pp.1–28.

29   See Donald Granberg's 'Pro-life or reflection of conservative ideology? An analysis of opposition to legalized abortion' (1978), *Sociology and Social Research*, vol. 62, no. 3, pp.414–29; 'Comparison of pro-choice and pro-life activists: their values, attitudes and beliefs' (1982), *Population and Environment*, vol. 5, no. 2, pp.75–94; 'The abortion activists' (1981), *Family Planning Perspectives*, vol. 13, no. 4, pp.157–63.

30   R. E. Morgan (1980), *The Politics of Religious Conflict*, 2nd edn, Lanham, MD: University Press of America.

31   W. A. McIntosh, L. T. Alston and J. P. Alston (1979), 'The differential impact of religious preference and church attendance on attitudes toward abortion', *Review of Religious Research*, vol. 20, no. 2, pp.195–213.

32   D. Burner (1967), *The Politics of Provincialism: The Democratic Party in Transition, 1918–1932*, New York: W.W. Norton.

33   S. Lubell (1965), *The Future of American Politics*, 3rd edn, New York: Harper & Row, Ch. 3.

34   P. R. Abramson, J. H. Aldrich and D. W. Rohde (1987), *Change and Continuity in the 1984 Elections*, rev. edn, Washington, D.C. Congressional Quarterly, p.146.

35   ibid., pp.263–4.

36   H. E. Quinley (1974), *The Prophetic Clergy: Social Activism among Protestant Ministers*, New York: Wiley-Interscience; 'The IEA/Roper Center theology faculty survey' (1982), *This World*, no. 2, pp.28–75; E. Kennedy (1985), *Re-imagining American Catholicism*, New York: Vintage; J. D. Hunter (1987), 'Religious elites in advanced industrial society', *Comparative Studies in Society and History*, vol. 29, no. 2, pp.360–74.

37   J. Guth (1985), 'The Christian right revisited: partisan realignment among southern Baptist ministers', paper presented to the Midwest Political Science Association, Chicago, IL; L.A. Kelistedt (1985), 'The Falwell "platform": an analysis of its causes and consequences', paper presented to the Society for the Scientific Study of Religion, Savannah, GA; S. Rothenberg an F. Newport (1984), *The Evangelical Voter*, Washington, DC: Free Congress Research and Education Foundation.

38   J. R. Petrocik and F. T. Steeper (1987), 'The political landscape in 1988', *Public Opinion*, vol. 10, no. 3, pp.41–4.

39   P. L. Benson and D. L. Williams (1982), *Religion on Capitol Hill*, San Francisco: Harper and Row; M. T. Hanna (1979), *Catholics and American Politics*, Cambridge, MA: Harvard University Press.

40   R. L. Gorsuch and D. Aleshire (1974), 'Christian faith and ethnic prejudice: a review and interpretation of research', *Journal for the Scientific Study of Religion*, vol. 13, no. 3, pp.281–307; T. J. Hoffman (1985), 'Religion and political imagery: the impacts of institutional connectedness and religious imagery', paper presented to the American Political Science Association, New Orleans, LA.

41 Roof and McKinney, op. cit., pp.48–57.
42 J. Guth (1981), 'The politics of the evangelical right', paper presented to the American Political Science Association, New York.
43 The poll data are reported in E. H. Hastings and P. K. Hastings (eds), *Index to International Public Opinion*, New York: Greenwood Press, various dates. See the 1986 edition, p.529 and the 1987 edition, pp.454–5, 459. Data on church membership have been calculated from C. H. Jacquet (ed.) (1986), *Yearbook of American and Canadian Churches 1986*, Nashville, TN: Abingdon Press, p.245.
44 A. Siegfried (1907), *The Race Question in Canada*, London: Evleigh Nash, p.11.
45 There are a number of illuminating essays on religious and political cultures in a special issue of the *Canadian Journal of Sociology* (1978), vol. 3, no. 2. See especially H. Fallding, 'Mainline Protestantism in Canada and the United States', pp.141–60; H. H. Hiller, 'Continentalism and the third force in religion', pp.183–208; and K. Wethue, 'Stars and stripes, the maple leaf, and the papal coat of arms', pp.245–61. There is a useful summary of research in S. M. Lipset, 'Canada and the United States: the cultural dimension' in C. F. Doran and J. H. Sigler (eds) (1985), *Canada and the United States: Enduring Friendship, Persisting Strains*, Englewood Cliffs, NJ: Prentice-Hall, pp.123–8.
46 F. C. Engelmann and M. A. Schwartz (1967), *Political Parties and the Canadian Social Structure*, Scarborough, ONT: Prentice-Hall of Canada, pp.228–31.
47 H. D. Clarke, J. Jenson, L. LeDuc and J. H. Pammett (1979), *Political Choice in Canada*, Toronto: McGraw-Hill, Ch. 4.
48 W. P. Irvine (1974), 'Explaining the religious basis of the Canadian partisan identify: success on the third try', *Canadian Journal of Political Science*, vol. 7, no. 3, pp.560–3.
49 R. J. Johnston (1985), 'The geography of class and religion in Canadian elections', paper delivered to the International Political Science Association, Oxford, England, p.31. See by the same author 'The reproduction of the religious cleavage in Canadian elections' (1985), *Canadian Journal of Political Science*, vol. 18, no. 1, pp.99–113.
50 M. Schwartz (1981), 'Politics and moral causes in Canada and the United States' in R. F. Tomasson (ed.), *Comparative Social Research*, Greenwich, CT: JAI Press, pp.65–90; J. H. Simpson (1986), 'Some elementary forms of authority and fundamentalist politics' in J. K. Hadden and A. Shupe (eds), *Prophetic Religions and Politics* vol. 1, New York: Paragon House, pp.391–409.
51 D. Martin (1978), *A General Theory of Secularization*, New York: Harper & Row, Ch. 1.
52 I. Lustick (1986), 'Review of *New nationalisms of the Developed West*', *American Political Science Review*, vol. 80, no. 4, pp.1408–9.
53 A. Lijphart (1979), 'Religious vs linguistic vs class voting: the "crucial experiment" of comparing Belgium, Canada, South Africa and Switzerland', *American Political Science Review*, vol. 73, no. 2, pp. 442–58; R. Rose and D. Urwin (1969), 'Social cohesion, political parties and strains in regimes', *Comparative Political Studies*, vol. 2, no. 1, pp.7–67.

54　J. J. Houska (1985), *Influencing Mass Political Behavior: Elites and Political Subcultures in the Netherlands and Austria*, Berkeley: Institute of International Studies, University of California.

55　L. Benson (1979), 'Marx's general and middle-range theories of social conflict' in R. K. Merton, J. S. Coleman and P. H. Rossi (eds), *Qualitative and Quantitative Social Research: Papers in Honor of Paul F. Lazarsfeld*, New York: Free Press, p.206.

Index